LECTIONARY FOR WORSHIP

REVISED COMMON LECTIONARY

Cycle C

Augsburg Fortress
Minneapolis

LECTIONARY FOR WORSHIP, CYCLE C
Study Edition

Design: Lecy Design
Typesetting: Peregrine Graphics Services

The paper used in this publication meets the minimum requirements of American National Standard for Information Sciences—Permanence of Paper for Printed Library Materials, ANSI Z329.48-1984. ⊗

Manufactured in U.S.A.   ISBN 0-8066-0196-5   AF 3-383
06   05   04   03   02   01   00   99   98   97   1   2   3   4   5   6   7   8   9   10

CONTENTS

INTRODUCTION

The word of God

The Scriptures speak of the word of God as light and lamp, imperishable seed, spiritual food and drink, healing balm, cleansing fire. The word sustains life, produces faith, strengthens hope, and inflames love. As the Bible attests, the word of God created the world and all living things. The word of the Lord liberated the Hebrew people from slavery and sustained them on their journey to the promised land. Throughout the history of Israel, this word inspired the judges and spoke to the prophets. In time, the great acts of God's mercy were written down and then proclaimed in the daily and weekly gatherings of the Jewish people. Through an annual cycle of lessons, the Hebrew Scriptures were read, sung, and interpreted in communal worship.

The word among us

"Long ago God spoke to our ancestors in many and various ways by the prophets, but in these last days he has spoken to us by a Son" (Hebrews 1:1-2). In the worship of his people, Jesus read the ancient scriptures and interpreted them anew: "Today this scripture has been fulfilled in your hearing" (Luke 4:21). In his own life, he proclaimed the good news of salvation in word and deed. To his disciples on the road, the risen Lord interpreted in all the scriptures the things concerning himself. In breaking open the word, he gave himself as the bread of life. Indeed, for the early Christian community, Jesus himself was the living Word to be proclaimed and interpreted in new places among new people. "We declare to you what was from the beginning, what we have heard, what we have seen with our eyes, what we have looked at and touched with our hands, concerning the word of life" (1 John 1:1).

The word proclaimed in worship

When the Scriptures are proclaimed in the worshiping assembly today, the living Word continues to speak to his disciples. Through the power of the Holy Spirit, the risen Christ is truly present when the Scriptures are read. Through the ministry of readers, the written word becomes a lively, spoken word addressed to all who listen with faith.

Gathered around the table of God's word, the church follows Christ's pattern of reading and interpreting the Scriptures, so that when the holy book is opened and read, Christ speaks anew this living and active word. In the hearing of this word the church is sustained in faith, drawn to the font and holy supper, and strengthened for witness in the world.

The proclamation of the word

In various ways the word of God is proclaimed in the liturgy by the worshiping assembly and its ministers. In particular, the word is proclaimed in the biblical readings (the Hebrew Scriptures, the New Testament letters, and the Gospels); in the singing of the psalms, hymns, and acclamations surrounding the readings; and in preaching.

The proclamation of the Gospel in reading and preaching is the high point of the word service. The other readings illuminate this central reading while the psalms, hymns, and acclamations offer musical responses to the readings. Because of the centrality of the Gospel reading, the assembly stands to welcome the Lord who speaks anew in this place and time.

In these varied actions, the dialogue between God and the worshiping assembly takes place. In order to take the word of God to heart and ponder its meaning, intervals of silence are often kept by the assembly and its readers. Just as haste hinders reflection on the word, so a tendency to wordiness on the part of worship leaders can detract from the clear and simple voice of the word proclaimed.

In most instances, baptized members of the worshiping assembly who have been trained in this ministry read the first and second readings. After brief silences, a cantor or choir leads the people in singing the psalm as well as the song or acclamation that greets the Gospel reading. Normally, the preacher reads the Gospel and then preaches the good news for the community and the world. A hymn responds to this word with thanksgiving. A proclamation of faith often continues the assembly's response, leading the community to pray for the church, the world, and those in need.

The medieval custom of two places for the word (lectern and pulpit) has yielded, in many congregations, to a single place (lectern or ambo) from which the readings are proclaimed and the sermon is preached. Here the book of life is opened; here the banquet of scripture is set forth; here the people of God are nourished on the word.

"He interpreted to them the things about himself in all the scriptures. He took bread, blessed and broke it, and gave it to them. Then their eyes were opened, and they recognized him" (Luke 24:27, 30-31). From the table of God's word, the worshiping assembly gathers at the table of the holy supper to receive the bread of life and the cup of blessing. In word and meal, the living Word welcomes, enlightens, and nourishes the people of God for service in the world.

The lectionary

The lectionary sets forth many of the stories, images, and actions through which the living Word sustains the Christian community gathered in public worship during the seasons of the year. It is ordered around the first reading, psalm, second reading, and Gospel reading. Appropriate introductions and conclusions to the readings are provided in this lectionary book. After announcing the reading with the introduction, the reader/minister pauses and then begins the proclamation. At the end of each of the first two readings, the reader pauses and then says, "The word of the Lord." The people respond, "Thanks be to God." At the conclusion of the Gospel reading, the minister says, "The Gospel of the Lord." The people respond with the words, "Praise to you, O Christ" or another appropriate acclamation.

In this lectionary book, the readings and psalms appointed for Lesser Festivals are printed after the Sunday and principal festival readings.

In places where the New Revised Standard Version versification for the psalms differs from that of the translation used in *Lutheran Book of Worship* and *Book of Common Prayer,* LBW/BCP alternate versification is noted in italics.

During the Sundays after Pentecost, an alternate set of semi-continuous first readings and psalms are provided in an appendix. Where it is the practice to read the semi-continuous first reading and psalm response, the lectionary should be opened first to the appropriate page in the appendix. The page in the body of the lectionary where the readings continue will need to be marked clearly.

In a few instances, the Revised Common Lectionary appoints readings and responses from selected books of the Apocrypha. These readings and responses are printed in a second appendix.

May this lectionary assist the worshiping assembly in the proclamation of the word and the preaching of the holy gospel.

SEASON OF ADVENT

First Sunday in Advent

NOVEMBER 30, 1997   DECEMBER 3, 2000   NOVEMBER 30, 2003

FIRST READING: JEREMIAH 33:14–16

A reading from Jeremiah:

¹⁴The days are surely coming, says the LORD,
when I will fulfill the promise I made to the house of Israel
and the house of Judah.
¹⁵In those days and at that time
I will cause a righteous Branch to spring up for David;
and he shall execute justice and righteousness in the land.
¹⁶In those days Judah will be saved
and Jerusalem will live in safety.
And this is the name by which it will be called:
"The LORD is our righteousness."

The word of the Lord.

PSALMODY: PSALM 25:1–10

Psalm 25:1–9 LBW/BCP

SECOND READING: 1 THESSALONIANS 3:9–13

A reading from First Thessalonians:

⁹How can we thank God enough for you
in return for all the joy that we feel before our God because of you?
¹⁰Night and day we pray most earnestly
that we may see you face to face
and restore whatever is lacking in your faith.

¹¹Now may our God and Father himself and our Lord Jesus
direct our way to you.
¹²And may the Lord make you increase and abound in love
for one another and for all,
just as we abound in love for you.
¹³And may he so strengthen your hearts in holiness
that you may be blameless before our God and Father
at the coming of our Lord Jesus with all his saints.

The word of the Lord.

GOSPEL: LUKE 21:25–36

The Holy Gospel according to Luke, the 21st chapter.

Jesus said:
25"There will be signs in the sun, the moon, and the stars,
and on the earth distress among nations
confused by the roaring of the sea and the waves.
26People will faint from fear and foreboding of what is coming upon the world,
for the powers of the heavens will be shaken.
27Then they will see 'the Son of Man coming in a cloud'
with power and great glory.
28Now when these things begin to take place,
stand up and raise your heads,
because your redemption is drawing near."

29Then he told them a parable:
"Look at the fig tree and all the trees;
30as soon as they sprout leaves
you can see for yourselves and know that summer is already near.
31So also, when you see these things taking place,
you know that the kingdom of God is near.
32Truly I tell you, this generation will not pass away
until all things have taken place.
33Heaven and earth will pass away, but my words will not pass away.

34"Be on guard so that your hearts are not weighed down
with dissipation and drunkenness and the worries of this life,
and that day does not catch you unexpectedly, 35like a trap.
For it will come upon all who live on the face of the whole earth.
36Be alert at all times,
praying that you may have the strength
to escape all these things that will take place,
and to stand before the Son of Man."

The Gospel of the Lord.

Second Sunday in Advent

DECEMBER 7, 1997　　DECEMBER 10, 2000　　DECEMBER 7, 2003

FIRST READING: MALACHI 3:1–4　　　　　　*Alternate Reading: Baruch 5:1–9 (p. 399)*

A reading from Malachi:

¹See, I am sending my messenger to prepare the way before me,
and the Lord whom you seek will suddenly come to his temple.
The messenger of the covenant in whom you delight—
indeed, he is coming, says the LORD of hosts.
²But who can endure the day of his coming,
and who can stand when he appears?

For he is like a refiner's fire and like fullers' soap;
³he will sit as a refiner and purifier of silver,
and he will purify the descendants of Levi
and refine them like gold and silver,
until they present offerings to the LORD in righteousness.
⁴Then the offering of Judah and Jerusalem will be pleasing to the LORD
as in the days of old and as in former years.

The word of the Lord.

PSALMODY: LUKE 1:68–79

SECOND READING: PHILIPPIANS 1:3–11

A reading from Philippians:

³I thank my God every time I remember you,
⁴constantly praying with joy in every one of my prayers for all of you,
⁵because of your sharing in the gospel from the first day until now.
⁶I am confident of this,
that the one who began a good work among you
will bring it to completion by the day of Jesus Christ.
⁷It is right for me to think this way about all of you,
because you hold me in your heart,
for all of you share in God's grace with me,
both in my imprisonment

and in the defense and confirmation of the gospel.
⁸For God is my witness,
how I long for all of you with the compassion of Christ Jesus.

⁹And this is my prayer,
that your love may overflow more and more with knowledge and full insight
¹⁰to help you to determine what is best,
so that in the day of Christ you may be pure and blameless,
¹¹having produced the harvest of righteousness
that comes through Jesus Christ for the glory and praise of God.

The word of the Lord.

GOSPEL: LUKE 3:1–6

The Holy Gospel according to Luke, the third chapter.

¹In the fifteenth year of the reign of Emperor Tiberius,
when Pontius Pilate was governor of Judea,
and Herod was ruler of Galilee,
and his brother Philip ruler of the region of Ituraea and Trachonitis,
and Lysanias ruler of Abilene,
²during the high priesthood of Annas and Caiaphas,
the word of God came to John son of Zechariah in the wilderness.
³He went into all the region around the Jordan,
proclaiming a baptism of repentance for the forgiveness of sins,
⁴as it is written in the book of the words of the prophet Isaiah,
    "The voice of one crying out in the wilderness:
    'Prepare the way of the Lord,
        make his paths straight.'
⁵'Every valley shall be filled,
        and every mountain and hill shall be made low,
    and the crooked shall be made straight,
        and the rough ways made smooth;
⁶and all flesh shall see the salvation of God.' "

The Gospel of the Lord.

FIRST READING: Zephaniah 3:14–20

A reading from Zephaniah:

¹⁴Sing aloud, O daughter Zion;
    shout, O Israel!
Rejoice and exult with all your heart,
    O daughter Jerusalem!
¹⁵The Lord has taken away the judgments against you,
    he has turned away your enemies.
The king of Israel, the Lord, is in your midst;
    you shall fear disaster no more.

¹⁶On that day it shall be said to Jerusalem:
Do not fear, O Zion;
    do not let your hands grow weak.
¹⁷The Lord, your God, is in your midst,
    a warrior who gives victory;
he will rejoice over you with gladness,
    he will renew you in his love;
he will exult over you with loud singing
    ¹⁸as on a day of festival.
I will remove disaster from you,
    so that you will not bear reproach for it.
¹⁹I will deal with all your oppressors
    at that time.
And I will save the lame
    and gather the outcast,
and I will change their shame into praise
    and renown in all the earth.
²⁰At that time I will bring you home,
    at the time when I gather you;
for I will make you renowned and praised
    among all the peoples of the earth,
when I restore your fortunes
    before your eyes, says the Lord.

The word of the Lord.

PSALMODY: Isaiah 12:2–6

SECOND READING: PHILIPPIANS 4:4–7

A reading from Philippians:

[4]Rejoice in the Lord always;
again I will say, Rejoice.
[5]Let your gentleness be known to everyone.
The Lord is near.
[6]Do not worry about anything,
but in everything by prayer and supplication with thanksgiving
let your requests be made known to God.
[7]And the peace of God, which surpasses all understanding,
will guard your hearts and your minds in Christ Jesus.

The word of the Lord.

GOSPEL: LUKE 3:7–18

The Holy Gospel according to Luke, the third chapter.

[7]John said to the crowds that came out to be baptized by him,
"You brood of vipers! Who warned you to flee from the wrath to come?
[8]Bear fruits worthy of repentance.
Do not begin to say to yourselves,
'We have Abraham as our ancestor';
for I tell you, God is able from these stones to raise up children to Abraham.
[9]Even now the ax is lying at the root of the trees;
every tree therefore that does not bear good fruit
is cut down and thrown into the fire."

[10]And the crowds asked him, "What then should we do?"
[11]In reply he said to them,
"Whoever has two coats must share with anyone who has none;
and whoever has food must do likewise."
[12]Even tax collectors came to be baptized, and they asked him,
"Teacher, what should we do?"
[13]He said to them, "Collect no more than the amount prescribed for you."
[14]Soldiers also asked him, "And we, what should we do?"
He said to them,
"Do not extort money from anyone by threats or false accusation,
and be satisfied with your wages."

[15]As the people were filled with expectation,
and all were questioning in their hearts concerning John,
whether he might be the Messiah,
[16]John answered all of them by saying,
"I baptize you with water;

but one who is more powerful than I is coming;
I am not worthy to untie the thong of his sandals.
He will baptize you with the Holy Spirit and fire.
[17]His winnowing fork is in his hand,
to clear his threshing floor and to gather the wheat into his granary;
but the chaff he will burn with unquenchable fire."

[18]So, with many other exhortations, he proclaimed the good news to
the people.

The Gospel of the Lord.

Fourth Sunday in Advent

DECEMBER 21, 1997   DECEMBER 24, 2000   DECEMBER 21, 2003

FIRST READING: MICAH 5:2–5a

A reading from Micah:

²But you, O Bethlehem of Ephrathah,
    who are one of the little clans of Judah,
from you shall come forth for me
    one who is to rule in Israel,
whose origin is from of old,
    from ancient days.
³Therefore he shall give them up until the time
    when she who is in labor has brought forth;
then the rest of his kindred shall return
    to the people of Israel.
⁴And he shall stand and feed his flock in the strength of the LORD,
    in the majesty of the name of the LORD his God.
And they shall live secure, for now he shall be great
    to the ends of the earth;
⁵and he shall be the one of peace.

The word of the Lord.

PSALMODY: LUKE 1:47–55 or PSALM 80:1–7

SECOND READING: HEBREWS 10:5–10

A reading from Hebrews:

⁵Consequently, when Christ came into the world, he said,
    "Sacrifices and offerings you have not desired,
        but a body you have prepared for me;
    ⁶in burnt offerings and sin offerings
        you have taken no pleasure.
    ⁷Then I said, 'See, God, I have come to do your will, O God'
        (in the scroll of the book it is written of me)."
⁸When he said above,
"You have neither desired nor taken pleasure in sacrifices and offerings

and burnt offerings and sin offerings"
(these are offered according to the law),
⁹then he added, "See, I have come to do your will."
He abolishes the first in order to establish the second.
¹⁰And it is by God's will that we have been sanctified
through the offering of the body of Jesus Christ once for all.

The word of the Lord.

GOSPEL: Luke 1:39–45 [46–55]

The Holy Gospel according to Luke, the first chapter.

³⁹In those days Mary set out
and went with haste to a Judean town in the hill country,
⁴⁰where she entered the house of Zechariah and greeted Elizabeth.
⁴¹When Elizabeth heard Mary's greeting, the child leaped in her womb.
And Elizabeth was filled with the Holy Spirit
⁴²and exclaimed with a loud cry,
"Blessed are you among women, and blessed is the fruit of your womb.
⁴³And why has this happened to me,
that the mother of my Lord comes to me?
⁴⁴For as soon as I heard the sound of your greeting,
the child in my womb leaped for joy.
⁴⁵And blessed is she who believed
that there would be a fulfillment of what was spoken to her by the Lord."

[⁴⁶And Mary said,
      "My soul magnifies the Lord,
            ⁴⁷and my spirit rejoices in God my Savior,
      ⁴⁸for he has looked with favor on the lowliness of his servant.
            Surely, from now on all generations will call me blessed;
      ⁴⁹for the Mighty One has done great things for me,
            and holy is his name.
      ⁵⁰His mercy is for those who fear him
            from generation to generation.
      ⁵¹He has shown strength with his arm;
            he has scattered the proud in the thoughts of their hearts.
      ⁵²He has brought down the powerful from their thrones,
            and lifted up the lowly;
      ⁵³he has filled the hungry with good things,
            and sent the rich away empty.
      ⁵⁴He has helped his servant Israel,
            in remembrance of his mercy,
      ⁵⁵according to the promise he made to our ancestors,
            to Abraham and to his descendants forever."]

The Gospel of the Lord.

SEASON OF CHRISTMAS

The Nativity of Our Lord
Christmas Eve (I)
DECEMBER 24

FIRST READING: ISAIAH 9:2–7

A reading from Isaiah:

²The people who walked in darkness
    have seen a great light;
those who lived in a land of deep darkness—
    on them light has shined.
³You have multiplied the nation,
    you have increased its joy;
they rejoice before you
    as with joy at the harvest,
    as people exult when dividing plunder.
⁴For the yoke of their burden,
    and the bar across their shoulders,
    the rod of their oppressor,
    you have broken as on the day of Midian.
⁵For all the boots of the tramping warriors
    and all the garments rolled in blood
    shall be burned as fuel for the fire.

⁶For a child has been born for us,
    a son given to us;
authority rests upon his shoulders;
    and he is named
Wonderful Counselor, Mighty God,
    Everlasting Father, Prince of Peace.
⁷His authority shall grow continually,
    and there shall be endless peace
for the throne of David and his kingdom.
    He will establish and uphold it
with justice and with righteousness
    from this time onward and forevermore.

The zeal of the LORD of hosts will do this.

The word of the Lord.

PSALMODY: PSALM 96

SECOND READING: Titus 2:11–14

A reading from Titus:

¹¹The grace of God has appeared,
bringing salvation to all,
¹²training us to renounce impiety and worldly passions,
and in the present age
to live lives that are self-controlled, upright, and godly,
¹³while we wait for the blessed hope
and the manifestation of the glory
of our great God and Savior, Jesus Christ.

¹⁴He it is who gave himself for us
that he might redeem us from all iniquity
and purify for himself a people of his own
who are zealous for good deeds.

The word of the Lord.

GOSPEL: Luke 2:1–14 [15–20]

The Holy Gospel according to Luke, the second chapter.

¹In those days a decree went out from Emperor Augustus
that all the world should be registered.
²This was the first registration
and was taken while Quirinius was governor of Syria.
³All went to their own towns to be registered.
⁴Joseph also went from the town of Nazareth in Galilee to Judea,
to the city of David called Bethlehem,
because he was descended from the house and family of David.
⁵He went to be registered with Mary,
to whom he was engaged and who was expecting a child.
⁶While they were there, the time came for her to deliver her child.
⁷And she gave birth to her firstborn son
and wrapped him in bands of cloth,
and laid him in a manger,
because there was no place for them in the inn.

[8]In that region there were shepherds living in the fields,
keeping watch over their flock by night.
[9]Then an angel of the Lord stood before them,
and the glory of the Lord shone around them,
and they were terrified.
[10]But the angel said to them,
"Do not be afraid;
for see—
I am bringing you good news of great joy for all the people:
[11]to you is born this day in the city of David
a Savior, who is the Messiah, the Lord.
[12]This will be a sign for you:
you will find a child wrapped in bands of cloth
and lying in a manger."
[13]And suddenly there was with the angel
a multitude of the heavenly host, praising God and saying,
> [14]"Glory to God in the highest heaven,
> and on earth peace among those whom he favors!"

[[15]When the angels had left them and gone into heaven,
the shepherds said to one another,
"Let us go now to Bethlehem
and see this thing that has taken place,
which the Lord has made known to us."
[16]So they went with haste
and found Mary and Joseph, and the child lying in the manger.
[17]When they saw this,
they made known what had been told them about this child;
[18]and all who heard it were amazed at what the shepherds told them.
[19]But Mary treasured all these words and pondered them in her heart.

[20]The shepherds returned,
glorifying and praising God for all they had heard and seen,
as it had been told them.]

The Gospel of the Lord.

The Nativity of Our Lord
Christmas Dawn (II)
DECEMBER 25

FIRST READING: ISAIAH 62:6–12

A reading from Isaiah:

⁶Upon your walls, O Jerusalem,
    I have posted sentinels;
all day and all night
    they shall never be silent.
You who remind the LORD,
    take no rest,
⁷and give him no rest
        until he establishes Jerusalem
        and makes it renowned throughout the earth.

⁸The LORD has sworn by his right hand
    and by his mighty arm:
I will not again give your grain
        to be food for your enemies,
and foreigners shall not drink the wine
        for which you have labored;
⁹but those who garner it shall eat it
        and praise the LORD,
and those who gather it shall drink it
        in my holy courts.

¹⁰Go through, go through the gates,
    prepare the way for the people;
build up, build up the highway,
        clear it of stones,
        lift up an ensign over the peoples.
¹¹The LORD has proclaimed
    to the end of the earth:
Say to daughter Zion,
    "See, your salvation comes;
his reward is with him,
        and his recompense before him."

^{12}They shall be called, "The Holy People,
   The Redeemed of the LORD";
and you shall be called, "Sought Out,
   A City Not Forsaken."

The word of the Lord.

PSALMODY: PSALM 97

SECOND READING: TITUS 3:4–7

A reading from Titus:

^{4}When the goodness and loving kindness of God our Savior appeared,
^{5}he saved us,
not because of any works of righteousness that we had done,
but according to his mercy,
through the water of rebirth
and renewal by the Holy Spirit.
^{6}This Spirit he poured out on us richly
through Jesus Christ our Savior,
^{7}so that, having been justified by his grace,
we might become heirs
according to the hope of eternal life.

The word of the Lord.

GOSPEL: LUKE 2:[1–7] 8–20

The Holy Gospel according to Luke, the second chapter.

[^{1}In those days a decree went out from Emperor Augustus
that all the world should be registered.
^{2}This was the first registration
and was taken while Quirinius was governor of Syria.
^{3}All went to their own towns to be registered.
^{4}Joseph also went from the town of Nazareth in Galilee to Judea,
to the city of David called Bethlehem,
because he was descended from the house and family of David.
^{5}He went to be registered with Mary,
to whom he was engaged and who was expecting a child.
^{6}While they were there, the time came for her to deliver her child.
^{7}And she gave birth to her firstborn son
and wrapped him in bands of cloth,
and laid him in a manger,
because there was no place for them in the inn.]

8In that region there were shepherds living in the fields,
keeping watch over their flock by night.
9Then an angel of the Lord stood before them,
and the glory of the Lord shone around them,
and they were terrified.
10But the angel said to them,
"Do not be afraid;
for see—
I am bringing you good news of great joy for all the people:
11to you is born this day in the city of David
a Savior, who is the Messiah, the Lord.
12This will be a sign for you:
you will find a child wrapped in bands of cloth
and lying in a manger."
13And suddenly there was with the angel
a multitude of the heavenly host, praising God and saying,
14"Glory to God in the highest heaven,
and on earth peace among those whom he favors!"

15When the angels had left them and gone into heaven,
the shepherds said to one another,
"Let us go now to Bethlehem
and see this thing that has taken place,
which the Lord has made known to us."
16So they went with haste
and found Mary and Joseph, and the child lying in the manger.
17When they saw this,
they made known what had been told them about this child;
18and all who heard it were amazed at what the shepherds told them.
19But Mary treasured all these words and pondered them in her heart.

20The shepherds returned,
glorifying and praising God for all they had heard and seen,
as it had been told them.

The Gospel of the Lord.

The Nativity of Our Lord
Christmas Day (III)
DECEMBER 25

FIRST READING: Isaiah 52:7–10

A reading from Isaiah:

⁷How beautiful upon the mountains
    are the feet of the messenger who announces peace,
who brings good news,
    who announces salvation,
    who says to Zion, "Your God reigns."

⁸Listen! Your sentinels lift up their voices,
    together they sing for joy;
for in plain sight they see
    the return of the LORD to Zion.

⁹Break forth together into singing,
    you ruins of Jerusalem;
for the LORD has comforted his people,
    he has redeemed Jerusalem.
¹⁰The LORD has bared his holy arm
    before the eyes of all the nations;
and all the ends of the earth shall see
    the salvation of our God.

The word of the Lord.

PSALMODY: Psalm 98

SECOND READING: HEBREWS 1:1–4 [5–12]

A reading from Hebrews:

¹Long ago God spoke to our ancestors
in many and various ways by the prophets,
²but in these last days
he has spoken to us by a Son,
whom he appointed heir of all things,
through whom he also created the worlds.
³He is the reflection of God's glory
and the exact imprint of God's very being,
and he sustains all things by his powerful word.
When he had made purification for sins,
he sat down at the right hand of the Majesty on high,
⁴having become as much superior to angels
as the name he has inherited is more excellent than theirs.

[⁵For to which of the angels did God ever say,
    "You are my Son;
        today I have begotten you"?
Or again,
    "I will be his Father,
        and he will be my Son"?
⁶And again, when he brings the firstborn into the world, he says,
    "Let all God's angels worship him."
⁷Of the angels he says,
    "He makes his angels winds,
        and his servants flames of fire."

⁸But of the Son he says,
    "Your throne, O God, is forever and ever,
        and the righteous scepter is the scepter of your kingdom.
    ⁹You have loved righteousness and hated wickedness;
    therefore God, your God, has anointed you
        with the oil of gladness beyond your companions."
¹⁰And,
    "In the beginning, Lord, you founded the earth,
        and the heavens are the work of your hands;
    ¹¹they will perish, but you remain;
        they will all wear out like clothing;
    ¹²like a cloak you will roll them up,
        and like clothing they will be changed.
    But you are the same,
        and your years will never end."]

The word of the Lord.

The Holy Gospel according to John, the first chapter.

[1]In the beginning was the Word,
and the Word was with God,
and the Word was God.
[2]He was in the beginning with God.
[3]All things came into being through him,
and without him not one thing came into being.
What has come into being [4]in him was life,
and the life was the light of all people.
[5]The light shines in the darkness,
and the darkness did not overcome it.

[6]There was a man sent from God, whose name was John.
[7]He came as a witness to testify to the light,
so that all might believe through him.
[8]He himself was not the light,
but he came to testify to the light.
[9]The true light, which enlightens everyone,
was coming into the world.

[10]He was in the world,
and the world came into being through him;
yet the world did not know him.
[11]He came to what was his own,
and his own people did not accept him.
[12]But to all who received him,
who believed in his name,
he gave power to become children of God,
[13]who were born,
not of blood or of the will of the flesh or of the will of man,
but of God.

[14]And the Word became flesh and lived among us,
and we have seen his glory,
the glory as of a father's only son,
full of grace and truth.

The Gospel of the Lord.

FIRST SUNDAY AFTER CHRISTMAS

DECEMBER 28, 1997   *DECEMBER 31, 2000*   *DECEMBER 28, 2003*

FIRST READING: 1 SAMUEL 2:18–20, 26

A reading from First Samuel:

18Samuel was ministering before the LORD,
a boy wearing a linen ephod.
19His mother used to make for him a little robe
and take it to him each year,
when she went up with her husband to offer the yearly sacrifice.
20Then Eli would bless Elkanah and his wife, and say,
"May the LORD repay you with children by this woman
for the gift that she made to the LORD";
and then they would return to their home.

26Now the boy Samuel continued to grow
both in stature and in favor with the LORD and with the people.

The word of the Lord.

PSALMODY: PSALM 148

SECOND READING: COLOSSIANS 3:12–17

A reading from Colossians:

12As God's chosen ones, holy and beloved,
clothe yourselves with compassion, kindness, humility, meekness,
    and patience.
13Bear with one another and,
if anyone has a complaint against another, forgive each other;
just as the Lord has forgiven you, so you also must forgive.
14Above all, clothe yourselves with love,
which binds everything together in perfect harmony.
15And let the peace of Christ rule in your hearts,
to which indeed you were called in the one body.
And be thankful.
16Let the word of Christ dwell in you richly;

teach and admonish one another in all wisdom;
and with gratitude in your hearts
sing psalms, hymns, and spiritual songs to God.
[17]And whatever you do, in word or deed,
do everything in the name of the Lord Jesus,
giving thanks to God the Father through him.

The word of the Lord.

GOSPEL: LUKE 2:41–52

The Holy Gospel according to Luke, the second chapter.

[41]Now every year Jesus' parents went to Jerusalem for the festival of the
       Passover.
[42]And when he was twelve years old, they went up as usual for the festival.
[43]When the festival was ended and they started to return,
the boy Jesus stayed behind in Jerusalem,
but his parents did not know it.
[44]Assuming that he was in the group of travelers, they went a day's journey.
Then they started to look for him among their relatives and friends.
[45]When they did not find him, they returned to Jerusalem to search for him.

[46]After three days they found him in the temple,
sitting among the teachers, listening to them and asking them questions.
[47]And all who heard him were amazed at his understanding and his answers.
[48]When his parents saw him they were astonished;
and his mother said to him,
"Child, why have you treated us like this?
Look, your father and I have been searching for you in great anxiety."
[49]He said to them, "Why were you searching for me?
Did you not know that I must be in my Father's house?"
[50]But they did not understand what he said to them.

[51]Then he went down with them and came to Nazareth,
and was obedient to them.
His mother treasured all these things in her heart.
[52]And Jesus increased in wisdom and in years,
and in divine and human favor.

The Gospel of the Lord.

SECOND SUNDAY AFTER CHRISTMAS

JANUARY 4, 1998   JANUARY 4, 2004

FIRST READING: JEREMIAH 31:7–14

Alternate Reading: Sirach 24:1–12 (p. 400)

A reading from Jeremiah:

⁷Thus says the LORD:
Sing aloud with gladness for Jacob,
    and raise shouts for the chief of the nations;
proclaim, give praise, and say,
    "Save, O LORD, your people,
    the remnant of Israel."

⁸See, I am going to bring them from the land of the north,
    and gather them from the farthest parts of the earth,
among them the blind and the lame,
    those with child and those in labor, together;
    a great company, they shall return here.
⁹With weeping they shall come,
    and with consolations I will lead them back,
I will let them walk by brooks of water,
    in a straight path in which they shall not stumble;
for I have become a father to Israel,
    and Ephraim is my firstborn.

¹⁰Hear the word of the LORD, O nations,
    and declare it in the coastlands far away;
say, "He who scattered Israel will gather him,
    and will keep him as a shepherd a flock."
¹¹For the LORD has ransomed Jacob,
    and has redeemed him from hands too strong for him.

¹²They shall come and sing aloud on the height of Zion,
    and they shall be radiant over the goodness of the LORD,
over the grain, the wine, and the oil,
    and over the young of the flock and the herd;
their life shall become like a watered garden,
    and they shall never languish again.

¹³Then shall the young women rejoice in the dance,
and the young men and the old shall be merry.
I will turn their mourning into joy,
I will comfort them, and give them gladness for sorrow.
¹⁴I will give the priests their fill of fatness,
and my people shall be satisfied with my bounty,

says the LORD.

The word of the Lord.

PSALMODY: PSALM 147:12–20

Psalm 147:13–21 LBW/BCP
Alternate Psalmody: Wisdom of Solomon 10:15–21

SECOND READING: EPHESIANS 1:3–14

A reading from Ephesians:

³Blessed be the God and Father of our Lord Jesus Christ,
who has blessed us in Christ
with every spiritual blessing in the heavenly places,
⁴just as he chose us in Christ before the foundation of the world
to be holy and blameless before him in love.
⁵He destined us for adoption as his children through Jesus Christ,
according to the good pleasure of his will,
⁶to the praise of his glorious grace
that he freely bestowed on us in the Beloved.

⁷In him we have redemption through his blood,
the forgiveness of our trespasses,
according to the riches of his grace ⁸that he lavished on us.

With all wisdom and insight
⁹he has made known to us the mystery of his will,
according to his good pleasure that he set forth in Christ,
¹⁰as a plan for the fullness of time,
to gather up all things in him,
things in heaven and things on earth.

¹¹In Christ we have also obtained an inheritance,
having been destined according to the purpose of him
who accomplishes all things according to his counsel and will,
¹²so that we, who were the first to set our hope on Christ,
might live for the praise of his glory.
¹³In him you also, when you had heard the word of truth,
the gospel of your salvation, and had believed in him,
were marked with the seal of the promised Holy Spirit;

¹⁴this is the pledge of our inheritance
toward redemption as God's own people,
to the praise of his glory.

The word of the Lord.

GOSPEL: John 1:[1–9] 10–18

The Holy Gospel according to John, the first chapter.

[¹In the beginning was the Word,
and the Word was with God,
and the Word was God.
²He was in the beginning with God.
³All things came into being through him,
and without him not one thing came into being.
What has come into being ⁴in him was life,
and the life was the light of all people.
⁵The light shines in the darkness,
and the darkness did not overcome it.

⁶There was a man sent from God, whose name was John.
⁷He came as a witness to testify to the light,
so that all might believe through him.
⁸He himself was not the light,
but he came to testify to the light.
⁹The true light, which enlightens everyone,
was coming into the world.]

¹⁰He was in the world,
and the world came into being through him;
yet the world did not know him.
¹¹He came to what was his own,
and his own people did not accept him.
¹²But to all who received him,
who believed in his name,
he gave power to become children of God,
¹³who were born, not of blood or of the will of the flesh
     or of the will of man,
but of God.

¹⁴And the Word became flesh and lived among us,
and we have seen his glory,
the glory as of a father's only son,
full of grace and truth.

^{15}(John testified to him and cried out,
"This was he of whom I said,
'He who comes after me ranks ahead of me because he was before me.' ")
^{16}From his fullness we have all received,
grace upon grace.
^{17}The law indeed was given through Moses;
grace and truth came through Jesus Christ.

^{18}No one has ever seen God.
It is God the only Son,
who is close to the Father's heart,
who has made him known.

The Gospel of the Lord.

SEASON OF EPIPHANY

The Epiphany of Our Lord

JANUARY 6

FIRST READING: Isaiah 60:1–6

A reading from Isaiah:

¹Arise, shine; for your light has come,
 and the glory of the Lord has risen upon you.
²For darkness shall cover the earth,
 and thick darkness the peoples;
but the Lord will arise upon you,
 and his glory will appear over you.
³Nations shall come to your light,
 and kings to the brightness of your dawn.

⁴Lift up your eyes and look around;
 they all gather together, they come to you;
your sons shall come from far away,
 and your daughters shall be carried on their nurses' arms.

⁵Then you shall see and be radiant;
 your heart shall thrill and rejoice,
because the abundance of the sea shall be brought to you,
 the wealth of the nations shall come to you.
⁶A multitude of camels shall cover you,
 the young camels of Midian and Ephah;
 all those from Sheba shall come.
They shall bring gold and frankincense,
 and shall proclaim the praise of the Lord.

The word of the Lord.

PSALMODY: Psalm 72:1–7, 10–14

SECOND READING: Ephesians 3:1–12

A reading from Ephesians:

^{1}This is the reason that I Paul am a prisoner for Christ Jesus
for the sake of you Gentiles—
^{2}for surely you have already heard of the commission of God's grace
that was given me for you,
^{3}and how the mystery was made known to me by revelation,
as I wrote above in a few words,
^{4}a reading of which will enable you
to perceive my understanding of the mystery of Christ.

^{5}In former generations this mystery was not made known to humankind,
as it has now been revealed to his holy apostles and prophets by the Spirit:
^{6}that is, the Gentiles have become fellow heirs,
members of the same body,
and sharers in the promise in Christ Jesus through the gospel.

^{7}Of this gospel I have become a servant
according to the gift of God's grace
that was given me by the working of his power.
^{8}Although I am the very least of all the saints,
this grace was given to me
to bring to the Gentiles the news of the boundless riches of Christ,
^{9}and to make everyone see
what is the plan of the mystery hidden for ages in God
who created all things;
^{10}so that through the church
the wisdom of God in its rich variety
might now be made known to the rulers and authorities
in the heavenly places.
^{11}This was in accordance with the eternal purpose
that he has carried out in Christ Jesus our Lord,
^{12}in whom we have access to God
in boldness and confidence through faith in him.

The word of the Lord.

The Holy Gospel according to Matthew, the second chapter.

[1]In the time of King Herod,
after Jesus was born in Bethlehem of Judea,
wise men from the East came to Jerusalem, [2]asking,
"Where is the child who has been born king of the Jews?
For we observed his star at its rising,
and have come to pay him homage."

[3]When King Herod heard this, he was frightened,
and all Jerusalem with him;
[4]and calling together all the chief priests and scribes of the people,
he inquired of them where the Messiah was to be born.
[5]They told him,
"In Bethlehem of Judea;
for so it has been written by the prophet:

> [6]'And you, Bethlehem, in the land of Judah,
>   are by no means least among the rulers of Judah;
> for from you shall come a ruler
>   who is to shepherd my people Israel.' "

[7]Then Herod secretly called for the wise men
and learned from them the exact time when the star had appeared.
[8]Then he sent them to Bethlehem, saying,
"Go and search diligently for the child;
and when you have found him,
bring me word so that I may also go and pay him homage."

[9]When they had heard the king, they set out;
and there, ahead of them,
went the star that they had seen at its rising,
until it stopped over the place where the child was.
[10]When they saw that the star had stopped,
they were overwhelmed with joy.

[11]On entering the house, they saw the child with Mary his mother;
and they knelt down and paid him homage.
Then, opening their treasure chests,
they offered him gifts of gold, frankincense, and myrrh.

[12]And having been warned in a dream not to return to Herod,
they left for their own country by another road.

The Gospel of the Lord.

THE BAPTISM OF OUR LORD
(First Sunday after the Epiphany)

JANUARY 11, 1998   JANUARY 7, 2001   JANUARY 11, 2004

FIRST READING: ISAIAH 43:1–7

A reading from Isaiah:

¹But now thus says the LORD,
 he who created you, O Jacob,
 he who formed you, O Israel:
Do not fear, for I have redeemed you;
 I have called you by name, you are mine.
²When you pass through the waters, I will be with you;
 and through the rivers, they shall not overwhelm you;
when you walk through fire you shall not be burned,
 and the flame shall not consume you.

³For I am the LORD your God,
 the Holy One of Israel, your Savior.
I give Egypt as your ransom,
 Ethiopia and Seba in exchange for you.
⁴Because you are precious in my sight,
 and honored, and I love you,
I give people in return for you,
 nations in exchange for your life.

⁵Do not fear, for I am with you;
 I will bring your offspring from the east,
 and from the west I will gather you;
⁶I will say to the north, "Give them up,"
 and to the south, "Do not withhold;
bring my sons from far away
 and my daughters from the end of the earth—
⁷everyone who is called by my name,
 whom I created for my glory,
 whom I formed and made."

The word of the Lord.

PSALMODY: PSALM 29

SECOND READING: ACTS 8:14–17

A reading from Acts:

¹⁴Now when the apostles at Jerusalem
heard that Samaria had accepted the word of God,
they sent Peter and John to them.
¹⁵The two went down and prayed for them
that they might receive the Holy Spirit
¹⁶(for as yet the Spirit had not come upon any of them;
they had only been baptized in the name of the Lord Jesus).
¹⁷Then Peter and John laid their hands on them,
and they received the Holy Spirit.

The word of the Lord.

GOSPEL: LUKE 3:15–17, 21–22

The Holy Gospel according to Luke, the third chapter.

¹⁵As the people were filled with expectation,
and all were questioning in their hearts concerning John,
whether he might be the Messiah,
¹⁶John answered all of them by saying,
"I baptize you with water;
but one who is more powerful than I is coming;
I am not worthy to untie the thong of his sandals.
He will baptize you with the Holy Spirit and fire.
¹⁷His winnowing fork is in his hand,
to clear his threshing floor and to gather the wheat into his granary;
but the chaff he will burn with unquenchable fire."

²¹Now when all the people were baptized,
and when Jesus also had been baptized and was praying,
the heaven was opened,
²²and the Holy Spirit descended upon him in bodily form like a dove.
And a voice came from heaven,
"You are my Son, the Beloved;
with you I am well pleased."

The Gospel of the Lord.

Second Sunday after the Epiphany

JANUARY 18, 1998   JANUARY 14, 2001   JANUARY 18, 2004

FIRST READING: Isaiah 62:1–5

A reading from Isaiah:

¹For Zion's sake I will not keep silent,
    and for Jerusalem's sake I will not rest,
until her vindication shines out like the dawn,
    and her salvation like a burning torch.
²The nations shall see your vindication,
    and all the kings your glory;
and you shall be called by a new name
    that the mouth of the Lord will give.

³You shall be a crown of beauty in the hand of the Lord,
    and a royal diadem in the hand of your God.
⁴You shall no more be termed Forsaken,
    and your land shall no more be termed Desolate;
but you shall be called My Delight Is in Her,
    and your land Married;
for the Lord delights in you,
    and your land shall be married.
⁵For as a young man marries a young woman,
    so shall your builder marry you,
and as the bridegroom rejoices over the bride,
    so shall your God rejoice over you.

The word of the Lord.

PSALMODY: Psalm 36:5–10

A reading from First Corinthians:

[1]Now concerning spiritual gifts, brothers and sisters,
I do not want you to be uninformed.
[2]You know that when you were pagans,
you were enticed and led astray to idols that could not speak.
[3]Therefore I want you to understand
that no one speaking by the Spirit of God ever says "Let Jesus be cursed!"
and no one can say "Jesus is Lord" except by the Holy Spirit.

[4]Now there are varieties of gifts, but the same Spirit;
[5]and there are varieties of services, but the same Lord;
[6]and there are varieties of activities,
but it is the same God who activates all of them in everyone.
[7]To each is given the manifestation of the Spirit for the common good.
[8]To one is given through the Spirit the utterance of wisdom,
and to another the utterance of knowledge according to the same Spirit,
[9]to another faith by the same Spirit,
to another gifts of healing by the one Spirit,
[10]to another the working of miracles,
to another prophecy,
to another the discernment of spirits,
to another various kinds of tongues,
to another the interpretation of tongues.
[11]All these are activated by one and the same Spirit,
who allots to each one individually just as the Spirit chooses.

The word of the Lord.

GOSPEL: JOHN 2:1–11

The Holy Gospel according to John, the second chapter.

^{1}On the third day there was a wedding in Cana of Galilee,
and the mother of Jesus was there.
^{2}Jesus and his disciples had also been invited to the wedding.
^{3}When the wine gave out, the mother of Jesus said to him,
"They have no wine."
^{4}And Jesus said to her, "Woman, what concern is that to you and to me?
My hour has not yet come."
^{5}His mother said to the servants, "Do whatever he tells you."

^{6}Now standing there were six stone water jars for the Jewish rites of
        purification,
each holding twenty or thirty gallons.
^{7}Jesus said to them, "Fill the jars with water."
And they filled them up to the brim.
^{8}He said to them, "Now draw some out, and take it to the chief steward."
So they took it.
^{9}When the steward tasted the water that had become wine,
and did not know where it came from
(though the servants who had drawn the water knew),
the steward called the bridegroom ^{10}and said to him,
"Everyone serves the good wine first,
and then the inferior wine after the guests have become drunk.
But you have kept the good wine until now."

^{11}Jesus did this, the first of his signs, in Cana of Galilee,
and revealed his glory;
and his disciples believed in him.

The Gospel of the Lord.

THIRD SUNDAY AFTER THE EPIPHANY

JANUARY 25, 1998   *JANUARY 21, 2001*   *JANUARY 25, 2004*

FIRST READING: NEHEMIAH 8:1–3, 5–6, 8–10

A reading from Nehemiah:

¹When the seventh month came—
the people of Israel being settled in their towns—
all the people gathered together into the square before the Water Gate.
They told the scribe Ezra to bring the book of the law of Moses,
which the LORD had given to Israel.
²Accordingly, the priest Ezra brought the law before the assembly,
both men and women and all who could hear with understanding.
This was on the first day of the seventh month.
³He read from it facing the square before the Water Gate
from early morning until midday,
in the presence of the men and the women and those who could understand;
and the ears of all the people were attentive to the book of the law.

⁵And Ezra opened the book in the sight of all the people,
for he was standing above all the people;
and when he opened it, all the people stood up.
⁶Then Ezra blessed the LORD, the great God,
and all the people answered, "Amen, Amen," lifting up their hands.
Then they bowed their heads
and worshiped the LORD with their faces to the ground.
⁸So they read from the book, from the law of God, with interpretation.
They gave the sense, so that the people understood the reading.

⁹And Nehemiah, who was the governor,
and Ezra the priest and scribe,
and the Levites who taught the people said to all the people,
"This day is holy to the LORD your God; do not mourn or weep."
For all the people wept when they heard the words of the law.
¹⁰Then he said to them,
"Go your way, eat the fat and drink sweet wine
and send portions of them to those for whom nothing is prepared,
for this day is holy to our LORD;

and do not be grieved,
for the joy of the LORD is your strength."

The word of the Lord.

PSALMODY: PSALM 19

SECOND READING: 1 CORINTHIANS 12:12–31a

A reading from First Corinthians:

¹²For just as the body is one and has many members,
and all the members of the body, though many, are one body,
so it is with Christ.
¹³For in the one Spirit we were all baptized into one body—
Jews or Greeks, slaves or free—
and we were all made to drink of one Spirit.

¹⁴Indeed, the body does not consist of one member but of many.
¹⁵If the foot would say, "Because I am not a hand, I do not belong to the body,"
that would not make it any less a part of the body.
¹⁶And if the ear would say, "Because I am not an eye, I do not belong to the
    body,"
that would not make it any less a part of the body.
¹⁷If the whole body were an eye, where would the hearing be?
If the whole body were hearing, where would the sense of smell be?
¹⁸But as it is, God arranged the members in the body,
each one of them, as he chose.
¹⁹If all were a single member, where would the body be?
²⁰As it is, there are many members, yet one body.
²¹The eye cannot say to the hand, "I have no need of you,"
nor again the head to the feet, "I have no need of you."
²²On the contrary,
the members of the body that seem to be weaker are indispensable,
²³and those members of the body that we think less honorable
we clothe with greater honor,
and our less respectable members are treated with greater respect;
²⁴whereas our more respectable members do not need this.
But God has so arranged the body,
giving the greater honor to the inferior member,
²⁵that there may be no dissension within the body,
but the members may have the same care for one another.
²⁶If one member suffers, all suffer together with it;
if one member is honored, all rejoice together with it.

²⁷Now you are the body of Christ and individually members of it.
²⁸And God has appointed in the church first apostles,

second prophets, third teachers;
then deeds of power, then gifts of healing,
forms of assistance, forms of leadership, various kinds of tongues.
29Are all apostles? Are all prophets? Are all teachers?
Do all work miracles? 30Do all possess gifts of healing?
Do all speak in tongues? Do all interpret?
31But strive for the greater gifts.

The word of the Lord.

GOSPEL: LUKE 4:14–21

The Holy Gospel according to Luke, the fourth chapter.

14Then Jesus, filled with the power of the Spirit, returned to Galilee,
and a report about him spread through all the surrounding country.
15He began to teach in their synagogues and was praised by everyone.

16When he came to Nazareth, where he had been brought up,
he went to the synagogue on the sabbath day, as was his custom.
He stood up to read, 17and the scroll of the prophet Isaiah was given to him.
He unrolled the scroll and found the place where it was written:
  18"The Spirit of the Lord is upon me,
      because he has anointed me
        to bring good news to the poor.
  He has sent me to proclaim release to the captives
      and recovery of sight to the blind,
        to let the oppressed go free,
  19to proclaim the year of the Lord's favor."

20And he rolled up the scroll, gave it back to the attendant, and sat down.
The eyes of all in the synagogue were fixed on him.
21Then he began to say to them,
"Today this scripture has been fulfilled in your hearing."

The Gospel of the Lord.

FOURTH SUNDAY AFTER THE EPIPHANY

FEBRUARY 1, 1998   JANUARY 28, 2001   FEBRUARY 1, 2004

FIRST READING: JEREMIAH 1:4–10

A reading from Jeremiah:

⁴Now the word of the LORD came to me saying,
⁵"Before I formed you in the womb I knew you,
and before you were born I consecrated you;
I appointed you a prophet to the nations."
⁶Then I said,
"Ah, Lord GOD! Truly I do not know how to speak, for I am only a boy."
⁷But the LORD said to me,
"Do not say, 'I am only a boy';
for you shall go to all to whom I send you,
and you shall speak whatever I command you.
⁸Do not be afraid of them,
for I am with you to deliver you,
                    says the LORD."
⁹Then the LORD put out his hand and touched my mouth;
and the LORD said to me,
"Now I have put my words in your mouth.
¹⁰See, today I appoint you over nations and over kingdoms,
to pluck up and to pull down,
to destroy and to overthrow,
to build and to plant."

The word of the Lord.

PSALMODY: PSALM 71:1–6

A reading from First Corinthians:

[1]If I speak in the tongues of mortals and of angels, but do not have love,
I am a noisy gong or a clanging cymbal.
[2]And if I have prophetic powers,
and understand all mysteries and all knowledge,
and if I have all faith, so as to remove mountains,
but do not have love, I am nothing.
[3]If I give away all my possessions,
and if I hand over my body so that I may boast,
but do not have love, I gain nothing.

[4]Love is patient; love is kind;
love is not envious or boastful or arrogant [5]or rude.
[6]It does not insist on its own way;
it is not irritable or resentful;
it does not rejoice in wrongdoing, but rejoices in the truth.
[7]It bears all things, believes all things, hopes all things, endures all things.

[8]Love never ends.
But as for prophecies, they will come to an end;
as for tongues, they will cease;
as for knowledge, it will come to an end.
[9]For we know only in part, and we prophesy only in part;
[10]but when the complete comes, the partial will come to an end.
[11]When I was a child, I spoke like a child,
I thought like a child, I reasoned like a child;
when I became an adult, I put an end to childish ways.
[12]For now we see in a mirror, dimly,
but then we will see face to face.
Now I know only in part;
then I will know fully, even as I have been fully known.
[13]And now faith, hope, and love abide, these three;
and the greatest of these is love.

The word of the Lord.

GOSPEL: LUKE 4:21–30

The Holy Gospel according to Luke, the fourth chapter.

[21]Then Jesus began to say to all in the synagogue in Nazareth,
"Today this scripture has been fulfilled in your hearing."
[22]All spoke well of him
and were amazed at the gracious words that came from his mouth.
They said, "Is not this Joseph's son?"
[23]He said to them,
"Doubtless you will quote to me this proverb, 'Doctor, cure yourself!'
And you will say, 'Do here also in your hometown
the things that we have heard you did at Capernaum.' "
[24]And he said,
"Truly I tell you, no prophet is accepted in the prophet's hometown.
[25]But the truth is, there were many widows in Israel in the time of Elijah,
when the heaven was shut up three years and six months,
and there was a severe famine over all the land;
[26]yet Elijah was sent to none of them except to a widow at Zarephath in Sidon.
[27]There were also many lepers in Israel in the time of the prophet Elisha,
and none of them was cleansed except Naaman the Syrian."

[28]When they heard this, all in the synagogue were filled with rage.
[29]They got up, drove him out of the town,
and led him to the brow of the hill on which their town was built,
so that they might hurl him off the cliff.
[30]But he passed through the midst of them and went on his way.

The Gospel of the Lord.

FIFTH SUNDAY AFTER THE EPIPHANY

FEBRUARY 8, 1998   FEBRUARY 4, 2001   FEBRUARY 8, 2004

FIRST READING: ISAIAH 6:1–8 [9–13]

A reading from Isaiah:

¹In the year that King Uzziah died,
I saw the Lord sitting on a throne, high and lofty;
and the hem of his robe filled the temple.
²Seraphs were in attendance above him;
each had six wings:
with two they covered their faces, and with two they covered their feet,
and with two they flew.
³And one called to another and said:
    "Holy, holy, holy is the LORD of hosts;
    the whole earth is full of his glory."
⁴The pivots on the thresholds shook at the voices of those who called,
and the house filled with smoke.
⁵And I said:
"Woe is me! I am lost, for I am a man of unclean lips,
and I live among a people of unclean lips;
yet my eyes have seen the King, the LORD of hosts!"

⁶Then one of the seraphs flew to me,
holding a live coal that had been taken from the altar with a pair of tongs.
⁷The seraph touched my mouth with it and said:
"Now that this has touched your lips,
your guilt has departed and your sin is blotted out."
⁸Then I heard the voice of the Lord saying,
"Whom shall I send, and who will go for us?"
And I said, "Here am I; send me!"

[⁹And he said, "Go and say to this people:
    'Keep listening, but do not comprehend;
    keep looking, but do not understand.'
    ¹⁰Make the mind of this people dull,
        and stop their ears,
        and shut their eyes,
    so that they may not look with their eyes,

> and listen with their ears,
>> and comprehend with their minds,
>>> and turn and be healed."
> ¹¹Then I said, "How long, O Lord?" And he said:
> "Until cities lie waste
>> without inhabitant,
> and houses without people,
>> and the land is utterly desolate;
> ¹²until the L ORD sends everyone far away,
>> and vast is the emptiness in the midst of the land.
> ¹³Even if a tenth part remain in it,
>> it will be burned again,
> like a terebinth or an oak
>> whose stump remains standing
>> when it is felled."
> The holy seed is its stump.]

The word of the Lord.

PSALMODY: P SALM 138

SECOND READING: 1 C ORINTHIANS 15:1–11

A reading from First Corinthians:

¹Now I would remind you, brothers and sisters,
of the good news that I proclaimed to you,
which you in turn received, in which also you stand,
²through which also you are being saved,
if you hold firmly to the message that I proclaimed to you—
unless you have come to believe in vain.

³For I handed on to you as of first importance what I in turn had received:
that Christ died for our sins in accordance with the scriptures,
⁴and that he was buried,
and that he was raised on the third day in accordance with the scriptures,
⁵and that he appeared to Cephas, then to the twelve.
⁶Then he appeared to more than five hundred brothers and sisters at one time,
most of whom are still alive, though some have died.
⁷Then he appeared to James, then to all the apostles.
⁸Last of all, as to one untimely born, he appeared also to me.
⁹For I am the least of the apostles,
unfit to be called an apostle, because I persecuted the church of God.
¹⁰But by the grace of God I am what I am,
and his grace toward me has not been in vain.
On the contrary, I worked harder than any of them—though it was not I,
but the grace of God that is with me.

[11]Whether then it was I or they,
so we proclaim and so you have come to believe.

The word of the Lord.

GOSPEL: LUKE 5:1–11

The Holy Gospel according to Luke, the fifth chapter.

[1]Once while Jesus was standing beside the lake of Gennesaret,
and the crowd was pressing in on him to hear the word of God,
[2]he saw two boats there at the shore of the lake;
the fishermen had gone out of them and were washing their nets.
[3]He got into one of the boats, the one belonging to Simon,
and asked him to put out a little way from the shore.
Then he sat down and taught the crowds from the boat.

[4]When he had finished speaking, he said to Simon,
"Put out into the deep water and let down your nets for a catch."
[5]Simon answered,
"Master, we have worked all night long but have caught nothing.
Yet if you say so, I will let down the nets."
[6]When they had done this,
they caught so many fish that their nets were beginning to break.
[7]So they signaled their partners in the other boat to come and help them.
And they came and filled both boats, so that they began to sink.
[8]But when Simon Peter saw it, he fell down at Jesus' knees, saying,
"Go away from me, Lord, for I am a sinful man!"
[9]For he and all who were with him
were amazed at the catch of fish that they had taken;
[10]and so also were James and John, sons of Zebedee, who were partners with
    Simon.
Then Jesus said to Simon,
"Do not be afraid; from now on you will be catching people."
[11]When they had brought their boats to shore,
they left everything and followed him.

The Gospel of the Lord.

Sixth Sunday after the Epiphany

PROPER 1

FEBRUARY 15, 1998   FEBRUARY 11, 2001   FEBRUARY 15, 2004

FIRST READING: JEREMIAH 17:5–10

A reading from Jeremiah:

⁵Thus says the LORD:
Cursed are those who trust in mere mortals
  and make mere flesh their strength,
  whose hearts turn away from the LORD.
⁶They shall be like a shrub in the desert,
  and shall not see when relief comes.
They shall live in the parched places of the wilderness,
  in an uninhabited salt land.

⁷Blessed are those who trust in the LORD,
  whose trust is the LORD.
⁸They shall be like a tree planted by water,
  sending out its roots by the stream.
It shall not fear when heat comes,
  and its leaves shall stay green;
in the year of drought it is not anxious,
  and it does not cease to bear fruit.

⁹The heart is devious above all else;
  it is perverse—
  who can understand it?
¹⁰I the LORD test the mind
  and search the heart,
to give to all according to their ways,
  according to the fruit of their doings.

The word of the Lord.

PSALMODY: PSALM 1

SECOND READING: 1 Corinthians 15:12–20

A reading from First Corinthians:

12Now if Christ is proclaimed as raised from the dead,
how can some of you say there is no resurrection of the dead?
13If there is no resurrection of the dead, then Christ has not been raised;
14and if Christ has not been raised,
then our proclamation has been in vain and your faith has been in vain.
15We are even found to be misrepresenting God,
because we testified of God that he raised Christ—
whom he did not raise if it is true that the dead are not raised.
16For if the dead are not raised, then Christ has not been raised.
17If Christ has not been raised,
your faith is futile and you are still in your sins.
18Then those also who have died in Christ have perished.
19If for this life only we have hoped in Christ,
we are of all people most to be pitied.

20But in fact Christ has been raised from the dead,
the first fruits of those who have died.

The word of the Lord.

GOSPEL: Luke 6:17–26

The Holy Gospel according to Luke, the sixth chapter.

17Jesus came down with the twelve and stood on a level place,
with a great crowd of his disciples and a great multitude of people
from all Judea, Jerusalem, and the coast of Tyre and Sidon.
18They had come to hear him and to be healed of their diseases;
and those who were troubled with unclean spirits were cured.
19And all in the crowd were trying to touch him,
for power came out from him and healed all of them.

20Then he looked up at his disciples and said:
    "Blessed are you who are poor,
        for yours is the kingdom of God.
    21"Blessed are you who are hungry now,
        for you will be filled.
    "Blessed are you who weep now,
        for you will laugh.
22"Blessed are you when people hate you,
and when they exclude you, revile you,
and defame you on account of the Son of Man.
23Rejoice in that day and leap for joy,

for surely your reward is great in heaven;
for that is what their ancestors did to the prophets.

    [24]"But woe to you who are rich,
        for you have received your consolation.
    [25]"Woe to you who are full now,
        for you will be hungry.
    "Woe to you who are laughing now,
        for you will mourn and weep.
[26]"Woe to you when all speak well of you,
for that is what their ancestors did to the false prophets."

The Gospel of the Lord.

Seventh Sunday after the Epiphany

PROPER 2

FEBRUARY 18, 2001

FIRST READING: Genesis 45:3–11, 15

A reading from Genesis:

³Joseph said to his brothers,
"I am Joseph. Is my father still alive?"
But his brothers could not answer him,
so dismayed were they at his presence.

⁴Then Joseph said to his brothers, "Come closer to me."
And they came closer.
He said, "I am your brother, Joseph, whom you sold into Egypt.
⁵And now do not be distressed,
or angry with yourselves, because you sold me here;
for God sent me before you to preserve life.
⁶For the famine has been in the land these two years;
and there are five more years in which there will be neither plowing
        nor harvest.
⁷God sent me before you to preserve for you a remnant on earth,
and to keep alive for you many survivors.
⁸So it was not you who sent me here, but God;
he has made me a father to Pharaoh,
and lord of all his house and ruler over all the land of Egypt.
⁹Hurry and go up to my father and say to him,
'Thus says your son Joseph, God has made me lord of all Egypt;
come down to me, do not delay.
¹⁰You shall settle in the land of Goshen, and you shall be near me,
you and your children and your children's children,
as well as your flocks, your herds, and all that you have.
¹¹I will provide for you there—
since there are five more years of famine to come—
so that you and your household, and all that you have,
will not come to poverty.' "

¹⁵And he kissed all his brothers and wept upon them;
and after that his brothers talked with him.

The word of the Lord.

PSALMODY: Psalm 37:1–11, 39–40   *Psalm 37:1–12, 41–42,* LBW/BCP

SECOND READING: 1 Corinthians 15:35–38, 42–50

A reading from First Corinthians:

[35]But someone will ask, "How are the dead raised?
With what kind of body do they come?"
[36]Fool! What you sow does not come to life unless it dies.
[37]And as for what you sow, you do not sow the body that is to be,
but a bare seed, perhaps of wheat or of some other grain.
[38]But God gives it a body as he has chosen,
and to each kind of seed its own body.

[42]So it is with the resurrection of the dead.
What is sown is perishable, what is raised is imperishable.
[43]It is sown in dishonor, it is raised in glory.
It is sown in weakness, it is raised in power.
[44]It is sown a physical body, it is raised a spiritual body.
If there is a physical body, there is also a spiritual body.
[45]Thus it is written, "The first man, Adam, became a living being";
the last Adam became a life-giving spirit.
[46]But it is not the spiritual that is first,
but the physical, and then the spiritual.
[47]The first man was from the earth, a man of dust;
the second man is from heaven.
[48]As was the man of dust, so are those who are of the dust;
and as is the man of heaven, so are those who are of heaven.
[49]Just as we have borne the image of the man of dust,
we will also bear the image of the man of heaven.

[50]What I am saying, brothers and sisters, is this:
flesh and blood cannot inherit the kingdom of God,
nor does the perishable inherit the imperishable.

The word of the Lord.

GOSPEL: Luke 6:27–38

The Holy Gospel according to Luke, the sixth chapter:

Jesus said:
[27]"But I say to you that listen,
Love your enemies,
do good to those who hate you,
[28]bless those who curse you,
pray for those who abuse you.
[29]If anyone strikes you on the cheek, offer the other also;
and from anyone who takes away your coat do not withhold even your shirt.
[30]Give to everyone who begs from you;

and if anyone takes away your goods, do not ask for them again. ³¹Do to others as you would have them do to you.

³²"If you love those who love you, what credit is that to you?
For even sinners love those who love them.
³³If you do good to those who do good to you, what credit is that to you?
For even sinners do the same.
³⁴If you lend to those from whom you hope to receive,
what credit is that to you?
Even sinners lend to sinners, to receive as much again.
³⁵But love your enemies,
do good, and lend, expecting nothing in return.
Your reward will be great, and you will be children of the Most High;
for he is kind to the ungrateful and the wicked.
³⁶Be merciful, just as your Father is merciful.

³⁷"Do not judge, and you will not be judged;
do not condemn, and you will not be condemned.
Forgive, and you will be forgiven;
³⁸give, and it will be given to you.
A good measure, pressed down, shaken together, running over,
will be put into your lap;
for the measure you give will be the measure you get back."

The Gospel of the Lord.

Eighth Sunday after the Epiphany

PROPER 3

FIRST READING: Isaiah 55:10–13   *Alternate Reading: Sirach 27:4–7 (p. 401)*

A reading from Isaiah:

¹⁰For as the rain and the snow come down from heaven,
    and do not return there until they have watered the earth,
making it bring forth and sprout,
    giving seed to the sower and bread to the eater,
¹¹so shall my word be that goes out from my mouth;
    it shall not return to me empty,
but it shall accomplish that which I purpose,
    and succeed in the thing for which I sent it.

¹²For you shall go out in joy,
    and be led back in peace;
the mountains and the hills before you
        shall burst into song,
    and all the trees of the field shall clap their hands.
¹³Instead of the thorn shall come up the cypress;
    instead of the brier shall come up the myrtle;
and it shall be to the LORD for a memorial,
    for an everlasting sign that shall not be cut off.

The word of the Lord.

PSALMODY: Psalm 92:1–4, 12–15   *Psalm 92:1–4, 11–14,* LBW/BCP

SECOND READING: 1 Corinthians 15:51–58

A reading from First Corinthians:

[51]Listen, I will tell you a mystery!
We will not all die, but we will all be changed,
[52]in a moment, in the twinkling of an eye, at the last trumpet.
For the trumpet will sound, and the dead will be raised imperishable,
and we will be changed.
[53]For this perishable body must put on imperishability,
and this mortal body must put on immortality.
[54]When this perishable body puts on imperishability,
and this mortal body puts on immortality,
then the saying that is written will be fulfilled:
    "Death has been swallowed up in victory."
    [55]"Where, O death, is your victory?
        Where, O death, is your sting?"
[56]The sting of death is sin, and the power of sin is the law.
[57]But thanks be to God,
who gives us the victory through our Lord Jesus Christ.

[58]Therefore, my beloved, be steadfast, immovable,
always excelling in the work of the Lord,
because you know that in the Lord your labor is not in vain.

The word of the Lord.

The Holy Gospel according to Luke, the sixth chapter.

[39]Jesus also told them a parable:
"Can a blind person guide a blind person?
Will not both fall into a pit?
[40]A disciple is not above the teacher,
but everyone who is fully qualified will be like the teacher.
[41]Why do you see the speck in your neighbor's eye,
but do not notice the log in your own eye?
[42]Or how can you say to your neighbor,
'Friend, let me take out the speck in your eye,'
when you yourself do not see the log in your own eye?
You hypocrite, first take the log out of your own eye,
and then you will see clearly to take the speck out of your neighbor's eye.

[43]"No good tree bears bad fruit,
nor again does a bad tree bear good fruit;
[44]for each tree is known by its own fruit.
Figs are not gathered from thorns,
nor are grapes picked from a bramble bush.
[45]The good person out of the good treasure of the heart produces good,
and the evil person out of evil treasure produces evil;
for it is out of the abundance of the heart that the mouth speaks.

[46]"Why do you call me 'Lord, Lord,' and do not do what I tell you?
[47]I will show you what someone is like who comes to me,
hears my words, and acts on them.
[48]That one is like a man building a house,
who dug deeply and laid the foundation on rock;
when a flood arose, the river burst against that house but could not shake it,
because it had been well built.
[49]But the one who hears and does not act
is like a man who built a house on the ground without a foundation.
When the river burst against it, immediately it fell,
and great was the ruin of that house."

The Gospel of the Lord.

The Transfiguration of Our Lord
(Last Sunday after the Epiphany)

FEBRUARY 22, 1998   *FEBRUARY 25, 2001*   *FEBRUARY 22, 2004*

FIRST READING: Exodus 34:29–35

A reading from Exodus:

²⁹Moses came down from Mount Sinai.
As he came down from the mountain
with the two tablets of the covenant in his hand,
Moses did not know that the skin of his face shone
because he had been talking with God.
³⁰When Aaron and all the Israelites saw Moses,
the skin of his face was shining,
and they were afraid to come near him.
³¹But Moses called to them;
and Aaron and all the leaders of the congregation returned to him,
and Moses spoke with them.
³²Afterward all the Israelites came near,
and he gave them in commandment
all that the LORD had spoken with him on Mount Sinai.
³³When Moses had finished speaking with them, he put a veil on his face;
³⁴but whenever Moses went in before the LORD to speak with him,
he would take the veil off, until he came out;
and when he came out,
and told the Israelites what he had been commanded,
³⁵the Israelites would see the face of Moses,
that the skin of his face was shining;
and Moses would put the veil on his face again,
until he went in to speak with him.

The word of the Lord.

PSALMODY: Psalm 99

A reading from Second Corinthians:

¹²Since, then, we have such a hope, we act with great boldness,
¹³not like Moses, who put a veil over his face
to keep the people of Israel from gazing at the end of the glory
      that was being set aside.
¹⁴But their minds were hardened.
Indeed, to this very day,
when they hear the reading of the old covenant,
that same veil is still there,
since only in Christ is it set aside.
¹⁵Indeed, to this very day whenever Moses is read,
a veil lies over their minds;
¹⁶but when one turns to the Lord, the veil is removed.
¹⁷Now the Lord is the Spirit,
and where the Spirit of the Lord is, there is freedom.
¹⁸And all of us, with unveiled faces,
seeing the glory of the Lord as though reflected in a mirror,
are being transformed into the same image from one degree of glory to an-
      other;
for this comes from the Lord, the Spirit.

⁴:¹Therefore, since it is by God's mercy that we are engaged in this ministry,
we do not lose heart.
²We have renounced the shameful things that one hides;
we refuse to practice cunning or to falsify God's word;
but by the open statement of the truth
we commend ourselves to the conscience of everyone in the sight of God.

The word of the Lord.

The Holy Gospel according to Luke, the ninth chapter.

28Now about eight days after these sayings
Jesus took with him Peter and John and James,
and went up on the mountain to pray.
29And while he was praying, the appearance of his face changed,
and his clothes became dazzling white.
30Suddenly they saw two men, Moses and Elijah, talking to him.
31They appeared in glory and were speaking of his departure,
which he was about to accomplish at Jerusalem.
32Now Peter and his companions were weighed down with sleep;
but since they had stayed awake,
they saw his glory and the two men who stood with him.
33Just as they were leaving him, Peter said to Jesus,
"Master, it is good for us to be here;
let us make three dwellings, one for you, one for Moses, and one for Elijah"—
not knowing what he said.
34While he was saying this, a cloud came and overshadowed them;
and they were terrified as they entered the cloud.
35Then from the cloud came a voice that said,
"This is my Son, my Chosen; listen to him!"
36When the voice had spoken, Jesus was found alone.
And they kept silent
and in those days told no one any of the things they had seen.

[37On the next day, when they had come down from the mountain,
a great crowd met him.
38Just then a man from the crowd shouted,
"Teacher, I beg you to look at my son; he is my only child.
39Suddenly a spirit seizes him, and all at once he shrieks.
It convulses him until he foams at the mouth;
it mauls him and will scarcely leave him.
40I begged your disciples to cast it out, but they could not."
41Jesus answered, "You faithless and perverse generation,
how much longer must I be with you and bear with you?
Bring your son here."
42While he was coming, the demon dashed him to the ground in convulsions.
But Jesus rebuked the unclean spirit,
healed the boy, and gave him back to his father.
43And all were astounded at the greatness of God.]

The Gospel of the Lord.

SEASON OF LENT

ASH WEDNESDAY

FIRST READING: JOEL 2:1–2, 12–17
Or Isaiah 58:1–12, following

A reading from Joel:

¹Blow the trumpet in Zion;
    sound the alarm on my holy mountain!
Let all the inhabitants of the land tremble,
    for the day of the LORD is coming, it is near—
²a day of darkness and gloom,
    a day of clouds and thick darkness!
Like blackness spread upon the mountains
    a great and powerful army comes;
their like has never been from of old,
    nor will be again after them
    in ages to come.

¹²Yet even now, says the LORD,
    return to me with all your heart,
with fasting, with weeping, and with mourning;
    ¹³rend your hearts and not your clothing.
Return to the LORD, your God,
    for he is gracious and merciful,
slow to anger, and abounding in steadfast love,
    and relents from punishing.
¹⁴Who knows whether he will not turn and relent,
    and leave a blessing behind him,
a grain offering and a drink offering
    for the LORD, your God?

¹⁵Blow the trumpet in Zion;
    sanctify a fast;
call a solemn assembly;
    ¹⁶gather the people.
Sanctify the congregation;
    assemble the aged;
gather the children,
    even infants at the breast.

Let the bridegroom leave his room,
    and the bride her canopy.

¹⁷Between the vestibule and the altar
    let the priests, the ministers of the LORD, weep.
Let them say, "Spare your people, O LORD,
    and do not make your heritage a mockery,
    a byword among the nations.
Why should it be said among the peoples,
    'Where is their God?' "

The word of the Lord.

OR: ISAIAH 58:1–12

A reading from Isaiah:

¹Shout out, do not hold back!
    Lift up your voice like a trumpet!
Announce to my people their rebellion,
    to the house of Jacob their sins.
²Yet day after day they seek me
    and delight to know my ways,
as if they were a nation that practiced righteousness
    and did not forsake the ordinance of their God;
they ask of me righteous judgments,
    they delight to draw near to God.

³"Why do we fast, but you do not see?
    Why humble ourselves, but you do not notice?"
Look, you serve your own interest on your fast day,
    and oppress all your workers.
⁴Look, you fast only to quarrel and to fight
    and to strike with a wicked fist.
Such fasting as you do today
    will not make your voice heard on high.

⁵Is such the fast that I choose,
    a day to humble oneself?
Is it to bow down the head like a bulrush,
    and to lie in sackcloth and ashes?
Will you call this a fast,
    a day acceptable to the LORD?

⁶Is not this the fast that I choose:
    to loose the bonds of injustice,
    to undo the thongs of the yoke,

to let the oppressed go free,
    and to break every yoke?
[7]Is it not to share your bread with the hungry,
    and bring the homeless poor into your house;
when you see the naked, to cover them,
    and not to hide yourself from your own kin?
[8]Then your light shall break forth like the dawn,
    and your healing shall spring up quickly;
your vindicator shall go before you,
    the glory of the LORD shall be your rear guard.
[9]Then you shall call, and the LORD will answer;
    you shall cry for help, and he will say, Here I am.

If you remove the yoke from among you,
    the pointing of the finger, the speaking of evil,
[10]if you offer your food to the hungry
    and satisfy the needs of the afflicted,
then your light shall rise in the darkness
    and your gloom be like the noonday.
[11]The LORD will guide you continually,
    and satisfy your needs in parched places,
    and make your bones strong;
and you shall be like a watered garden,
    like a spring of water,
    whose waters never fail.
[12]Your ancient ruins shall be rebuilt;
    you shall raise up the foundations of many generations;
you shall be called the repairer of the breach,
    the restorer of streets to live in.

The word of the Lord.

PSALMODY: PSALM 51:1–17

Psalm 51:1–18 LBW/BCP

A reading from Second Corinthians:

20bWe entreat you on behalf of Christ,
be reconciled to God.
21For our sake he made him to be sin who knew no sin,
so that in him we might become the righteousness of God.

6:1As we work together with him,
we urge you also not to accept the grace of God in vain.
2For he says,
    "At an acceptable time I have listened to you,
        and on a day of salvation I have helped you."
See, now is the acceptable time;
see, now is the day of salvation!

3We are putting no obstacle in anyone's way,
so that no fault may be found with our ministry,
4but as servants of God we have commended ourselves in every way:
through great endurance,
in afflictions, hardships, calamities,
5beatings, imprisonments, riots,
labors, sleepless nights, hunger;
6by purity, knowledge, patience,
kindness, holiness of spirit, genuine love,
7truthful speech, and the power of God;
with the weapons of righteousness for the right hand and for the left;
8in honor and dishonor,
in ill repute and good repute.
We are treated as impostors, and yet are true;
9as unknown, and yet are well known;
as dying, and see—we are alive;
as punished, and yet not killed;
10as sorrowful, yet always rejoicing;
as poor, yet making many rich;
as having nothing, and yet possessing everything.

The word of the Lord.

GOSPEL: MATTHEW 6:1–6, 16–21

The Holy Gospel according to Matthew, the sixth chapter.

Jesus said to the disciples:
[1]"Beware of practicing your piety before others
in order to be seen by them;
for then you have no reward from your Father in heaven.
[2]So whenever you give alms, do not sound a trumpet before you,
as the hypocrites do in the synagogues and in the streets,
so that they may be praised by others.
Truly I tell you,
they have received their reward.
[3]But when you give alms,
do not let your left hand know what your right hand is doing,
[4]so that your alms may be done in secret;
and your Father who sees in secret will reward you.

[5]"And whenever you pray, do not be like the hypocrites;
for they love to stand and pray in the synagogues and at the street corners,
so that they may be seen by others.
Truly I tell you,
they have received their reward.
[6]But whenever you pray,
go into your room and shut the door
and pray to your Father who is in secret;
and your Father who sees in secret will reward you.

[16]"And whenever you fast, do not look dismal, like the hypocrites,
for they disfigure their faces so as to show others that they are fasting.
Truly I tell you,
they have received their reward.
[17]But when you fast,
put oil on your head and wash your face,
[18]so that your fasting may be seen not by others
but by your Father who is in secret;
and your Father who sees in secret will reward you.

[19]"Do not store up for yourselves treasures on earth,
where moth and rust consume
and where thieves break in and steal;
[20]but store up for yourselves treasures in heaven,
where neither moth nor rust consumes
and where thieves do not break in and steal.
[21]For where your treasure is,
there your heart will be also."

The Gospel of the Lord.

First Sunday in Lent

MARCH 1, 1998   MARCH 4, 2001   FEBRUARY 29, 2004

FIRST READING: Deuteronomy 26:1–11

A reading from Deuteronomy:

¹When you have come into the land
that the Lord your God is giving you as an inheritance to possess,
and you possess it, and settle in it,
²you shall take some of the first of all the fruit of the ground,
which you harvest from the land that the Lord your God is giving you,
and you shall put it in a basket
and go to the place that the Lord your God will choose as a dwelling for his name.
³You shall go to the priest who is in office at that time, and say to him,
"Today I declare to the Lord your God
that I have come into the land that the Lord swore to our ancestors to give us."

⁴When the priest takes the basket from your hand
and sets it down before the altar of the Lord your God,
⁵you shall make this response before the Lord your God:
"A wandering Aramean was my ancestor;
he went down into Egypt and lived there as an alien, few in number,
and there he became a great nation, mighty and populous.
⁶When the Egyptians treated us harshly and afflicted us,
by imposing hard labor on us,
⁷we cried to the Lord, the God of our ancestors;
the Lord heard our voice and saw our affliction, our toil, and our oppression.
⁸The Lord brought us out of Egypt with a mighty hand and an outstretched arm,
with a terrifying display of power, and with signs and wonders;
⁹and he brought us into this place and gave us this land,
a land flowing with milk and honey.
¹⁰So now I bring the first of the fruit of the ground that you, O Lord, have
    given me."
You shall set it down before the Lord your God
and bow down before the Lord your God.
¹¹Then you, together with the Levites and the aliens who reside among you,
shall celebrate with all the bounty
that the Lord your God has given to you and to your house.

The word of the Lord.

PSALMODY: Psalm 91:1–2, 9–16

SECOND READING: ROMANS 10:8b–13

A reading from Romans:

^{8b}"The word is near you,
     on your lips and in your heart"
(that is, the word of faith that we proclaim);
⁹because if you confess with your lips that Jesus is Lord
and believe in your heart that God raised him from the dead,
you will be saved.
¹⁰For one believes with the heart and so is justified,
and one confesses with the mouth and so is saved.
¹¹The scripture says,
"No one who believes in him will be put to shame."
¹²For there is no distinction between Jew and Greek;
the same Lord is Lord of all and is generous to all who call on him.
¹³For, "Everyone who calls on the name of the Lord shall be saved."

The word of the Lord.

GOSPEL: LUKE 4:1–13

The Holy Gospel according to Luke, the fourth chapter.

[1]Jesus, full of the Holy Spirit, returned from the Jordan
and was led by the Spirit in the wilderness,
[2]where for forty days he was tempted by the devil.
He ate nothing at all during those days,
and when they were over, he was famished.
[3]The devil said to him, "If you are the Son of God,
command this stone to become a loaf of bread."
[4]Jesus answered him, "It is written,
'One does not live by bread alone.' "

[5]Then the devil led him up
and showed him in an instant all the kingdoms of the world.
[6]And the devil said to him,
"To you I will give their glory and all this authority;
for it has been given over to me, and I give it to anyone I please.
[7]If you, then, will worship me, it will all be yours."
[8]Jesus answered him,
"It is written,
        'Worship the Lord your God,
            and serve only him.' "

[9]Then the devil took him to Jerusalem,
and placed him on the pinnacle of the temple, saying to him,
"If you are the Son of God, throw yourself down from here,
[10]for it is written,
        'He will command his angels concerning you,
            to protect you,'
[11]and
        'On their hands they will bear you up,
            so that you will not dash your foot against a stone.' "
[12]Jesus answered him, "It is said,
'Do not put the Lord your God to the test.' "
[13]When the devil had finished every test,
he departed from him until an opportune time.

The Gospel of the Lord.

Second Sunday in Lent

MARCH 8, 1998   MARCH 11, 2001   MARCH 7, 2004

FIRST READING: Genesis 15:1–12, 17–18

A reading from Genesis:

¹After these things the word of the Lord came to Abram in a vision,
"Do not be afraid, Abram, I am your shield;
your reward shall be very great."
²But Abram said, "O Lord God,
what will you give me, for I continue childless,
and the heir of my house is Eliezer of Damascus?"
³And Abram said, "You have given me no offspring,
and so a slave born in my house is to be my heir."
⁴But the word of the Lord came to him,
"This man shall not be your heir;
no one but your very own issue shall be your heir."
⁵He brought him outside and said,
"Look toward heaven and count the stars,
if you are able to count them."
Then he said to him,
"So shall your descendants be."
⁶And he believed the Lord;
and the Lord reckoned it to him as righteousness.

⁷Then he said to him,
"I am the Lord who brought you from Ur of the Chaldeans,
to give you this land to possess."
⁸But he said, "O Lord God, how am I to know that I shall possess it?"
⁹He said to him, "Bring me a heifer three years old,
a female goat three years old, a ram three years old,
a turtledove, and a young pigeon."
¹⁰He brought him all these and cut them in two,
laying each half over against the other;
but he did not cut the birds in two.
¹¹And when birds of prey came down on the carcasses,
Abram drove them away.
¹²As the sun was going down, a deep sleep fell upon Abram,
and a deep and terrifying darkness descended upon him.

¹⁷When the sun had gone down and it was dark,

SECOND SUNDAY IN LENT   73

a smoking fire pot and a flaming torch passed between these pieces. ¹⁸On that day the Lord made a covenant with Abram, saying, "To your descendants I give this land, from the river of Egypt to the great river, the river Euphrates."

The word of the Lord.

PSALMODY: Psalm 27

SECOND READING: Philippians 3:17—4:1

A reading from Philippians:

¹⁷Brothers and sisters, join in imitating me, and observe those who live according to the example you have in us. ¹⁸For many live as enemies of the cross of Christ; I have often told you of them, and now I tell you even with tears. ¹⁹Their end is destruction; their god is the belly; and their glory is in their shame; their minds are set on earthly things. ²⁰But our citizenship is in heaven, and it is from there that we are expecting a Savior, the Lord Jesus Christ. ²¹He will transform the body of our humiliation that it may be conformed to the body of his glory, by the power that also enables him to make all things subject to himself.

⁴:¹Therefore, my brothers and sisters, whom I love and long for, my joy and crown, stand firm in the Lord in this way, my beloved.

The word of the Lord.

The Holy Gospel according to Luke, the 13th chapter.

[31]At that very hour some Pharisees came and said to Jesus,
"Get away from here, for Herod wants to kill you."
[32]He said to them, "Go and tell that fox for me,
'Listen, I am casting out demons and performing cures today and tomorrow,
and on the third day I finish my work.
[33]Yet today, tomorrow, and the next day I must be on my way,
because it is impossible for a prophet to be killed outside of Jerusalem.'

[34]"Jerusalem, Jerusalem,
the city that kills the prophets and stones those who are sent to it!
How often have I desired to gather your children together
as a hen gathers her brood under her wings,
and you were not willing!
[35]See, your house is left to you.
And I tell you, you will not see me until the time comes when you say,
'Blessed is the one who comes in the name of the Lord.'"

The Gospel of the Lord.

THIRD SUNDAY IN LENT

MARCH 15, 1998   MARCH 18, 2001   MARCH 14, 2004

FIRST READING: Isaiah 55:1–9

A reading from Isaiah:

¹Ho, everyone who thirsts,
     come to the waters;
and you that have no money,
     come, buy and eat!
Come, buy wine and milk
     without money and without price.
²Why do you spend your money for that which is not bread,
     and your labor for that which does not satisfy?
Listen carefully to me, and eat what is good,
     and delight yourselves in rich food.
³Incline your ear, and come to me;
     listen, so that you may live.
I will make with you an everlasting covenant,
     my steadfast, sure love for David.
⁴See, I made him a witness to the peoples,
     a leader and commander for the peoples.
⁵See, you shall call nations that you do not know,
     and nations that do not know you shall run to you,
because of the Lord your God, the Holy One of Israel,
     for he has glorified you.

⁶Seek the Lord while he may be found,
     call upon him while he is near;
⁷let the wicked forsake their way,
     and the unrighteous their thoughts;
let them return to the Lord, that he may have mercy on them,
     and to our God, for he will abundantly pardon.
⁸For my thoughts are not your thoughts,
     nor are your ways my ways, says the Lord.
⁹For as the heavens are higher than the earth,
     so are my ways higher than your ways
     and my thoughts than your thoughts.

The word of the Lord.

PSALMODY: Psalm 63:1–8

SECOND READING: 1 CORINTHIANS 10:1–13

A reading from First Corinthians:

¹I do not want you to be unaware, brothers and sisters,
that our ancestors were all under the cloud,
and all passed through the sea,
²and all were baptized into Moses in the cloud and in the sea,
³and all ate the same spiritual food,
⁴and all drank the same spiritual drink.
For they drank from the spiritual rock that followed them,
and the rock was Christ.
⁵Nevertheless, God was not pleased with most of them,
and they were struck down in the wilderness.

⁶Now these things occurred as examples for us,
so that we might not desire evil as they did.
⁷Do not become idolaters as some of them did;
as it is written, "The people sat down to eat and drink,
and they rose up to play."
⁸We must not indulge in sexual immorality as some of them did,
and twenty-three thousand fell in a single day.
⁹We must not put Christ to the test, as some of them did,
and were destroyed by serpents.
¹⁰And do not complain as some of them did,
and were destroyed by the destroyer.
¹¹These things happened to them to serve as an example,
and they were written down to instruct us,
on whom the ends of the ages have come.
¹²So if you think you are standing, watch out that you do not fall.
¹³No testing has overtaken you that is not common to everyone.
God is faithful,
and he will not let you be tested beyond your strength,
but with the testing he will also provide the way out
so that you may be able to endure it.

The word of the Lord.

GOSPEL: LUKE 13:1–9

The Holy Gospel according to Luke, the 13th chapter.

[1]At that very time there were some present who told him about the Galileans whose blood Pilate had mingled with their sacrifices.
[2]Jesus asked them,
"Do you think that because these Galileans suffered in this way
they were worse sinners than all other Galileans?
[3]No, I tell you; but unless you repent, you will all perish as they did.
[4]Or those eighteen who were killed when the tower of Siloam fell on them—
do you think that they were worse offenders than all the others living in
       Jerusalem?
[5]No, I tell you; but unless you repent, you will all perish just as they did."

[6]Then he told this parable:
"A man had a fig tree planted in his vineyard;
and he came looking for fruit on it and found none.
[7]So he said to the gardener, 'See here!
For three years I have come looking for fruit on this fig tree,
and still I find none.
Cut it down! Why should it be wasting the soil?'
[8]He replied, 'Sir, let it alone for one more year,
until I dig around it and put manure on it.
[9]If it bears fruit next year, well and good;
but if not, you can cut it down.' "

The Gospel of the Lord.

FOURTH SUNDAY IN LENT

MARCH 22, 1998　　*MARCH 25, 2001*　　*MARCH 21, 2004*

FIRST READING: JOSHUA 5:9–12

A reading from Joshua:

⁹The LORD said to Joshua,
"Today I have rolled away from you the disgrace of Egypt."
And so that place is called Gilgal to this day.

¹⁰While the Israelites were camped in Gilgal
they kept the passover in the evening on the fourteenth day of the month
in the plains of Jericho.
¹¹On the day after the passover, on that very day,
they ate the produce of the land, unleavened cakes and parched grain.
¹²The manna ceased on the day they ate the produce of the land,
and the Israelites no longer had manna;
they ate the crops of the land of Canaan that year.

The word of the Lord.

PSALMODY: PSALM 32

SECOND READING: 2 Corinthians 5:16–21

A reading from Second Corinthians:

16From now on, therefore, we regard no one from a human point of view;
even though we once knew Christ from a human point of view,
we know him no longer in that way.
17So if anyone is in Christ, there is a new creation:
everything old has passed away;
see, everything has become new!
18All this is from God, who reconciled us to himself through Christ,
and has given us the ministry of reconciliation;
19that is, in Christ God was reconciling the world to himself,
not counting their trespasses against them,
and entrusting the message of reconciliation to us.
20So we are ambassadors for Christ,
since God is making his appeal through us;
we entreat you on behalf of Christ,
be reconciled to God.
21For our sake he made him to be sin who knew no sin,
so that in him we might become the righteousness of God.

The word of the Lord.

GOSPEL: Luke 15:1–3, 11b–32

The Holy Gospel according to Luke, the 15th chapter.

1Now all the tax collectors and sinners were coming near to listen to Jesus.
2And the Pharisees and the scribes were grumbling and saying,
"This fellow welcomes sinners and eats with them."

3So he told them this parable:
11"There was a man who had two sons.
12The younger of them said to his father,
'Father, give me the share of the property that will belong to me.'
So he divided his property between them.
13A few days later the younger son gathered all he had
and traveled to a distant country,
and there he squandered his property in dissolute living.
14When he had spent everything,
a severe famine took place throughout that country,
and he began to be in need.
15So he went and hired himself out to one of the citizens of that country,
who sent him to his fields to feed the pigs.
16He would gladly have filled himself with the pods that the pigs were eating;
and no one gave him anything.
17But when he came to himself he said,

'How many of my father's hired hands have bread enough and to spare,
but here I am dying of hunger!
[18]I will get up and go to my father, and I will say to him,
"Father, I have sinned against heaven and before you;
[19]I am no longer worthy to be called your son;
treat me like one of your hired hands." '
[20]So he set off and went to his father.
But while he was still far off,
his father saw him and was filled with compassion;
he ran and put his arms around him and kissed him.
[21]Then the son said to him,
'Father, I have sinned against heaven and before you;
I am no longer worthy to be called your son.'
[22]But the father said to his slaves,
'Quickly, bring out a robe—the best one—and put it on him;
put a ring on his finger and sandals on his feet.
[23]And get the fatted calf and kill it, and let us eat and celebrate;
[24]for this son of mine was dead and is alive again;
he was lost and is found!'
And they began to celebrate.

[25]"Now his elder son was in the field;
and when he came and approached the house, he heard music and dancing.
[26]He called one of the slaves and asked what was going on.
[27]He replied, 'Your brother has come,
and your father has killed the fatted calf,
because he has got him back safe and sound.'
[28]Then he became angry and refused to go in.
His father came out and began to plead with him.
[29]But he answered his father,
'Listen! For all these years I have been working like a slave for you,
and I have never disobeyed your command;
yet you have never given me even a young goat
so that I might celebrate with my friends.
[30]But when this son of yours came back,
who has devoured your property with prostitutes,
you killed the fatted calf for him!'
[31]Then the father said to him,
'Son, you are always with me, and all that is mine is yours.
[32]But we had to celebrate and rejoice,
because this brother of yours was dead and has come to life;
he was lost and has been found.' "

The Gospel of the Lord.

FIFTH SUNDAY IN LENT

MARCH 29, 1998 • APRIL 1, 2001 • MARCH 28, 2004

FIRST READING: Isaiah 43:16–21

A reading from Isaiah:

¹⁶Thus says the LORD,
  who makes a way in the sea,
  a path in the mighty waters,
¹⁷who brings out chariot and horse,
  army and warrior;
they lie down, they cannot rise,
  they are extinguished, quenched like a wick:
¹⁸Do not remember the former things,
  or consider the things of old.
¹⁹I am about to do a new thing;
  now it springs forth, do you not perceive it?
I will make a way in the wilderness
  and rivers in the desert.
²⁰The wild animals will honor me,
  the jackals and the ostriches;
for I give water in the wilderness,
  rivers in the desert,
to give drink to my chosen people,
  ²¹the people whom I formed for myself
so that they might declare my praise.

The word of the Lord.

PSALMODY: Psalm 126

SECOND READING: PHILIPPIANS 3:4b–14

A reading from Philippians:

[4b]If anyone else has reason to be confident in the flesh, I have more:
[5]circumcised on the eighth day,
a member of the people of Israel, of the tribe of Benjamin,
a Hebrew born of Hebrews;
as to the law, a Pharisee; [6]as to zeal, a persecutor of the church;
as to righteousness under the law, blameless.

[7]Yet whatever gains I had,
these I have come to regard as loss because of Christ.
[8]More than that, I regard everything as loss
because of the surpassing value of knowing Christ Jesus my Lord.
For his sake I have suffered the loss of all things,
and I regard them as rubbish,
in order that I may gain Christ [9]and be found in him,
not having a righteousness of my own that comes from the law,
but one that comes through faith in Christ,
the righteousness from God based on faith.
[10]I want to know Christ and the power of his resurrection
and the sharing of his sufferings by becoming like him in his death,
[11]if somehow I may attain the resurrection from the dead.

[12]Not that I have already obtained this or have already reached the goal
but I press on to make it my own,
because Christ Jesus has made me his own.
[13]Beloved, I do not consider that I have made it my own but this one thing I do:
forgetting what lies behind and straining forward to what lies ahead,
[14]I press on toward the goal for the prize of the heavenly call of God in Christ
   Jesus.

The word of the Lord.

GOSPEL: JOHN 12:1–8

The Holy Gospel according to John, the twelfth chapter.

[1]Six days before the Passover Jesus came to Bethany,
the home of Lazarus, whom he had raised from the dead.
[2]There they gave a dinner for him.
Martha served, and Lazarus was one of those at the table with him.
[3]Mary took a pound of costly perfume made of pure nard,
anointed Jesus' feet, and wiped them with her hair.
The house was filled with the fragrance of the perfume.
[4]But Judas Iscariot, one of his disciples
(the one who was about to betray him), said,
[5]"Why was this perfume not sold for three hundred denarii
and the money given to the poor?"
[6](He said this not because he cared about the poor,
but because he was a thief;
he kept the common purse and used to steal what was put into it.)
[7]Jesus said, "Leave her alone.
She bought it so that she might keep it for the day of my burial.
[8]You always have the poor with you,
but you do not always have me."

The Gospel of the Lord.

HOLY WEEK

SUNDAY OF THE PASSION/PALM SUNDAY
Liturgy of the Palms

APRIL 5, 1998   APRIL 8, 2001   APRIL 4, 2004

GOSPEL: LUKE 19:28–40

The Holy Gospel according to Luke, the 19th chapter.

28Jesus went on ahead, going up to Jerusalem.
29When he had come near Bethphage and Bethany,
at the place called the Mount of Olives,
he sent two of the disciples, 30saying,
"Go into the village ahead of you,
and as you enter it you will find tied there a colt that has never been ridden.
Untie it and bring it here.
31If anyone asks you, 'Why are you untying it?'
just say this, 'The Lord needs it.' "
32So those who were sent departed and found it as he had told them.
33As they were untying the colt, its owners asked them,
"Why are you untying the colt?"
34They said, "The Lord needs it."

35Then they brought it to Jesus;
and after throwing their cloaks on the colt, they set Jesus on it.
36As he rode along, people kept spreading their cloaks on the road.
37As he was now approaching the path down from the Mount of Olives,
the whole multitude of the disciples began to praise God joyfully with a loud
        voice
for all the deeds of power that they had seen, 38saying,
    "Blessed is the king
        who comes in the name of the Lord!
    Peace in heaven,
        and glory in the highest heaven!"
39Some of the Pharisees in the crowd said to him,
"Teacher, order your disciples to stop."
40He answered,
"I tell you, if these were silent, the stones would shout out."

The Gospel of the Lord.

SUNDAY OF THE PASSION/PALM SUNDAY
Liturgy of the Passion

APRIL 5, 1998   APRIL 8, 2001   APRIL 4, 2004

FIRST READING: ISAIAH 50:4–9a

A reading from Isaiah:

⁴The Lord GOD has given me
  the tongue of a teacher,
that I may know how to sustain
  the weary with a word.
Morning by morning he wakens—
  wakens my ear
  to listen as those who are taught.
⁵The Lord GOD has opened my ear,
  and I was not rebellious,
  I did not turn backward.
⁶I gave my back to those who struck me,
  and my cheeks to those who pulled out the beard;
I did not hide my face
  from insult and spitting.

⁷The Lord GOD helps me;
  therefore I have not been disgraced;
therefore I have set my face like flint,
  and I know that I shall not be put to shame;
  ⁸he who vindicates me is near.
Who will contend with me?
  Let us stand up together.
Who are my adversaries?
  Let them confront me.
⁹It is the Lord GOD who helps me;
  who will declare me guilty?

The word of the Lord.

PSALMODY: PSALM 31:9–16

SECOND READING: PHILIPPIANS 2:5–11

A reading from Philippians:

[5]Let the same mind be in you that was in Christ Jesus,
    [6]who, though he was in the form of God,
        did not regard equality with God
        as something to be exploited,
    [7]but emptied himself,
        taking the form of a slave,
        being born in human likeness.
And being found in human form,
    [8]he humbled himself
        and became obedient to the point of death —
        even death on a cross.

[9]Therefore God also highly exalted him
    and gave him the name
    that is above every name,
[10]so that at the name of Jesus
    every knee should bend,
    in heaven and on earth and under the earth,
[11]and every tongue should confess
    that Jesus Christ is Lord,
    to the glory of God the Father.

The word of the Lord.

GOSPEL: LUKE 22:14—23:56

Or Luke 23:1–49, following

The Holy Gospel according to Luke, the 22nd and 23rd chapters.

[14]When the hour came, Jesus took his place at the table,
and the apostles with him.
[15]He said to them,
"I have eagerly desired to eat this Passover with you before I suffer;
[16]for I tell you, I will not eat it until it is fulfilled in the kingdom of God."
[17]Then he took a cup, and after giving thanks he said,
"Take this and divide it among yourselves;
[18]for I tell you that from now on
I will not drink of the fruit of the vine until the kingdom of God comes."
[19]Then he took a loaf of bread,
and when he had given thanks, he broke it and gave it to them, saying,
"This is my body, which is given for you.
Do this in remembrance of me."
[20]And he did the same with the cup after supper, saying,
"This cup that is poured out for you is the new covenant in my blood.
[21]But see, the one who betrays me is with me, and his hand is on the table.
[22]For the Son of Man is going as it has been determined,
but woe to that one by whom he is betrayed!"
[23]Then they began to ask one another which one of them it could be who
would do this.

[24]A dispute also arose among them
as to which one of them was to be regarded as the greatest.
[25]But he said to them, "The kings of the Gentiles lord it over them;
and those in authority over them are called benefactors.
[26]But not so with you;
rather the greatest among you must become like the youngest,
and the leader like one who serves.
[27]For who is greater, the one who is at the table or the one who serves?
Is it not the one at the table?
But I am among you as one who serves.

[28]"You are those who have stood by me in my trials;
[29]and I confer on you, just as my Father has conferred on me, a kingdom,
[30]so that you may eat and drink at my table in my kingdom,
and you will sit on thrones judging the twelve tribes of Israel.

[31]"Simon, Simon, listen!
Satan has demanded to sift all of you like wheat,
[32]but I have prayed for you that your own faith may not fail;
and you, when once you have turned back, strengthen your brothers."
[33]And he said to him,
"Lord, I am ready to go with you to prison and to death!"
[34]Jesus said, "I tell you, Peter, the cock will not crow this day,
until you have denied three times that you know me."

35He said to them,
"When I sent you out without a purse, bag, or sandals,
did you lack anything?"
They said, "No, not a thing."
36He said to them, "But now, the one who has a purse must take it,
and likewise a bag.
And the one who has no sword must sell his cloak and buy one.
37For I tell you, this scripture must be fulfilled in me,
'And he was counted among the lawless';
and indeed what is written about me is being fulfilled."
38They said, "Lord, look, here are two swords."
He replied, "It is enough."

39He came out and went, as was his custom, to the Mount of Olives;
and the disciples followed him.
40When he reached the place, he said to them,
"Pray that you may not come into the time of trial."
41Then he withdrew from them about a stone's throw, knelt down, and prayed,
42"Father, if you are willing, remove this cup from me;
yet, not my will but yours be done."
[43Then an angel from heaven appeared to him and gave him strength.
44In his anguish he prayed more earnestly,
and his sweat became like great drops of blood falling down on the ground.]
45When he got up from prayer,
he came to the disciples and found them sleeping because of grief,
46and he said to them, "Why are you sleeping?
Get up and pray that you may not come into the time of trial."

47While he was still speaking, suddenly a crowd came,
and the one called Judas, one of the twelve, was leading them.
He approached Jesus to kiss him;
48but Jesus said to him,
"Judas, is it with a kiss that you are betraying the Son of Man?"
49When those who were around him saw what was coming, they asked,
"Lord, should we strike with the sword?"
50Then one of them struck the slave of the high priest and cut off his right ear.
51But Jesus said, "No more of this!"
And he touched his ear and healed him.
52Then Jesus said to the chief priests, the officers of the temple police,
and the elders who had come for him,
"Have you come out with swords and clubs as if I were a bandit?
53When I was with you day after day in the temple,
you did not lay hands on me.
But this is your hour, and the power of darkness!"

54Then they seized him and led him away,
bringing him into the high priest's house.
But Peter was following at a distance.

⁵⁵When they had kindled a fire in the middle of the courtyard
and sat down together, Peter sat among them.
⁵⁶Then a servant-girl, seeing him in the firelight, stared at him and said,
"This man also was with him."
⁵⁷But he denied it, saying, "Woman, I do not know him."
⁵⁸A little later someone else, on seeing him, said,
"You also are one of them."
But Peter said, "Man, I am not!"
⁵⁹Then about an hour later still another kept insisting,
"Surely this man also was with him; for he is a Galilean."
⁶⁰But Peter said, "Man, I do not know what you are talking about!"
At that moment, while he was still speaking, the cock crowed.
⁶¹The Lord turned and looked at Peter.
Then Peter remembered the word of the Lord, how he had said to him,
"Before the cock crows today, you will deny me three times."
⁶²And he went out and wept bitterly.

⁶³Now the men who were holding Jesus began to mock him and beat him;
⁶⁴they also blindfolded him and kept asking him,
"Prophesy! Who is it that struck you?"
⁶⁵They kept heaping many other insults on him.

⁶⁶When day came, the assembly of the elders of the people,
both chief priests and scribes, gathered together,
and they brought him to their council.
⁶⁷They said, "If you are the Messiah, tell us."
He replied, "If I tell you, you will not believe;
⁶⁸and if I question you, you will not answer.
⁶⁹But from now on
the Son of Man will be seated at the right hand of the power of God."
⁷⁰All of them asked, "Are you, then, the Son of God?"
He said to them, "You say that I am."
⁷¹Then they said, "What further testimony do we need?
We have heard it ourselves from his own lips!"

²³:¹Then the assembly rose as a body and brought Jesus before Pilate.
²They began to accuse him, saying,
"We found this man perverting our nation,
forbidding us to pay taxes to the emperor,
and saying that he himself is the Messiah, a king."
³Then Pilate asked him, "Are you the king of the Jews?"
He answered, "You say so."
⁴Then Pilate said to the chief priests and the crowds,
"I find no basis for an accusation against this man."
⁵But they were insistent and said,
"He stirs up the people by teaching throughout all Judea,
from Galilee where he began even to this place."

⁶When Pilate heard this, he asked whether the man was a Galilean.
⁷And when he learned that he was under Herod's jurisdiction,
he sent him off to Herod, who was himself in Jerusalem at that time.
⁸When Herod saw Jesus, he was very glad,
for he had been wanting to see him for a long time,
because he had heard about him and was hoping to see him perform
        some sign.
⁹He questioned him at some length, but Jesus gave him no answer.
¹⁰The chief priests and the scribes stood by, vehemently accusing him.
¹¹Even Herod with his soldiers treated him with contempt and mocked him;
then he put an elegant robe on him, and sent him back to Pilate.
¹²That same day Herod and Pilate became friends with each other;
before this they had been enemies.

¹³Pilate then called together the chief priests, the leaders, and the people,
¹⁴and said to them,
"You brought me this man as one who was perverting the people;
and here I have examined him in your presence
and have not found this man guilty of any of your charges against him.
¹⁵Neither has Herod, for he sent him back to us.
Indeed, he has done nothing to deserve death.
¹⁶I will therefore have him flogged and release him."

¹⁸Then they all shouted out together,
"Away with this fellow! Release Barabbas for us!"
¹⁹(This was a man who had been put in prison
for an insurrection that had taken place in the city, and for murder.)
²⁰Pilate, wanting to release Jesus, addressed them again;
²¹but they kept shouting, "Crucify, crucify him!"
²²A third time he said to them, "Why, what evil has he done?
I have found in him no ground for the sentence of death;
I will therefore have him flogged and then release him."
²³But they kept urgently demanding with loud shouts that he should be
        crucified;
and their voices prevailed.
²⁴So Pilate gave his verdict that their demand should be granted.
²⁵He released the man they asked for,
the one who had been put in prison for insurrection and murder,
and he handed Jesus over as they wished.

²⁶As they led him away,
they seized a man, Simon of Cyrene, who was coming from the country,
and they laid the cross on him, and made him carry it behind Jesus.
²⁷A great number of the people followed him,
and among them were women who were beating their breasts and wailing
        for him.
²⁸But Jesus turned to them and said,
"Daughters of Jerusalem, do not weep for me,

but weep for yourselves and for your children.
29For the days are surely coming when they will say,
'Blessed are the barren, and the wombs that never bore,
and the breasts that never nursed.'
30Then they will begin to say to the mountains, 'Fall on us';
and to the hills, 'Cover us.'
31For if they do this when the wood is green, what will happen when it is dry?"

32Two others also, who were criminals, were led away to be put to death
        with him.
33When they came to the place that is called The Skull,
they crucified Jesus there with the criminals,
one on his right and one on his left.
[34Then Jesus said, "Father, forgive them;
for they do not know what they are doing."]
And they cast lots to divide his clothing.
35And the people stood by, watching;
but the leaders scoffed at him, saying,
"He saved others;
let him save himself if he is the Messiah of God, his chosen one!"
36The soldiers also mocked him,
coming up and offering him sour wine, 37and saying,
"If you are the King of the Jews, save yourself!"
38There was also an inscription over him,
"This is the King of the Jews."

39One of the criminals who were hanged there kept deriding him
and saying, "Are you not the Messiah?
Save yourself and us!"
40But the other rebuked him, saying, "Do you not fear God,
since you are under the same sentence of condemnation?
41And we indeed have been condemned justly,
for we are getting what we deserve for our deeds,
but this man has done nothing wrong."
42Then he said,
"Jesus, remember me when you come into your kingdom."
43He replied, "Truly I tell you, today you will be with me in Paradise."

44It was now about noon,
and darkness came over the whole land until three in the afternoon,
45while the sun's light failed; and the curtain of the temple was torn in two.
46Then Jesus, crying with a loud voice, said,
"Father, into your hands I commend my spirit."
Having said this, he breathed his last.
47When the centurion saw what had taken place, he praised God and said,
"Certainly this man was innocent."
48And when all the crowds who had gathered there for this spectacle
saw what had taken place,

they returned home, beating their breasts.
⁴⁹But all his acquaintances,
including the women who had followed him from Galilee,
stood at a distance, watching these things.

⁵⁰Now there was a good and righteous man named Joseph,
who, though a member of the council,
⁵¹had not agreed to their plan and action.
He came from the Jewish town of Arimathea,
and he was waiting expectantly for the kingdom of God.
⁵²This man went to Pilate and asked for the body of Jesus.
⁵³Then he took it down, wrapped it in a linen cloth,
and laid it in a rock-hewn tomb where no one had ever been laid.
⁵⁴It was the day of Preparation, and the sabbath was beginning.
⁵⁵The women who had come with him from Galilee followed,
and they saw the tomb and how his body was laid.
⁵⁶Then they returned, and prepared spices and ointments.

On the sabbath they rested according to the commandment.

The Gospel of the Lord.

OR: LUKE 23:1–49

The Holy Gospel according to Luke, the 23rd chapter.

¹Then the assembly rose as a body and brought Jesus before Pilate.
²They began to accuse him, saying,
"We found this man perverting our nation,
forbidding us to pay taxes to the emperor,
and saying that he himself is the Messiah, a king."
³Then Pilate asked him, "Are you the king of the Jews?"
He answered, "You say so."
⁴Then Pilate said to the chief priests and the crowds,
"I find no basis for an accusation against this man."
⁵But they were insistent and said,
"He stirs up the people by teaching throughout all Judea,
from Galilee where he began even to this place."

⁶When Pilate heard this, he asked whether the man was a Galilean.
⁷And when he learned that he was under Herod's jurisdiction,
he sent him off to Herod, who was himself in Jerusalem at that time.
⁸When Herod saw Jesus, he was very glad,
for he had been wanting to see him for a long time,
because he had heard about him and was hoping to see him perform some
        sign.
⁹He questioned him at some length, but Jesus gave him no answer.
¹⁰The chief priests and the scribes stood by, vehemently accusing him.
¹¹Even Herod with his soldiers treated him with contempt and mocked him;

then he put an elegant robe on him, and sent him back to Pilate.
¹²That same day Herod and Pilate became friends with each other;
before this they had been enemies.

¹³Pilate then called together the chief priests, the leaders, and the people,
¹⁴and said to them,
"You brought me this man as one who was perverting the people;
and here I have examined him in your presence
and have not found this man guilty of any of your charges against him.
¹⁵Neither has Herod, for he sent him back to us.
Indeed, he has done nothing to deserve death.
¹⁶I will therefore have him flogged and release him."

¹⁸Then they all shouted out together,
"Away with this fellow! Release Barabbas for us!"
¹⁹(This was a man who had been put in prison
for an insurrection that had taken place in the city, and for murder.)
²⁰Pilate, wanting to release Jesus, addressed them again;
²¹but they kept shouting, "Crucify, crucify him!"
²²A third time he said to them, "Why, what evil has he done?
I have found in him no ground for the sentence of death;
I will therefore have him flogged and then release him."
²³But they kept urgently demanding with loud shouts that he should be
    crucified;
and their voices prevailed.
²⁴So Pilate gave his verdict that their demand should be granted.
²⁵He released the man they asked for,
the one who had been put in prison for insurrection and murder,
and he handed Jesus over as they wished.

²⁶As they led him away,
they seized a man, Simon of Cyrene, who was coming from the country,
and they laid the cross on him, and made him carry it behind Jesus.
²⁷A great number of the people followed him,
and among them were women who were beating their breasts and wailing
    for him.
²⁸But Jesus turned to them and said,
"Daughters of Jerusalem, do not weep for me,
but weep for yourselves and for your children.
²⁹For the days are surely coming when they will say,
'Blessed are the barren, and the wombs that never bore,
and the breasts that never nursed.'
³⁰Then they will begin to say to the mountains, 'Fall on us';
and to the hills, 'Cover us.'
³¹For if they do this when the wood is green, what will happen when it is dry?"

³²Two others also, who were criminals, were led away to be put to death
    with him.

³³When they came to the place that is called The Skull,
they crucified Jesus there with the criminals,
one on his right and one on his left.
[³⁴Then Jesus said, "Father, forgive them;
for they do not know what they are doing."]
And they cast lots to divide his clothing.
³⁵And the people stood by, watching;
but the leaders scoffed at him, saying,
"He saved others;
let him save himself if he is the Messiah of God, his chosen one!"
³⁶The soldiers also mocked him,
coming up and offering him sour wine, ³⁷and saying,
"If you are the King of the Jews, save yourself!"
³⁸There was also an inscription over him,
"This is the King of the Jews."

³⁹One of the criminals who were hanged there kept deriding him
and saying, "Are you not the Messiah?
Save yourself and us!"
⁴⁰But the other rebuked him, saying, "Do you not fear God,
since you are under the same sentence of condemnation?
⁴¹And we indeed have been condemned justly,
for we are getting what we deserve for our deeds,
but this man has done nothing wrong."
⁴²Then he said,
"Jesus, remember me when you come into your kingdom."
⁴³He replied, "Truly I tell you, today you will be with me in Paradise."

⁴⁴It was now about noon,
and darkness came over the whole land until three in the afternoon,
⁴⁵while the sun's light failed; and the curtain of the temple was torn in two.
⁴⁶Then Jesus, crying with a loud voice, said,
"Father, into your hands I commend my spirit."
Having said this, he breathed his last.
⁴⁷When the centurion saw what had taken place, he praised God and said,
"Certainly this man was innocent."
⁴⁸And when all the crowds who had gathered there for this spectacle
saw what had taken place,
they returned home, beating their breasts.
⁴⁹But all his acquaintances,
including the women who had followed him from Galilee,
stood at a distance, watching these things.

The Gospel of the Lord.

Monday in Holy Week

APRIL 6, 1998   *APRIL 9, 2001*   *APRIL 5, 2004*

FIRST READING: Isaiah 42:1–9

A reading from Isaiah:

¹Here is my servant, whom I uphold,
    my chosen, in whom my soul delights;
I have put my spirit upon him;
    he will bring forth justice to the nations.
²He will not cry or lift up his voice,
    or make it heard in the street;
³a bruised reed he will not break,
    and a dimly burning wick he will not quench;
    he will faithfully bring forth justice.
⁴He will not grow faint or be crushed
    until he has established justice in the earth;
    and the coastlands wait for his teaching.

⁵Thus says God, the Lord,
    who created the heavens and stretched them out,
    who spread out the earth and what comes from it,
who gives breath to the people upon it
    and spirit to those who walk in it:
⁶I am the Lord, I have called you in righteousness,
    I have taken you by the hand and kept you;
I have given you as a covenant to the people,
    a light to the nations,
        ⁷to open the eyes that are blind,
to bring out the prisoners from the dungeon,
    from the prison those who sit in darkness.
⁸I am the Lord, that is my name;
    my glory I give to no other,
    nor my praise to idols.
⁹See, the former things have come to pass,
    and new things I now declare;
before they spring forth,
    I tell you of them.

The word of the Lord.

PSALMODY: Psalm 36:5–11

SECOND READING: HEBREWS 9:11–15

A reading from Hebrews:

[11]When Christ came as a high priest of the good things that have come,
then through the greater and perfect tent
(not made with hands, that is, not of this creation),
[12]he entered once for all into the Holy Place,
not with the blood of goats and calves,
but with his own blood, thus obtaining eternal redemption.

[13]For if the blood of goats and bulls,
with the sprinkling of the ashes of a heifer,
sanctifies those who have been defiled so that their flesh is purified,
[14]how much more will the blood of Christ,
who through the eternal Spirit offered himself without blemish to God,
purify our conscience from dead works to worship the living God!

[15]For this reason he is the mediator of a new covenant,
so that those who are called may receive the promised eternal inheritance,
because a death has occurred
that redeems them from the transgressions under the first covenant.

The word of the Lord.

GOSPEL: JOHN 12:1–11

The Holy Gospel according to John, the twelfth chapter.

[1]Six days before the Passover Jesus came to Bethany,
the home of Lazarus, whom he had raised from the dead.
[2]There they gave a dinner for him.
Martha served, and Lazarus was one of those at the table with him.
[3]Mary took a pound of costly perfume made of pure nard,
anointed Jesus' feet, and wiped them with her hair.
The house was filled with the fragrance of the perfume.

[4]But Judas Iscariot, one of his disciples
(the one who was about to betray him), said,
[5]"Why was this perfume not sold for three hundred denarii
and the money given to the poor?"
[6](He said this not because he cared about the poor,
but because he was a thief;
he kept the common purse and used to steal what was put into it.)
[7]Jesus said,
"Leave her alone.
She bought it so that she might keep it for the day of my burial.
[8]You always have the poor with you,
but you do not always have me."

[9]When the great crowd of the Jews learned that he was there,
they came not only because of Jesus
but also to see Lazarus, whom he had raised from the dead.
[10]So the chief priests planned to put Lazarus to death as well,
[11]since it was on account of him that many of the Jews were deserting
and were believing in Jesus.

The Gospel of the Lord.

TUESDAY IN HOLY WEEK

APRIL 7, 1998   APRIL 10, 2001   APRIL 6, 2004

FIRST READING: Isaiah 49:1–7

A reading from Isaiah:

[1]Listen to me, O coastlands,
   pay attention, you peoples from far away!
The Lord called me before I was born,
   while I was in my mother's womb he named me.
[2]He made my mouth like a sharp sword,
   in the shadow of his hand he hid me;
he made me a polished arrow,
   in his quiver he hid me away.
[3]And he said to me, "You are my servant,
   Israel, in whom I will be glorified."
[4]But I said, "I have labored in vain,
   I have spent my strength for nothing and vanity;
yet surely my cause is with the Lord,
   and my reward with my God."

[5]And now the Lord says,
   who formed me in the womb to be his servant,
to bring Jacob back to him,
   and that Israel might be gathered to him,
for I am honored in the sight of the Lord,
   and my God has become my strength—
[6]he says,
"It is too light a thing that you should be my servant
   to raise up the tribes of Jacob
   and to restore the survivors of Israel;
I will give you as a light to the nations,
   that my salvation may reach to the end of the earth."

[7]Thus says the Lord,
   the Redeemer of Israel and his Holy One,
to one deeply despised, abhorred by the nations,
   the slave of rulers,

"Kings shall see and stand up,
    princes, and they shall prostrate themselves,
because of the LORD, who is faithful,
    the Holy One of Israel, who has chosen you."

The word of the Lord.

PSALMODY: PSALM 71:1–14

SECOND READING: 1 CORINTHIANS 1:18–31

A reading from First Corinthians:

18The message about the cross is foolishness to those who are perishing,
but to us who are being saved it is the power of God.
19For it is written,
    "I will destroy the wisdom of the wise,
        and the discernment of the discerning I will thwart."
20Where is the one who is wise?
Where is the scribe?
Where is the debater of this age?
Has not God made foolish the wisdom of the world?

21For since, in the wisdom of God,
the world did not know God through wisdom,
God decided, through the foolishness of our proclamation,
to save those who believe.
22For Jews demand signs and Greeks desire wisdom,
23but we proclaim Christ crucified,
a stumbling block to Jews and foolishness to Gentiles,
24but to those who are the called, both Jews and Greeks,
Christ the power of God and the wisdom of God.
25For God's foolishness is wiser than human wisdom,
and God's weakness is stronger than human strength.

26Consider your own call, brothers and sisters:
not many of you were wise by human standards,
not many were powerful,
not many were of noble birth.
27But God chose what is foolish in the world to shame the wise;
God chose what is weak in the world to shame the strong;
28God chose what is low and despised in the world,
things that are not,
to reduce to nothing things that are,
29so that no one might boast in the presence of God.

³⁰He is the source of your life in Christ Jesus,
who became for us wisdom from God,
and righteousness and sanctification and redemption,
³¹in order that, as it is written,
"Let the one who boasts, boast in the Lord."

The word of the Lord.

GOSPEL: JOHN 12:20–36

The Holy Gospel according to John, the twelfth chapter.

²⁰Now among those who went up to worship at the festival were some Greeks.
²¹They came to Philip, who was from Bethsaida in Galilee,
and said to him, "Sir, we wish to see Jesus."
²²Philip went and told Andrew;
then Andrew and Philip went and told Jesus.
²³Jesus answered them,
"The hour has come for the Son of Man to be glorified.
²⁴Very truly, I tell you,
unless a grain of wheat falls into the earth and dies,
it remains just a single grain;
but if it dies, it bears much fruit.
²⁵Those who love their life lose it,
and those who hate their life in this world will keep it for eternal life.
²⁶Whoever serves me must follow me,
and where I am, there will my servant be also.
Whoever serves me, the Father will honor.

²⁷"Now my soul is troubled.
And what should I say—'Father, save me from this hour'?
No, it is for this reason that I have come to this hour.
²⁸Father, glorify your name."
Then a voice came from heaven,
"I have glorified it, and I will glorify it again."
²⁹The crowd standing there heard it and said that it was thunder.
Others said, "An angel has spoken to him."
³⁰Jesus answered,
"This voice has come for your sake, not for mine.
³¹Now is the judgment of this world;
now the ruler of this world will be driven out.
³²And I, when I am lifted up from the earth,
will draw all people to myself."
³³He said this to indicate the kind of death he was to die.
³⁴The crowd answered him,
"We have heard from the law that the Messiah remains forever.

How can you say that the Son of Man must be lifted up?
Who is this Son of Man?"
[35]Jesus said to them,
"The light is with you for a little longer.
Walk while you have the light,
so that the darkness may not overtake you.
If you walk in the darkness, you do not know where you are going.
[36]While you have the light, believe in the light,
so that you may become children of light."

After Jesus had said this, he departed and hid from them.

The Gospel of the Lord.

WEDNESDAY IN HOLY WEEK

APRIL 8, 1998   APRIL 11, 2001   APRIL 7, 2004

FIRST READING: Isaiah 50:4–9a

A reading from Isaiah:

⁴The Lord GOD has given me
     the tongue of a teacher,
that I may know how to sustain
     the weary with a word.
Morning by morning he wakens—
     wakens my ear
     to listen as those who are taught.
⁵The Lord GOD has opened my ear,
     and I was not rebellious,
     I did not turn backward.
⁶I gave my back to those who struck me,
     and my cheeks to those who pulled out the beard;
I did not hide my face
     from insult and spitting.

⁷The Lord GOD helps me;
     therefore I have not been disgraced;
therefore I have set my face like flint,
     and I know that I shall not be put to shame;
     ⁸he who vindicates me is near.
Who will contend with me?
     Let us stand up together.
Who are my adversaries?
     Let them confront me.
⁹It is the Lord GOD who helps me;
     who will declare me guilty?

The word of the Lord.

PSALMODY: Psalm 70

SECOND READING: Hebrews 12:1–3

A reading from Hebrews:

¹Since we are surrounded by so great a cloud of witnesses,
let us also lay aside every weight and the sin that clings so closely,
and let us run with perseverance the race that is set before us,

²looking to Jesus the pioneer and perfecter of our faith,
who for the sake of the joy that was set before him
endured the cross, disregarding its shame,
and has taken his seat at the right hand of the throne of God.

³Consider him who endured such hostility against himself from sinners,
so that you may not grow weary or lose heart.

The word of the Lord.

GOSPEL: JOHN 13:21–32

The Holy Gospel according to John, the 13th chapter.

²¹Jesus was troubled in spirit, and declared,
"Very truly, I tell you, one of you will betray me."
²²The disciples looked at one another,
uncertain of whom he was speaking.

²³One of his disciples—the one whom Jesus loved—was reclining next to him;
²⁴Simon Peter therefore motioned to him to ask Jesus of whom he was speaking.
²⁵So while reclining next to Jesus, he asked him,
"Lord, who is it?"
²⁶Jesus answered,
"It is the one to whom I give this piece of bread
when I have dipped it in the dish."
So when he had dipped the piece of bread,
he gave it to Judas son of Simon Iscariot.
²⁷After he received the piece of bread, Satan entered into him.
Jesus said to him,
"Do quickly what you are going to do."
²⁸Now no one at the table knew why he said this to him.
²⁹Some thought that, because Judas had the common purse,
Jesus was telling him, "Buy what we need for the festival";
or, that he should give something to the poor.
³⁰So, after receiving the piece of bread, he immediately went out.
And it was night.

³¹When he had gone out, Jesus said,
"Now the Son of Man has been glorified,
and God has been glorified in him.
³²If God has been glorified in him,
God will also glorify him in himself and will glorify him at once."

The Gospel of the Lord.

THE THREE DAYS

Maundy Thursday

APRIL 9, 1998   APRIL 12, 2001   APRIL 8, 2004

FIRST READING: Exodus 12:1–4 [5–10] 11–14

A reading from Exodus:

¹The Lord said to Moses and Aaron in the land of Egypt:
²This month shall mark for you the beginning of months;
it shall be the first month of the year for you.
³Tell the whole congregation of Israel
that on the tenth of this month they are to take a lamb for each family,
a lamb for each household.
⁴If a household is too small for a whole lamb,
it shall join its closest neighbor in obtaining one;
the lamb shall be divided in proportion to the number of people who eat of it.

[⁵Your lamb shall be without blemish, a year-old male;
you may take it from the sheep or from the goats.
⁶You shall keep it until the fourteenth day of this month;
then the whole assembled congregation of Israel shall slaughter it at twilight.
⁷They shall take some of the blood and put it on the two doorposts
and the lintel of the houses in which they eat it.
⁸They shall eat the lamb that same night;
they shall eat it roasted over the fire
with unleavened bread and bitter herbs.
⁹Do not eat any of it raw or boiled in water,
but roasted over the fire, with its head, legs, and inner organs.
¹⁰You shall let none of it remain until the morning;
anything that remains until the morning you shall burn.]

¹¹This is how you shall eat it:
your loins girded, your sandals on your feet, and your staff in your hand;
and you shall eat it hurriedly.
It is the passover of the Lord.
¹²For I will pass through the land of Egypt that night,
and I will strike down every firstborn in the land of Egypt,
both human beings and animals;
on all the gods of Egypt I will execute judgments:
I am the Lord.
¹³The blood shall be a sign for you on the houses where you live:
when I see the blood, I will pass over you,

and no plague shall destroy you when I strike the land of Egypt.

14This day shall be a day of remembrance for you.
You shall celebrate it as a festival to the LORD;
throughout your generations you shall observe it as a perpetual ordinance.

The word of the Lord.

PSALMODY: PSALM 116:1–2, 12–19   *Psalm 116:1, 10–17*   LBW/BCP

SECOND READING: 1 CORINTHIANS 11:23–26

A reading from First Corinthians:

23For I received from the Lord what I also handed on to you,
that the Lord Jesus on the night when he was betrayed
took a loaf of bread,
24and when he had given thanks, he broke it and said,
"This is my body that is for you.
Do this in remembrance of me."
25In the same way he took the cup also, after supper, saying,
"This cup is the new covenant in my blood.
Do this, as often as you drink it, in remembrance of me."

26For as often as you eat this bread and drink the cup,
you proclaim the Lord's death until he comes.

The word of the Lord.

GOSPEL: JOHN 13:1–17, 31b–35

The Holy Gospel according to John, the 13th chapter.

1Now before the festival of the Passover,
Jesus knew that his hour had come to depart from this world
and go to the Father.
Having loved his own who were in the world,
he loved them to the end.
2The devil had already put it into the heart of Judas son of Simon Iscariot
to betray him.

And during supper
3Jesus, knowing that the Father had given all things into his hands,
and that he had come from God and was going to God,
4got up from the table,
took off his outer robe, and tied a towel around himself.
5Then he poured water into a basin
and began to wash the disciples' feet
and to wipe them with the towel that was tied around him.

⁶He came to Simon Peter, who said to him,
"Lord, are you going to wash my feet?"
⁷Jesus answered,
"You do not know now what I am doing,
but later you will understand."
⁸Peter said to him,
"You will never wash my feet."
Jesus answered,
"Unless I wash you, you have no share with me."
⁹Simon Peter said to him,
"Lord, not my feet only but also my hands and my head!"
¹⁰Jesus said to him,
"One who has bathed does not need to wash, except for the feet,
but is entirely clean.
And you are clean, though not all of you."
¹¹For he knew who was to betray him;
for this reason he said, "Not all of you are clean."

¹²After he had washed their feet, had put on his robe,
and had returned to the table, he said to them,
"Do you know what I have done to you?
¹³You call me Teacher and Lord—
and you are right, for that is what I am.
¹⁴So if I, your Lord and Teacher, have washed your feet,
you also ought to wash one another's feet.
¹⁵For I have set you an example,
that you also should do as I have done to you.
¹⁶Very truly, I tell you,
servants are not greater than their master,
nor are messengers greater than the one who sent them.
¹⁷If you know these things,
you are blessed if you do them.

^{31b}"Now the Son of Man has been glorified,
and God has been glorified in him.
³²If God has been glorified in him,
God will also glorify him in himself and will glorify him at once.
³³Little children, I am with you only a little longer.
You will look for me;
and as I said to the Jews so now I say to you,
'Where I am going, you cannot come.'

³⁴"I give you a new commandment,
that you love one another.
Just as I have loved you, you also should love one another.
³⁵By this everyone will know that you are my disciples,
if you have love for one another."

The Gospel of the Lord.

GOOD FRIDAY

FIRST READING: Isaiah 52:13—53:12

A reading from Isaiah:

¹³See, my servant shall prosper;
    he shall be exalted and lifted up,
    and shall be very high.
¹⁴Just as there were many who were astonished at him
    —so marred was his appearance, beyond human semblance,
    and his form beyond that of mortals—
¹⁵so he shall startle many nations;
    kings shall shut their mouths because of him;
for that which had not been told them they shall see,
    and that which they had not heard they shall contemplate.

53:1Who has believed what we have heard?
    And to whom has the arm of the Lord been revealed?
²For he grew up before him like a young plant,
    and like a root out of dry ground;
he had no form or majesty that we should look at him,
    nothing in his appearance that we should desire him.
³He was despised and rejected by others;
    a man of suffering and acquainted with infirmity;
and as one from whom others hide their faces
    he was despised, and we held him of no account.

⁴Surely he has borne our infirmities
    and carried our diseases;
yet we accounted him stricken,
    struck down by God, and afflicted.
⁵But he was wounded for our transgressions,
    crushed for our iniquities;
upon him was the punishment that made us whole,
    and by his bruises we are healed.
⁶All we like sheep have gone astray;
    we have all turned to our own way,
and the Lord has laid on him
    the iniquity of us all.

7He was oppressed, and he was afflicted,
yet he did not open his mouth;
like a lamb that is led to the slaughter,
and like a sheep that before its shearers is silent,
so he did not open his mouth.
8By a perversion of justice he was taken away.
Who could have imagined his future?
For he was cut off from the land of the living,
stricken for the transgression of my people.
9They made his grave with the wicked
and his tomb with the rich,
although he had done no violence,
and there was no deceit in his mouth.

10Yet it was the will of the LORD to crush him with pain.
When you make his life an offering for sin,
he shall see his offspring, and shall prolong his days;
through him the will of the LORD shall prosper.
11Out of his anguish he shall see light;
he shall find satisfaction through his knowledge.
The righteous one, my servant, shall make many righteous,
and he shall bear their iniquities.
12Therefore I will allot him a portion with the great,
and he shall divide the spoil with the strong;
because he poured out himself to death,
and was numbered with the transgressors;
yet he bore the sin of many,
and made intercession for the transgressors.

The word of the Lord.

PSALMODY: PSALM 22

SECOND READING: HEBREWS 10:16–25
Or Hebrews 4:14–16; 5:7–9, following

A reading from Hebrews:

16"This is the covenant that I will make with them
after those days, says the Lord:
I will put my laws in their hearts,
and I will write them on their minds,"
17he also adds,
"I will remember their sins and their lawless deeds no more."
18Where there is forgiveness of these,
there is no longer any offering for sin.

¹⁹Therefore, my friends,
since we have confidence to enter the sanctuary by the blood of Jesus,
²⁰by the new and living way that he opened for us through the curtain
(that is, through his flesh),
²¹and since we have a great priest over the house of God,
²²let us approach with a true heart in full assurance of faith,
with our hearts sprinkled clean from an evil conscience
and our bodies washed with pure water.
²³Let us hold fast to the confession of our hope without wavering,
for he who has promised is faithful.
²⁴And let us consider how to provoke one another to love and good deeds,
²⁵not neglecting to meet together, as is the habit of some,
but encouraging one another,
and all the more as you see the Day approaching.

The word of the Lord.

OR: Hebrews 4:14–16; 5:7–9

A reading from Hebrews:

¹⁴Since, then, we have a great high priest
    who has passed through the heavens,
Jesus, the Son of God,
let us hold fast to our confession.
¹⁵For we do not have a high priest who is unable to sympathize with our
    weaknesses,
but we have one who in every respect has been tested as we are,
yet without sin.
¹⁶Let us therefore approach the throne of grace with boldness,
so that we may receive mercy and find grace
to help in time of need.

⁵:⁷In the days of his flesh, Jesus offered up prayers and supplications,
with loud cries and tears,
to the one who was able to save him from death,
and he was heard because of his reverent submission.
⁸Although he was a Son,
he learned obedience through what he suffered;
⁹and having been made perfect,
he became the source of eternal salvation for all who obey him.

The word of the Lord.

The Passion of our Lord Jesus Christ according to John.

[1]Jesus went out with his disciples across the Kidron valley
to a place where there was a garden, which he and his disciples entered.
[2]Now Judas, who betrayed him, also knew the place,
because Jesus often met there with his disciples.
[3]So Judas brought a detachment of soldiers together
with police from the chief priests and the Pharisees,
and they came there with lanterns and torches and weapons.
[4]Then Jesus, knowing all that was to happen to him,
came forward and asked them,
"Whom are you looking for?"
[5]They answered, "Jesus of Nazareth."
Jesus replied, "I am he."
Judas, who betrayed him, was standing with them.
[6]When Jesus said to them, "I am he,"
they stepped back and fell to the ground.
[7]Again he asked them, "Whom are you looking for?"
And they said, "Jesus of Nazareth."
[8]Jesus answered, "I told you that I am he.
So if you are looking for me, let these men go."
[9]This was to fulfill the word that he had spoken,
"I did not lose a single one of those whom you gave me."
[10]Then Simon Peter, who had a sword, drew it,
struck the high priest's slave, and cut off his right ear.
The slave's name was Malchus.
[11]Jesus said to Peter,
"Put your sword back into its sheath.
Am I not to drink the cup that the Father has given me?"

[12]So the soldiers, their officer, and the Jewish police
arrested Jesus and bound him.
[13]First they took him to Annas,
who was the father-in-law of Caiaphas, the high priest that year.
[14]Caiaphas was the one who had advised the Jews
that it was better to have one person die for the people.

[15]Simon Peter and another disciple followed Jesus.
Since that disciple was known to the high priest,
he went with Jesus into the courtyard of the high priest,
[16]but Peter was standing outside at the gate.
So the other disciple, who was known to the high priest,
went out, spoke to the woman who guarded the gate,
and brought Peter in.

¹⁷The woman said to Peter,
"You are not also one of this man's disciples, are you?"
He said, "I am not."
¹⁸Now the slaves and the police had made a charcoal fire because it was cold,
and they were standing around it and warming themselves.
Peter also was standing with them and warming himself.

¹⁹Then the high priest questioned Jesus about his disciples
                and about his teaching.
²⁰Jesus answered, "I have spoken openly to the world;
I have always taught in synagogues and in the temple,
where all the Jews come together.
I have said nothing in secret.
²¹Why do you ask me?
Ask those who heard what I said to them; they know what I said."
²²When he had said this,
one of the police standing nearby struck Jesus on the face, saying,
"Is that how you answer the high priest?"
²³Jesus answered, "If I have spoken wrongly, testify to the wrong.
But if I have spoken rightly, why do you strike me?"
²⁴Then Annas sent him bound to Caiaphas the high priest.

²⁵Now Simon Peter was standing and warming himself.
They asked him, "You are not also one of his disciples, are you?"
He denied it and said, "I am not."
²⁶One of the slaves of the high priest,
a relative of the man whose ear Peter had cut off, asked,
"Did I not see you in the garden with him?"
²⁷Again Peter denied it, and at that moment the cock crowed.

²⁸Then they took Jesus from Caiaphas to Pilate's headquarters.
It was early in the morning.
They themselves did not enter the headquarters,
so as to avoid ritual defilement
and to be able to eat the Passover.
²⁹So Pilate went out to them and said,
"What accusation do you bring against this man?"
³⁰They answered, "If this man were not a criminal,
we would not have handed him over to you."
³¹Pilate said to them,
"Take him yourselves and judge him according to your law."
The Jews replied,
"We are not permitted to put anyone to death."
³²(This was to fulfill what Jesus had said
when he indicated the kind of death he was to die.)

³³Then Pilate entered the headquarters again,
summoned Jesus, and asked him,
"Are you the King of the Jews?"

[34]Jesus answered,
"Do you ask this on your own, or did others tell you about me?"
[35]Pilate replied, "I am not a Jew, am I?
Your own nation and the chief priests have handed you over to me.
What have you done?"
[36]Jesus answered,
"My kingdom is not from this world.
If my kingdom were from this world,
my followers would be fighting to keep me from being handed over
          to the Jews.
But as it is, my kingdom is not from here."
[37]Pilate asked him, "So you are a king?"
Jesus answered,
"You say that I am a king. For this I was born,
and for this I came into the world, to testify to the truth.
Everyone who belongs to the truth listens to my voice."
[38]Pilate asked him, "What is truth?"

After he had said this, he went out to the Jews again and told them,
"I find no case against him.
[39]But you have a custom that I release someone for you at the Passover.
Do you want me to release for you the King of the Jews?"
[40]They shouted in reply,
"Not this man, but Barabbas!"
Now Barabbas was a bandit.

[19:1]Then Pilate took Jesus and had him flogged.
[2]And the soldiers wove a crown of thorns and put it on his head,
and they dressed him in a purple robe.
[3]They kept coming up to him, saying,
"Hail, King of the Jews!" and striking him on the face.
[4]Pilate went out again and said to them,
"Look, I am bringing him out to you
to let you know that I find no case against him."
[5]So Jesus came out, wearing the crown of thorns and the purple robe.
Pilate said to them, "Here is the man!"
[6]When the chief priests and the police saw him, they shouted,
"Crucify him! Crucify him!"
Pilate said to them,
"Take him yourselves and crucify him; I find no case against him."
[7]The Jews answered him,
"We have a law, and according to that law
he ought to die because he has claimed to be the Son of God."

[8]Now when Pilate heard this, he was more afraid than ever.
[9]He entered his headquarters again and asked Jesus,
"Where are you from?"
But Jesus gave him no answer.

¹⁰Pilate therefore said to him,
"Do you refuse to speak to me?
Do you not know that I have power to release you, and power to crucify you?"
¹¹Jesus answered him,
"You would have no power over me unless it had been given you from above;
therefore the one who handed me over to you is guilty of a greater sin."
¹²From then on Pilate tried to release him,
but the Jews cried out,
"If you release this man, you are no friend of the emperor.
Everyone who claims to be a king sets himself against the emperor."

¹³When Pilate heard these words, he brought Jesus outside
and sat on the judge's bench at a place called The Stone Pavement,
or in Hebrew Gabbatha.
¹⁴Now it was the day of Preparation for the Passover; and it was about noon.
He said to the Jews, "Here is your King!"
¹⁵They cried out,
"Away with him! Away with him! Crucify him!"
Pilate asked them, "Shall I crucify your King?"
The chief priests answered,
"We have no king but the emperor."
¹⁶Then he handed him over to them to be crucified.

So they took Jesus; ¹⁷and carrying the cross by himself,
he went out to what is called The Place of the Skull,
which in Hebrew is called Golgotha.
¹⁸There they crucified him,
and with him two others, one on either side, with Jesus between them.
¹⁹Pilate also had an inscription written and put on the cross.
It read, "Jesus of Nazareth, the King of the Jews."
²⁰Many of the Jews read this inscription,
because the place where Jesus was crucified was near the city;
and it was written in Hebrew, in Latin, and in Greek.
²¹Then the chief priests of the Jews said to Pilate,
"Do not write, 'The King of the Jews,' but,
'This man said, I am King of the Jews.' "
²²Pilate answered,
"What I have written I have written."
²³When the soldiers had crucified Jesus,
they took his clothes and divided them into four parts, one for each soldier.
They also took his tunic;
now the tunic was seamless, woven in one piece from the top.
²⁴So they said to one another,
"Let us not tear it, but cast lots for it to see who will get it."
This was to fulfill what the scripture says,
        "They divided my clothes among themselves,
            and for my clothing they cast lots."
²⁵And that is what the soldiers did.

Meanwhile, standing near the cross of Jesus were his mother,
and his mother's sister, Mary the wife of Clopas, and Mary Magdalene.
[26]When Jesus saw his mother
and the disciple whom he loved standing beside her,
he said to his mother, "Woman, here is your son."
[27]Then he said to the disciple, "Here is your mother."
And from that hour the disciple took her into his own home.

[28]After this, when Jesus knew that all was now finished,
he said (in order to fulfill the scripture),
"I am thirsty."
[29]A jar full of sour wine was standing there.
So they put a sponge full of the wine on a branch of hyssop
and held it to his mouth.
[30]When Jesus had received the wine, he said,
"It is finished."
Then he bowed his head and gave up his spirit.

[31]Since it was the day of Preparation,
the Jews did not want the bodies left on the cross during the sabbath,
especially because that sabbath was a day of great solemnity.
So they asked Pilate to have the legs of the crucified men broken
and the bodies removed.
[32]Then the soldiers came and broke the legs of the first
and of the other who had been crucified with him.
[33]But when they came to Jesus and saw that he was already dead,
they did not break his legs.
[34]Instead, one of the soldiers pierced his side with a spear,
and at once blood and water came out.
[35](He who saw this has testified so that you also may believe.
His testimony is true, and he knows that he tells the truth.)
[36]These things occurred so that the scripture might be fulfilled,
"None of his bones shall be broken."
[37]And again another passage of scripture says,
"They will look on the one whom they have pierced."

[38]After these things, Joseph of Arimathea, who was a disciple of Jesus,
though a secret one because of his fear of the Jews,
asked Pilate to let him take away the body of Jesus.
Pilate gave him permission; so he came and removed his body.
[39]Nicodemus, who had at first come to Jesus by night, also came,
bringing a mixture of myrrh and aloes, weighing about a hundred pounds.
[40]They took the body of Jesus and wrapped it with the spices in linen cloths,
according to the burial custom of the Jews.
[41]Now there was a garden in the place where he was crucified,
and in the garden there was a new tomb in which no one had ever been laid.
[42]And so, because it was the Jewish day of Preparation,
and the tomb was nearby, they laid Jesus there.

The Gospel of the Lord.

Saturday in Holy Week

(for services other than the Vigil of Easter)

APRIL 11, 1998   APRIL 14, 2001   APRIL 10, 2004

FIRST READING: Job 14:1–14

Or Lamentations 3:1–9, 19–24, following

A reading from Job:

¹"A mortal, born of woman, few of days and full of trouble,
²comes up like a flower and withers,
    flees like a shadow and does not last.
³Do you fix your eyes on such a one?
    Do you bring me into judgment with you?
⁴Who can bring a clean thing out of an unclean?
    No one can.
⁵Since their days are determined,
    and the number of their months is known to you,
    and you have appointed the bounds that they cannot pass,
⁶look away from them, and desist,
    that they may enjoy, like laborers, their days.

⁷"For there is hope for a tree,
    if it is cut down,that it will sprout again,
    and that its shoots will not cease.
⁸Though its root grows old in the earth,
    and its stump dies in the ground,
⁹yet at the scent of water it will bud
    and put forth branches like a young plant.
¹⁰But mortals die, and are laid low;
    humans expire, and where are they?
¹¹As waters fail from a lake,
    and a river wastes away and dries up,
¹²so mortals lie down and do not rise again;
    until the heavens are no more, they will not awake
    or be roused out of their sleep.
¹³O that you would hide me in Sheol,
    that you would conceal me until your wrath is past,
    that you would appoint me a set time, and remember me!
¹⁴If mortals die, will they live again?
    All the days of my service I would wait
    until my release should come."

The word of the Lord.

A reading from Lamentations:

¹I am one who has seen affliction
    under the rod of God's wrath;
²he has driven and brought me
    into darkness without any light;
³against me alone he turns his hand,
    again and again, all day long.

⁴He has made my flesh and my skin waste away,
    and broken my bones;
⁵he has besieged and enveloped me
    with bitterness and tribulation;
⁶he has made me sit in darkness
    like the dead of long ago.

⁷He has walled me about so that I cannot escape;
    he has put heavy chains on me;
⁸though I call and cry for help,
    he shuts out my prayer;
⁹he has blocked my ways with hewn stones,
    he has made my paths crooked.

¹⁹The thought of my affliction and my homelessness
    is wormwood and gall!
²⁰My soul continually thinks of it
    and is bowed down within me.
²¹But this I call to mind,
    and therefore I have hope:

²²The steadfast love of the LORD never ceases,
    his mercies never come to an end;
²³they are new every morning;
    great is your faithfulness.
²⁴"The LORD is my portion," says my soul,
    "therefore I will hope in him."

The word of the Lord.

PSALMODY: PSALM 31:1–4, 15–16

A reading from First Peter:

¹Since therefore Christ suffered in the flesh,
arm yourselves also with the same intention
(for whoever has suffered in the flesh has finished with sin),
²so as to live for the rest of your earthly life
no longer by human desires but by the will of God.
³You have already spent enough time in doing what the Gentiles like to do,
living in licentiousness, passions, drunkenness,
revels, carousing, and lawless idolatry.
⁴They are surprised that you no longer join them
in the same excesses of dissipation, and so they blaspheme.

⁵But they will have to give an accounting to him who stands ready
to judge the living and the dead.
⁶For this is the reason the gospel was proclaimed even to the dead,
 so that, though they had been judged in the flesh as everyone is judged,
they might live in the spirit as God does.

⁷The end of all things is near;
therefore be serious and discipline yourselves for the sake of your prayers.
⁸Above all, maintain constant love for one another,
for love covers a multitude of sins.

The word of the Lord.

GOSPEL: MATTHEW 27:57–66

Or John 19:38–42, following

The Holy Gospel according to Matthew, the 27th chapter:

⁵⁷When it was evening, there came a rich man from Arimathea, named Joseph,
who was also a disciple of Jesus.
⁵⁸He went to Pilate and asked for the body of Jesus;
then Pilate ordered it to be given to him.
⁵⁹So Joseph took the body and wrapped it in a clean linen cloth
⁶⁰and laid it in his own new tomb, which he had hewn in the rock.
He then rolled a great stone to the door of the tomb and went away.
⁶¹Mary Magdalene and the other Mary were there, sitting opposite the tomb.

⁶²The next day, that is, after the day of Preparation,
the chief priests and the Pharisees gathered before Pilate ⁶³and said,
"Sir, we remember what that impostor said while he was still alive,
'After three days I will rise again.'
⁶⁴Therefore command the tomb to be made secure until the third day;
otherwise his disciples may go and steal him away,

and tell the people, 'He has been raised from the dead,'
and the last deception would be worse than the first."
⁶⁵Pilate said to them,
"You have a guard of soldiers;
go, make it as secure as you can."
⁶⁶So they went with the guard and made the tomb secure by sealing the stone.

The Gospel of the Lord.

OR: JOHN 19:38–42

The Holy Gospel according to John, the 19th chapter.

³⁸Joseph of Arimathea, who was a disciple of Jesus,
though a secret one because of his fear of the Jews,
asked Pilate to let him take away the body of Jesus.
Pilate gave him permission; so he came and removed his body.
³⁹Nicodemus, who had at first come to Jesus by night, also came,
bringing a mixture of myrrh and aloes, weighing about a hundred pounds.
⁴⁰They took the body of Jesus
and wrapped it with the spices in linen cloths,
according to the burial custom of the Jews.
⁴¹Now there was a garden in the place where he was crucified,
and in the garden there was a new tomb in which no one had ever been laid.
⁴²And so, because it was the Jewish day of Preparation,
and the tomb was nearby, they laid Jesus there.

The Gospel of the Lord.

THE RESURRECTION OF OUR LORD
VIGIL OF EASTER

APRIL 11, 1998   APRIL 14, 2001   APRIL 10, 2004

FIRST READING: GENESIS 1:1—2:4a
Creation

A reading from Genesis:

¹In the beginning when God created the heavens and the earth,
²the earth was a formless void and darkness covered the face of the deep,
while a wind from God swept over the face of the waters.
³Then God said,
"Let there be light"; and there was light.
⁴And God saw that the light was good;
and God separated the light from the darkness.
⁵God called the light Day,
and the darkness he called Night.
And there was evening and there was morning, the first day.

⁶And God said,
"Let there be a dome in the midst of the waters,
and let it separate the waters from the waters."
⁷So God made the dome
and separated the waters that were under the dome
from the waters that were above the dome.
And it was so.
⁸God called the dome Sky.
And there was evening and there was morning, the second day.

⁹And God said,
"Let the waters under the sky be gathered together into one place,
and let the dry land appear."
And it was so.
¹⁰God called the dry land Earth,
and the waters that were gathered together he called Seas.
And God saw that it was good.
¹¹Then God said,
"Let the earth put forth vegetation:
plants yielding seed,
and fruit trees of every kind on earth that bear fruit with the seed in it."
And it was so.
¹²The earth brought forth vegetation:

plants yielding seed of every kind,
and trees of every kind bearing fruit with the seed in it.
And God saw that it was good.
¹³And there was evening and there was morning, the third day.

¹⁴And God said,
"Let there be lights in the dome of the sky
to separate the day from the night;
and let them be for signs and for seasons and for days and years,
¹⁵and let them be lights in the dome of the sky to give light upon the earth."
And it was so.
¹⁶God made the two great lights—
the greater light to rule the day
and the lesser light to rule the night—and the stars.
¹⁷God set them in the dome of the sky to give light upon the earth,
¹⁸to rule over the day and over the night,
and to separate the light from the darkness.
And God saw that it was good.
¹⁹And there was evening and there was morning, the fourth day.

²⁰And God said,
"Let the waters bring forth swarms of living creatures,
and let birds fly above the earth across the dome of the sky."
²¹So God created the great sea monsters
and every living creature that moves,
of every kind, with which the waters swarm,
and every winged bird of every kind.
And God saw that it was good.
²²God blessed them, saying,
"Be fruitful and multiply and fill the waters in the seas,
and let birds multiply on the earth."
²³And there was evening and there was morning, the fifth day.

²⁴And God said,
"Let the earth bring forth living creatures of every kind:
cattle and creeping things and wild animals of the earth of every kind."
And it was so.
²⁵God made the wild animals of the earth of every kind,
and the cattle of every kind,
and everything that creeps upon the ground of every kind.
And God saw that it was good.

²⁶Then God said,
"Let us make humankind in our image, according to our likeness;
and let them have dominion over the fish of the sea,
and over the birds of the air,
and over the cattle, and over all the wild animals of the earth,
and over every creeping thing that creeps upon the earth."

²⁷So God created humankind in his image,
  in the image of God he created them;
  male and female he created them.
²⁸God blessed them, and God said to them,
"Be fruitful and multiply,
and fill the earth and subdue it;
and have dominion over the fish of the sea
and over the birds of the air
and over every living thing that moves upon the earth."
²⁹God said,
"See, I have given you every plant yielding seed
that is upon the face of all the earth,
and every tree with seed in its fruit;
you shall have them for food.
³⁰And to every beast of the earth,
and to every bird of the air,
and to everything that creeps on the earth,
everything that has the breath of life,
I have given every green plant for food."
And it was so.
³¹God saw everything that he had made,
and indeed, it was very good.
And there was evening and there was morning, the sixth day.

2:1Thus the heavens and the earth were finished, and all their multitude.
²And on the seventh day God finished the work that he had done,
and he rested on the seventh day from all the work that he had done.
³So God blessed the seventh day and hallowed it,
because on it God rested from all the work that he had done in creation.

⁴These are the generations of the heavens and the earth
  when they were created.

The word of the Lord.

RESPONSE: PSALM 136:1–9, 23–26

SECOND READING: Genesis 7:1–5, 11–18; 8:6–18; 9:8–13
The Flood

A reading from Genesis:

¹The LORD said to Noah,
"Go into the ark, you and all your household,
for I have seen that you alone are righteous before me in this generation.
²Take with you seven pairs of all clean animals,
the male and its mate;
and a pair of the animals that are not clean,
the male and its mate;
³and seven pairs of the birds of the air also, male and female,
to keep their kind alive on the face of all the earth.
⁴For in seven days I will send rain on the earth
for forty days and forty nights;
and every living thing that I have made
I will blot out from the face of the ground."
⁵And Noah did all that the LORD had commanded him.

¹¹In the six hundredth year of Noah's life,
in the second month, on the seventeenth day of the month,
on that day all the fountains of the great deep burst forth,
and the windows of the heavens were opened.
¹²The rain fell on the earth forty days and forty nights.
¹³On the very same day Noah with his sons,
Shem and Ham and Japheth,
and Noah's wife and the three wives of his sons entered the ark,
¹⁴they and every wild animal of every kind,
and all domestic animals of every kind,
and every creeping thing that creeps on the earth,
and every bird of every kind—every bird, every winged creature.
¹⁵They went into the ark with Noah,
two and two of all flesh in which there was the breath of life.
¹⁶And those that entered, male and female of all flesh,
went in as God had commanded him;
and the LORD shut him in.

¹⁷The flood continued forty days on the earth;
and the waters increased,
and bore up the ark, and it rose high above the earth.
¹⁸The waters swelled and increased greatly on the earth;
and the ark floated on the face of the waters.

⁸:⁶At the end of forty days
Noah opened the window of the ark that he had made
⁷and sent out the raven;
and it went to and fro until the waters were dried up from the earth.
⁸Then he sent out the dove from him,
to see if the waters had subsided from the face of the ground;
⁹but the dove found no place to set its foot,

and it returned to him to the ark,
for the waters were still on the face of the whole earth.
So he put out his hand and took it
and brought it into the ark with him.
¹⁰He waited another seven days,
and again he sent out the dove from the ark;
¹¹and the dove came back to him in the evening,
and there in its beak was a freshly plucked olive leaf;
so Noah knew that the waters had subsided from the earth.
¹²Then he waited another seven days, and sent out the dove;
and it did not return to him any more.

¹³In the six hundred first year,
in the first month, on the first day of the month,
the waters were dried up from the earth;
and Noah removed the covering of the ark,
and looked, and saw that the face of the ground was drying.
¹⁴In the second month, on the twenty-seventh day of the month,
the earth was dry.
¹⁵Then God said to Noah,
¹⁶"Go out of the ark, you and your wife,
and your sons and your sons' wives with you.
¹⁷Bring out with you every living thing that is with you of all flesh—
birds and animals and every creeping thing that creeps on the earth—
so that they may abound on the earth,
and be fruitful and multiply on the earth."
¹⁸So Noah went out with his sons and his wife and his sons' wives.

⁹:⁸Then God said to Noah and to his sons with him,
⁹"As for me,
I am establishing my covenant with you and your descendants after you,
¹⁰and with every living creature that is with you,
the birds, the domestic animals,
and every animal of the earth with you,
as many as came out of the ark.
¹¹I establish my covenant with you,
that never again shall all flesh be cut off by the waters of a flood,
and never again shall there be a flood to destroy the earth."
¹²God said,
"This is the sign of the covenant that I make
between me and you and every living creature that is with you,
for all future generations:
¹³I have set my bow in the clouds,
and it shall be a sign of the covenant between me and the earth."

The word of the Lord.

RESPONSE: PSALM 46

THIRD READING: Genesis 22:1–18
The Testing of Abraham

A reading from Genesis:

¹God tested Abraham.
He said to him, "Abraham!"
And he said, "Here I am."
²God said,
"Take your son, your only son Isaac, whom you love,
and go to the land of Moriah, and offer him there as a burnt offering
on one of the mountains that I shall show you."

³So Abraham rose early in the morning,
saddled his donkey, and took two of his young men with him,
and his son Isaac;
he cut the wood for the burnt offering,
and set out and went to the place in the distance that God had shown him.
⁴On the third day Abraham looked up and saw the place far away.
⁵Then Abraham said to his young men,
"Stay here with the donkey;
the boy and I will go over there;
we will worship, and then we will come back to you."

⁶Abraham took the wood of the burnt offering
and laid it on his son Isaac,
and he himself carried the fire and the knife.
So the two of them walked on together.
⁷Isaac said to his father Abraham, "Father!"
And he said, "Here I am, my son."
He said, "The fire and the wood are here,
but where is the lamb for a burnt offering?"
⁸Abraham said,
"God himself will provide the lamb for a burnt offering, my son."
So the two of them walked on together.

⁹When they came to the place that God had shown him,
Abraham built an altar there and laid the wood in order.
He bound his son Isaac,
and laid him on the altar, on top of the wood.
¹⁰Then Abraham reached out his hand
and took the knife to kill his son.
¹¹But the angel of the LORD called to him from heaven, and said,
"Abraham, Abraham!"
And he said, "Here I am."
¹²He said,
"Do not lay your hand on the boy or do anything to him;
for now I know that you fear God,
since you have not withheld your son, your only son, from me."

¹³And Abraham looked up and saw a ram, caught in a thicket by its horns. Abraham went and took the ram
and offered it up as a burnt offering instead of his son.
¹⁴So Abraham called that place "The LORD will provide";
as it is said to this day,
"On the mount of the LORD it shall be provided."

¹⁵The angel of the LORD called to Abraham a second time from heaven,
¹⁶and said,
"By myself I have sworn, says the LORD:
Because you have done this,
and have not withheld your son, your only son,
¹⁷I will indeed bless you,
and I will make your offspring as numerous as the stars of heaven
and as the sand that is on the seashore.
And your offspring shall possess the gate of their enemies,
¹⁸and by your offspring shall all the nations of the earth
gain blessing for themselves,
because you have obeyed my voice."

The word of the Lord.

RESPONSE: PSALM 16

FOURTH READING: EXODUS 14:10–31; 15:20–21
Israel's Deliverance at the Red Sea

A reading from Exodus:

^{10}As Pharaoh drew near, the Israelites looked back,
and there were the Egyptians advancing on them.
In great fear the Israelites cried out to the LORD.
^{11}They said to Moses,
"Was it because there were no graves in Egypt
that you have taken us away to die in the wilderness?
What have you done to us, bringing us out of Egypt?
^{12}Is this not the very thing we told you in Egypt,
'Let us alone and let us serve the Egyptians'?
For it would have been better for us to serve the Egyptians
than to die in the wilderness."
^{13}But Moses said to the people,
"Do not be afraid, stand firm,
and see the deliverance that the LORD will accomplish for you today;
for the Egyptians whom you see today you shall never see again.
^{14}The LORD will fight for you,
 and you have only to keep still."

^{15}Then the LORD said to Moses,
"Why do you cry out to me?
Tell the Israelites to go forward.
^{16}But you lift up your staff,
and stretch out your hand over the sea and divide it,
that the Israelites may go into the sea on dry ground.
^{17}Then I will harden the hearts of the Egyptians
so that they will go in after them;
and so I will gain glory for myself over Pharaoh and all his army,
his chariots, and his chariot drivers.
^{18}And the Egyptians shall know that I am the LORD,
when I have gained glory for myself over Pharaoh,
his chariots, and his chariot drivers."

^{19}The angel of God who was going before the Israelite army moved
and went behind them;
and the pillar of cloud moved from in front of them
and took its place behind them.
^{20}It came between the army of Egypt and the army of Israel.
And so the cloud was there with the darkness,
and it lit up the night;
one did not come near the other all night.

^{21}Then Moses stretched out his hand over the sea.
The LORD drove the sea back by a strong east wind all night,
and turned the sea into dry land;

and the waters were divided.
²²The Israelites went into the sea on dry ground,
the waters forming a wall for them on their right and on their left.
²³The Egyptians pursued, and went into the sea after them,
all of Pharaoh's horses, chariots, and chariot drivers.
²⁴At the morning watch
the Lᴏʀᴅ in the pillar of fire and cloud looked down upon the Egyptian army,
and threw the Egyptian army into panic.
²⁵He clogged their chariot wheels so that they turned with difficulty.
The Egyptians said,
"Let us flee from the Israelites,
for the Lᴏʀᴅ is fighting for them against Egypt."

²⁶Then the Lᴏʀᴅ said to Moses,
"Stretch out your hand over the sea,
so that the water may come back upon the Egyptians,
upon their chariots and chariot drivers."
²⁷So Moses stretched out his hand over the sea,
and at dawn the sea returned to its normal depth.
As the Egyptians fled before it,
the Lᴏʀᴅ tossed the Egyptians into the sea.
²⁸The waters returned and covered the chariots and the chariot drivers,
the entire army of Pharaoh that had followed them into the sea;
not one of them remained.
²⁹But the Israelites walked on dry ground through the sea,
the waters forming a wall for them on their right and on their left.

³⁰Thus the Lᴏʀᴅ saved Israel that day from the Egyptians;
and Israel saw the Egyptians dead on the seashore.
³¹Israel saw the great work that the Lᴏʀᴅ did against the Egyptians.
So the people feared the Lᴏʀᴅ
and believed in the Lᴏʀᴅ and in his servant Moses.

¹⁵:²⁰Then the prophet Miriam, Aaron's sister, took a tambourine in her hand;
and all the women went out after her with tambourines and with dancing.
²¹And Miriam sang to them:
    "Sing to the Lᴏʀᴅ, for he has triumphed gloriously;
    horse and rider he has thrown into the sea."

The word of the Lord.

RESPONSE: Exᴏᴅᴜs 15:1b–13, 17–18

FIFTH READING: ISAIAH 55:1–11
Salvation Freely Offered to All

A reading from Isaiah:

¹Ho, everyone who thirsts,
  come to the waters;
and you that have no money,
  come, buy and eat!
Come, buy wine and milk
  without money and without price.
²Why do you spend your money for that which is not bread,
  and your labor for that which does not satisfy?
Listen carefully to me, and eat what is good,
  and delight yourselves in rich food.

³Incline your ear, and come to me;
  listen, so that you may live.
I will make with you an everlasting covenant,
  my steadfast, sure love for David.
⁴See, I made him a witness to the peoples,
  a leader and commander for the peoples.
⁵See, you shall call nations that you do not know,
  and nations that do not know you shall run to you,
because of the LORD your God, the Holy One of Israel,
  for he has glorified you.

⁶Seek the LORD while he may be found,
  call upon him while he is near;
⁷let the wicked forsake their way,
  and the unrighteous their thoughts;
let them return to the LORD, that he may have mercy on them,
  and to our God, for he will abundantly pardon.
⁸For my thoughts are not your thoughts,
  nor are your ways my ways, says the LORD.
⁹For as the heavens are higher than the earth,
  so are my ways higher than your ways
  and my thoughts than your thoughts.

¹⁰For as the rain and the snow come down from heaven,
  and do not return there until they have watered the earth,
making it bring forth and sprout,
  giving seed to the sower and bread to the eater,
¹¹so shall my word be that goes out from my mouth;
  it shall not return to me empty,
but it shall accomplish that which I purpose,
  and succeed in the thing for which I sent it.

The word of the Lord.

RESPONSE: ISAIAH 12:2–6

SIXTH READING: Proverbs 8:1–8, 19–21; 9:4b–6

The Wisdom of God   *Alternate Reading: Baruch 3:9–15, 32—4:4 (p. 402)*

A reading from Proverbs:

1Does not wisdom call,
    and does not understanding raise her voice?
2On the heights, beside the way,
    at the crossroads she takes her stand;
3beside the gates in front of the town,
    at the entrance of the portals she cries out:
4"To you, O people, I call,
    and my cry is to all that live.
5O simple ones, learn prudence;
    acquire intelligence, you who lack it.
6Hear, for I will speak noble things,
    and from my lips will come what is right;
7for my mouth will utter truth;
    wickedness is an abomination to my lips.
8All the words of my mouth are righteous;
    there is nothing twisted or crooked in them.

19My fruit is better than gold, even fine gold,
    and my yield than choice silver.
20I walk in the way of righteousness,
    along the paths of justice,
21endowing with wealth those who love me,
    and filling their treasuries.

9:4bTo those without sense she says,
5"Come, eat of my bread
    and drink of the wine I have mixed.
6Lay aside immaturity, and live,
    and walk in the way of insight."

The word of the Lord.

RESPONSE: Psalm 19

SEVENTH READING: Ezekiel 36:24–28
A New Heart and a New Spirit

A reading from Ezekiel:

Thus says the Lord GOD:
24I will take you from the nations,
and gather you from all the countries,
and bring you into your own land.
25I will sprinkle clean water upon you,
and you shall be clean from all your uncleannesses,
and from all your idols I will cleanse you.
26A new heart I will give you,
and a new spirit I will put within you;
and I will remove from your body the heart of stone
and give you a heart of flesh.
27I will put my spirit within you,
and make you follow my statutes and be careful to observe my ordinances.
28Then you shall live in the land that I gave to your ancestors;
and you shall be my people, and I will be your God.

The word of the Lord.

RESPONSE: PSALM 42 and PSALM 43

EIGHTH READING: Ezekiel 37:1–14
The Valley of the Dry Bones

A reading from Ezekiel:

1The hand of the LORD came upon me,
and he brought me out by the spirit of the LORD
and set me down in the middle of a valley;
it was full of bones.
2He led me all around them;
there were very many lying in the valley, and they were very dry.
3He said to me,
"Mortal, can these bones live?"
I answered, "O Lord GOD, you know."

4Then he said to me,
"Prophesy to these bones, and say to them:
O dry bones, hear the word of the LORD.
5Thus says the Lord GOD to these bones:
I will cause breath to enter you, and you shall live.
6I will lay sinews on you,
and will cause flesh to come upon you, and cover you with skin,

and put breath in you, and you shall live;
and you shall know that I am the LORD."

⁷So I prophesied as I had been commanded;
and as I prophesied, suddenly there was a noise, a rattling,
and the bones came together, bone to its bone.
⁸I looked, and there were sinews on them,
and flesh had come upon them, and skin had covered them;
but there was no breath in them.
⁹Then he said to me,
"Prophesy to the breath, prophesy, mortal, and say to the breath:
Thus says the Lord GOD:
Come from the four winds, O breath,
and breathe upon these slain, that they may live."
¹⁰I prophesied as he commanded me,
and the breath came into them,
and they lived, and stood on their feet, a vast multitude.

¹¹Then he said to me,
"Mortal, these bones are the whole house of Israel.
They say, 'Our bones are dried up, and our hope is lost;
we are cut off completely.'
¹²Therefore prophesy, and say to them,
Thus says the Lord GOD:
I am going to open your graves,
and bring you up from your graves, O my people;
and I will bring you back to the land of Israel.
¹³And you shall know that I am the LORD,
when I open your graves,
and bring you up from your graves, O my people.
¹⁴I will put my spirit within you, and you shall live,
and I will place you on your own soil;
then you shall know that I, the LORD, have spoken and will act,"
says the LORD.

The word of the Lord.

RESPONSE: PSALM 143

NINTH READING: Zephaniah 3:14–20
The Gathering of God's People

A reading from Zephaniah:

¹⁴Sing aloud, O daughter Zion;
>   shout, O Israel!
Rejoice and exult with all your heart,
>   O daughter Jerusalem!
¹⁵The LORD has taken away the judgments against you,
>   he has turned away your enemies.
The king of Israel, the LORD, is in your midst;
>   you shall fear disaster no more.
¹⁶On that day it shall be said to Jerusalem:
Do not fear, O Zion;
>   do not let your hands grow weak.
¹⁷The LORD, your God, is in your midst,
>   a warrior who gives victory;
he will rejoice over you with gladness,
>   he will renew you in his love;
he will exult over you with loud singing
>   ¹⁸as on a day of festival.

I will remove disaster from you,
>   so that you will not bear reproach for it.
¹⁹I will deal with all your oppressors
>   at that time.
And I will save the lame
>   and gather the outcast,
and I will change their shame into praise
>   and renown in all the earth.
²⁰At that time I will bring you home,
>   at the time when I gather you;
for I will make you renowned and praised
>   among all the peoples of the earth,
when I restore your fortunes
>   before your eyes, says the LORD.

The word of the Lord.

RESPONSE: Psalm 98

Three additional readings from the Hebrew Scriptures follow on pp. 138–142.
The New Testament and Gospel readings continue on p. 143.

TENTH READING: Jonah 3:1–10
The Call of Jonah

A reading from Jonah.

¹The word of the Lord came to Jonah a second time, saying,
²"Get up, go to Nineveh, that great city,
and proclaim to it the message that I tell you."
³So Jonah set out and went to Nineveh, according to the word of the Lord.

Now Nineveh was an exceedingly large city, a three days' walk across.
⁴Jonah began to go into the city, going a day's walk.
And he cried out,
"Forty days more, and Nineveh shall be overthrown!"
⁵And the people of Nineveh believed God;
they proclaimed a fast,
and everyone, great and small, put on sackcloth.

⁶When the news reached the king of Nineveh,
he rose from his throne, removed his robe,
covered himself with sackcloth, and sat in ashes.
⁷Then he had a proclamation made in Nineveh:
"By the decree of the king and his nobles:
No human being or animal, no herd or flock, shall taste anything.
They shall not feed, nor shall they drink water.
⁸Human beings and animals shall be covered with sackcloth,
and they shall cry mightily to God.
All shall turn from their evil ways
and from the violence that is in their hands.
⁹Who knows? God may relent and change his mind;
he may turn from his fierce anger, so that we do not perish."

¹⁰When God saw what they did,
how they turned from their evil ways,
God changed his mind about the calamity
that he had said he would bring upon them;
and he did not do it.

The word of the Lord.

RESPONSE: Jonah 2:1–3 [4–6] 7–9

ELEVENTH READING: DEUTERONOMY 31:19–30
The Song of Moses

A reading from Deuteronomy.

¹⁹"Now therefore write this song,
and teach it to the Israelites;
put it in their mouths,
in order that this song may be a witness for me against the Israelites.

²⁰For when I have brought them into the land flowing with milk and honey,
which I promised on oath to their ancestors,
and they have eaten their fill and grown fat,
they will turn to other gods and serve them,
despising me and breaking my covenant.
²¹And when many terrible troubles come upon them,
this song will confront them as a witness,
because it will not be lost from the mouths of their descendants.
For I know what they are inclined to do even now,
before I have brought them into the land that I promised them on oath."
²²That very day Moses wrote this song and taught it to the Israelites.

²³Then the LORD commissioned Joshua son of Nun and said,
"Be strong and bold,
for you shall bring the Israelites into the land that I promised them;
I will be with you."

²⁴When Moses had finished writing down in a book
the words of this law to the very end,
²⁵Moses commanded the Levites who carried the ark of the covenant of the
        LORD, saying,
²⁶"Take this book of the law
and put it beside the ark of the covenant of the LORD your God;
let it remain there as a witness against you.
²⁷For I know well how rebellious and stubborn you are.
If you already have been so rebellious toward the LORD
while I am still alive among you,
how much more after my death!
²⁸Assemble to me all the elders of your tribes and your officials,
so that I may recite these words in their hearing
and call heaven and earth to witness against them.
²⁹For I know that after my death you will surely act corruptly,
turning aside from the way that I have commanded you.
In time to come trouble will befall you,
because you will do what is evil in the sight of the LORD,
provoking him to anger through the work of your hands."

³⁰Then Moses recited the words of this song, to the very end,
in the hearing of the whole assembly of Israel.

The word of the Lord.

RESPONSE: DEUTERONOMY 32:1–4, 7, 36a, 43a

TWELFTH READING: DANIEL 3:1–29
The Fiery Furnace

A reading from Daniel.

¹King Nebuchadnezzar made a golden statue whose height was sixty cubits
and whose width was six cubits;
he set it up on the plain of Dura in the province of Babylon.
²Then King Nebuchadnezzar sent for the satraps, the prefects,
        and the governors,
the counselors, the treasurers, the justices, the magistrates,
and all the officials of the provinces,
to assemble and come to the dedication of the statue
that King Nebuchadnezzar had set up.

³So the satraps, the prefects, and the governors,
the counselors, the treasurers, the justices, the magistrates,
and all the officials of the provinces,
assembled for the dedication of the statue
that King Nebuchadnezzar had set up.
When they were standing before the statue that Nebuchadnezzar had set up,
⁴the herald proclaimed aloud,
"You are commanded, O peoples, nations, and languages,
⁵that when you hear the sound of the horn, pipe, lyre,
trigon, harp, drum, and entire musical ensemble,
you are to fall down and worship the golden statue
that King Nebuchadnezzar has set up.
⁶Whoever does not fall down and worship
shall immediately be thrown into a furnace of blazing fire."
⁷Therefore, as soon as all the peoples heard the sound of the horn, pipe, lyre,
trigon, harp, drum, and entire musical ensemble,
all the peoples, nations, and languages fell down
and worshiped the golden statue that King Nebuchadnezzar had set up.

⁸Accordingly, at this time
certain Chaldeans came forward and denounced the Jews.
⁹They said to King Nebuchadnezzar,
"O king, live forever!
¹⁰You, O king, have made a decree,
that everyone who hears the sound of the horn, pipe, lyre,
trigon, harp, drum, and entire musical ensemble,
shall fall down and worship the golden statue,

¹¹and whoever does not fall down and worship
shall be thrown into a furnace of blazing fire.
¹²There are certain Jews
whom you have appointed over the affairs of the province of Babylon:
Shadrach, Meshach, and Abednego.
These pay no heed to you, O king.
They do not serve your gods
and they do not worship the golden statue that you have set up.”

¹³Then Nebuchadnezzar in furious rage
commanded that Shadrach, Meshach, and Abednego be brought in;
so they brought those men before the king.
¹⁴Nebuchadnezzar said to them,
“Is it true, O Shadrach, Meshach, and Abednego,
that you do not serve my gods
and you do not worship the golden statue that I have set up?
¹⁵Now if you are ready when you hear the sound of the horn, pipe, lyre,
trigon, harp, drum, and entire musical ensemble
to fall down and worship the statue that I have made,
well and good.
But if you do not worship,
you shall immediately be thrown into a furnace of blazing fire,
and who is the god that will deliver you out of my hands?”

¹⁶Shadrach, Meshach, and Abednego answered the king,
“O Nebuchadnezzar,
we have no need to present a defense to you in this matter.
¹⁷If our God whom we serve is able to deliver us
from the furnace of blazing fire and out of your hand, O king,
let him deliver us.
¹⁸But if not, be it known to you, O king,
that we will not serve your gods
and we will not worship the golden statue that you have set up.”

¹⁹Then Nebuchadnezzar was so filled with rage
against Shadrach, Meshach, and Abednego
that his face was distorted.
He ordered the furnace heated up seven times more than was customary,
²⁰and ordered some of the strongest guards in his army
to bind Shadrach, Meshach, and Abednego
and to throw them into the furnace of blazing fire.
²¹So the men were bound, still wearing their tunics,
their trousers, their hats, and their other garments,
and they were thrown into the furnace of blazing fire.
²²Because the king's command was urgent and the furnace was so overheated,
the raging flames killed the men who lifted Shadrach, Meshach, and
      Abednego.

²³But the three men, Shadrach, Meshach, and Abednego, fell down,
bound, into the furnace of blazing fire.

²⁴Then King Nebuchadnezzar was astonished and rose up quickly.
He said to his counselors,
"Was it not three men that we threw bound into the fire?"
They answered the king, "True, O king."
²⁵He replied, "But I see four men unbound,
walking in the middle of the fire,
and they are not hurt;
and the fourth has the appearance of a god."

²⁶Nebuchadnezzar then approached the door of the furnace of blazing fire
        and said,
"Shadrach, Meshach, and Abednego,
servants of the Most High God,
come out! Come here!"
So Shadrach, Meshach, and Abednego came out from the fire.
²⁷And the satraps, the prefects, the governors,
and the king's counselors gathered together
and saw that the fire had not had any power over the bodies of those men;
the hair of their heads was not singed,
their tunics were not harmed,
and not even the smell of fire came from them.

²⁸Nebuchadnezzar said,
"Blessed be the God of Shadrach, Meshach, and Abednego,
who has sent his angel and delivered his servants who trusted in him.
They disobeyed the king's command and yielded up their bodies
rather than serve and worship any god except their own God.
²⁹Therefore I make a decree:
Any people, nation, or language that utters blasphemy
against the God of Shadrach, Meshach, and Abednego
shall be torn limb from limb,
and their houses laid in ruins;
for there is no other god who is able to deliver in this way."

The word of the Lord.

RESPONSE: SONG OF THE THREE YOUNG MEN 35–65

NEW TESTAMENT READING: ROMANS 6:3–11

A reading from Romans:

³Do you not know that all of us who have been baptized into Christ Jesus
were baptized into his death?
⁴Therefore we have been buried with him by baptism into death,
so that, just as Christ was raised from the dead by the glory of the Father,
so we too might walk in newness of life.

⁵For if we have been united with him in a death like his,
we will certainly be united with him in a resurrection like his.
⁶We know that our old self was crucified with him
so that the body of sin might be destroyed,
and we might no longer be enslaved to sin.
⁷For whoever has died is freed from sin.
⁸But if we have died with Christ,
we believe that we will also live with him.
⁹We know that Christ, being raised from the dead, will never die again;
death no longer has dominion over him.
¹⁰The death he died, he died to sin, once for all;
but the life he lives, he lives to God.

¹¹So you also must consider yourselves dead to sin
and alive to God in Christ Jesus.

The word of the Lord.

RESPONSE: PSALM 114

The Holy Gospel according to Luke, the 24th chapter.

¹But on the first day of the week, at early dawn,
they came to the tomb, taking the spices that they had prepared.
²They found the stone rolled away from the tomb,
³but when they went in, they did not find the body.
⁴While they were perplexed about this,
suddenly two men in dazzling clothes stood beside them.
⁵The women were terrified and bowed their faces to the ground,
but the men said to them,
"Why do you look for the living among the dead?
He is not here, but has risen.
⁶Remember how he told you, while he was still in Galilee,
⁷that the Son of Man must be handed over to sinners,
and be crucified, and on the third day rise again."

⁸Then they remembered his words,
⁹and returning from the tomb,
they told all this to the eleven and to all the rest.
¹⁰Now it was Mary Magdalene, Joanna, Mary the mother of James,
and the other women with them who told this to the apostles.
¹¹But these words seemed to them an idle tale,
and they did not believe them.
¹²But Peter got up and ran to the tomb;
stooping and looking in, he saw the linen cloths by themselves;
then he went home, amazed at what had happened.

The Gospel of the Lord.

SEASON OF EASTER

The Resurrection of Our Lord
Easter Day

APRIL 12, 1998   APRIL 15, 2001   APRIL 11, 2004

FIRST READING: Acts 10:34–43
Or Isaiah 65:17–25, following

A reading from Acts:

[34]Then Peter began to speak to them:
"I truly understand that God shows no partiality,
[35]but in every nation anyone who fears him and does what is right
is acceptable to him.

[36]"You know the message he sent to the people of Israel,
preaching peace by Jesus Christ—
he is Lord of all.
[37]That message spread throughout Judea,
beginning in Galilee after the baptism that John announced:
[38]how God anointed Jesus of Nazareth with the Holy Spirit and with power;
how he went about doing good and healing all who were oppressed by the
      devil,
for God was with him.
[39]We are witnesses to all that he did both in Judea and in Jerusalem.
They put him to death by hanging him on a tree;
[40]but God raised him on the third day and allowed him to appear,
[41]not to all the people but to us who were chosen by God as witnesses,
and who ate and drank with him after he rose from the dead.

[42]"He commanded us to preach to the people
and to testify that he is the one ordained by God
as judge of the living and the dead.
[43]All the prophets testify about him that everyone who believes in him
receives forgiveness of sins through his name."

The word of the Lord.

A reading from Isaiah:

¹⁷For I am about to create new heavens
 and a new earth;
the former things shall not be remembered
 or come to mind.
¹⁸But be glad and rejoice forever
 in what I am creating;
for I am about to create Jerusalem as a joy,
 and its people as a delight.
¹⁹I will rejoice in Jerusalem,
 and delight in my people;
no more shall the sound of weeping be heard in it,
 or the cry of distress.
²⁰No more shall there be in it
 an infant that lives but a few days,
 or an old person who does not live out a lifetime;
for one who dies at a hundred years will be considered a youth,
 and one who falls short of a hundred will be considered accursed.
²¹They shall build houses and inhabit them;
 they shall plant vineyards and eat their fruit.
²²They shall not build and another inhabit;
 they shall not plant and another eat;
for like the days of a tree shall the days of my people be,
 and my chosen shall long enjoy the work of their hands.
²³They shall not labor in vain,
 or bear children for calamity;
for they shall be offspring blessed by the LORD—
 and their descendants as well.
²⁴Before they call I will answer,
 while they are yet speaking I will hear.
²⁵The wolf and the lamb shall feed together,
 the lion shall eat straw like the ox;
 but the serpent—its food shall be dust!
They shall not hurt or destroy
 on all my holy mountain,
     says the LORD.

The word of the Lord.

PSALMODY: PSALM 118:1–2, 14–24

A reading from First Corinthians:

[19]If for this life only we have hoped in Christ,
we are of all people most to be pitied.
[20]But in fact Christ has been raised from the dead,
the first fruits of those who have died.
[21]For since death came through a human being,
the resurrection of the dead has also come through a human being;
[22]for as all die in Adam,
so all will be made alive in Christ.
[23]But each in his own order:
Christ the first fruits,
then at his coming those who belong to Christ.
[24]Then comes the end,
when he hands over the kingdom to God the Father,
after he has destroyed every ruler and every authority and power.
[25]For he must reign until he has put all his enemies under his feet.
[26]The last enemy to be destroyed is death.

The word of the Lord.

OR: Acts 10:34–43

A reading from Acts:

[34]Then Peter began to speak to them:
"I truly understand that God shows no partiality,
[35]but in every nation anyone who fears him and does what is right
is acceptable to him.

[36]"You know the message he sent to the people of Israel,
preaching peace by Jesus Christ—
he is Lord of all.
[37]That message spread throughout Judea,
beginning in Galilee after the baptism that John announced:
[38]how God anointed Jesus of Nazareth with the Holy Spirit and with power;
how he went about doing good
and healing all who were oppressed by the devil,
for God was with him.
[39]We are witnesses to all that he did both in Judea and in Jerusalem.
They put him to death by hanging him on a tree;
[40]but God raised him on the third day
and allowed him to appear, [41]not to all the people
but to us who were chosen by God as witnesses,
and who ate and drank with him after he rose from the dead.

[2]"He commanded us to preach to the people
and to testify that he is the one ordained by God
as judge of the living and the dead.
[43]All the prophets testify about him that everyone who believes in him
receives forgiveness of sins through his name."

The word of the Lord.

GOSPEL: JOHN 20:1–18
Or Luke 24:1–12, following

The Holy Gospel according to John, the 20th chapter.

[1]Early on the first day of the week, while it was still dark,
Mary Magdalene came to the tomb
and saw that the stone had been removed from the tomb.
[2]So she ran and went to Simon Peter and the other disciple,
the one whom Jesus loved, and said to them,
"They have taken the Lord out of the tomb,
and we do not know where they have laid him."

[3]Then Peter and the other disciple set out and went toward the tomb.
[4]The two were running together,
but the other disciple outran Peter and reached the tomb first.
[5]He bent down to look in and saw the linen wrappings lying there,
but he did not go in.
[6]Then Simon Peter came, following him, and went into the tomb.
He saw the linen wrappings lying there,
[7]and the cloth that had been on Jesus' head,
not lying with the linen wrappings but rolled up in a place by itself.
[8]Then the other disciple, who reached the tomb first,
also went in, and he saw and believed;
[9]for as yet they did not understand the scripture,
that he must rise from the dead.
[10]Then the disciples returned to their homes.

[11]But Mary stood weeping outside the tomb.
As she wept, she bent over to look into the tomb;
[12]and she saw two angels in white,
sitting where the body of Jesus had been lying,
one at the head and the other at the feet.
[13]They said to her, "Woman, why are you weeping?"
She said to them,
"They have taken away my Lord,
and I do not know where they have laid him."
[14]When she had said this, she turned around and saw Jesus standing there,
but she did not know that it was Jesus.
[15]Jesus said to her,
"Woman, why are you weeping? Whom are you looking for?"

Supposing him to be the gardener, she said to him,
"Sir, if you have carried him away,
tell me where you have laid him, and I will take him away."
[16]Jesus said to her, "Mary!"
She turned and said to him in Hebrew,
"Rabbouni!" (which means Teacher).
[17]Jesus said to her,
"Do not hold on to me, because I have not yet ascended to the Father.
But go to my brothers and say to them,
'I am ascending to my Father and your Father,
to my God and your God.' "

[18]Mary Magdalene went and announced to the disciples,
"I have seen the Lord";
and she told them that he had said these things to her.

The Gospel of the Lord.

OR: LUKE 24:1–12

The Holy Gospel according to Luke, the 24th chapter.

[1]But on the first day of the week, at early dawn,
they came to the tomb, taking the spices that they had prepared.
[2]They found the stone rolled away from the tomb,
[3]but when they went in, they did not find the body.
[4]While they were perplexed about this,
suddenly two men in dazzling clothes stood beside them.
[5]The women were terrified and bowed their faces to the ground,
but the men said to them,
"Why do you look for the living among the dead?
He is not here, but has risen.
[6]Remember how he told you, while he was still in Galilee,
[7]that the Son of Man must be handed over to sinners,
and be crucified, and on the third day rise again."

[8]Then they remembered his words,
[9]and returning from the tomb,
they told all this to the eleven and to all the rest.
[10]Now it was Mary Magdalene, Joanna, Mary the mother of James,
and the other women with them who told this to the apostles.
[11]But these words seemed to them an idle tale,
and they did not believe them.
[12]But Peter got up and ran to the tomb;
stooping and looking in, he saw the linen cloths by themselves;
then he went home, amazed at what had happened.

The Gospel of the Lord.

The Resurrection of Our Lord
Easter Evening

APRIL 12, 1998   APRIL 15, 2001   APRIL 11, 2004

FIRST READING: Isaiah 25:6–9

A reading from Isaiah:

⁶On this mountain the Lord of hosts will make for all peoples
    a feast of rich food, a feast of well-aged wines,
    of rich food filled with marrow, of well-aged wines strained clear.
⁷And he will destroy on this mountain
    the shroud that is cast over all peoples,
    the sheet that is spread over all nations;
    he will swallow up death forever.
⁸Then the Lord God will wipe away the tears from all faces,
    and the disgrace of his people he will take away from all the earth,
    for the Lord has spoken.

⁹It will be said on that day,
    Lo, this is our God; we have waited for him, so that he might save us.
    This is the Lord for whom we have waited;
    let us be glad and rejoice in his salvation.

The word of the Lord.

PSALMODY: Psalm 114

SECOND READING: 1 Corinthians 5:6b–8

A reading from First Corinthians:

⁶ᵇDo you not know that a little yeast leavens the whole batch of dough?
⁷Clean out the old yeast so that you may be a new batch,
as you really are unleavened.
For our paschal lamb, Christ, has been sacrificed.
⁸Therefore, let us celebrate the festival,
not with the old yeast, the yeast of malice and evil,
but with the unleavened bread of sincerity and truth.

The word of the Lord.

The Holy Gospel according to Luke, the 24th chapter.

[13]Now on that same day when Jesus had appeared to Mary Magdalene,
two of them were going to a village called Emmaus,
about seven miles from Jerusalem,
[14]and talking with each other about all these things that had happened.
[15]While they were talking and discussing,
Jesus himself came near and went with them,
[16]but their eyes were kept from recognizing him.
[17]And he said to them,
"What are you discussing with each other while you walk along?"
They stood still, looking sad.
[18]Then one of them, whose name was Cleopas, answered him,
"Are you the only stranger in Jerusalem
who does not know the things that have taken place there in these days?"
[19]He asked them, "What things?"
They replied, "The things about Jesus of Nazareth,
who was a prophet mighty in deed and word before God and all the people,
[20]and how our chief priests and leaders
handed him over to be condemned to death and crucified him.
[21]But we had hoped that he was the one to redeem Israel.
Yes, and besides all this,
it is now the third day since these things took place.
[22]Moreover, some women of our group astounded us.
They were at the tomb early this morning,
[23]and when they did not find his body there, they came back
and told us that they had indeed seen a vision of angels
who said that he was alive.
[24]Some of those who were with us went to the tomb
and found it just as the women had said;
but they did not see him."

[25]Then he said to them,
"Oh, how foolish you are,
and how slow of heart to believe all that the prophets have declared!
[26]Was it not necessary that the Messiah should suffer these things
and then enter into his glory?"
[27]Then beginning with Moses and all the prophets,
he interpreted to them the things about himself in all the scriptures.

[28]As they came near the village to which they were going,
he walked ahead as if he were going on.
[29]But they urged him strongly, saying,
"Stay with us,
because it is almost evening and the day is now nearly over."
So he went in to stay with them.

^{30}When he was at the table with them,
he took bread, blessed and broke it, and gave it to them.
^{31}Then their eyes were opened, and they recognized him;
and he vanished from their sight.
^{32}They said to each other,
"Were not our hearts burning within us
while he was talking to us on the road,
while he was opening the scriptures to us?"

^{33}That same hour they got up and returned to Jerusalem;
and they found the eleven and their companions gathered together.
^{34}They were saying,
"The Lord has risen indeed, and he has appeared to Simon!"
^{35}Then they told what had happened on the road,
and how he had been made known to them in the breaking of the bread.

^{36}While they were talking about this,
Jesus himself stood among them and said to them,
"Peace be with you."
^{37}They were startled and terrified,
and thought that they were seeing a ghost.
^{38}He said to them,
"Why are you frightened, and why do doubts arise in your hearts?
^{39}Look at my hands and my feet; see that it is I myself.
Touch me and see;
for a ghost does not have flesh and bones as you see that I have."
^{40}And when he had said this, he showed them his hands and his feet.
^{41}While in their joy they were disbelieving and still wondering,
he said to them,
"Have you anything here to eat?"
^{42}They gave him a piece of broiled fish,
^{43}and he took it and ate in their presence.

^{44}Then he said to them,
"These are my words that I spoke to you while I was still with you—
that everything written about me
in the law of Moses, the prophets, and the psalms must be fulfilled."
^{45}Then he opened their minds to understand the scriptures,
^{46}and he said to them,
"Thus it is written,
that the Messiah is to suffer and to rise from the dead on the third day,
^{47}and that repentance and forgiveness of sins
is to be proclaimed in his name to all nations, beginning from Jerusalem.
^{48}You are witnesses of these things.
^{49}And see, I am sending upon you what my Father promised;
so stay here in the city until you have been clothed with power from on high."

The Gospel of the Lord.

SECOND SUNDAY OF EASTER

APRIL 19, 1998   APRIL 22, 2001   APRIL 18, 2004

FIRST READING: ACTS 5:27–32

A reading from Acts:

²⁷When they had brought the apostles,
they had them stand before the council.
The high priest questioned them, ²⁸saying,
"We gave you strict orders not to teach in this name,
yet here you have filled Jerusalem with your teaching
and you are determined to bring this man's blood on us."
²⁹But Peter and the apostles answered,
"We must obey God rather than any human authority.
³⁰The God of our ancestors raised up Jesus,
whom you had killed by hanging him on a tree.
³¹God exalted him at his right hand as Leader and Savior
that he might give repentance to Israel and forgiveness of sins.
³²And we are witnesses to these things,
and so is the Holy Spirit whom God has given to those who obey him."

The word of the Lord.

PSALMODY: PSALM 118:14–29 or PSALM 150

SECOND READING: Revelation 1:4–8

A reading from Revelation:

⁴John to the seven churches that are in Asia:
Grace to you and peace
from him who is and who was and who is to come,
and from the seven spirits who are before his throne,
⁵and from Jesus Christ, the faithful witness, the firstborn of the dead,
and the ruler of the kings of the earth.
To him who loves us and freed us from our sins by his blood,
⁶and made us to be a kingdom, priests serving his God and Father,
to him be glory and dominion forever and ever. Amen.
⁷Look! He is coming with the clouds;
every eye will see him,
even those who pierced him;
and on his account all the tribes of the earth will wail.
So it is to be. Amen.

⁸"I am the Alpha and the Omega," says the Lord God,
who is and who was and who is to come, the Almighty.

The word of the Lord.

GOSPEL: JOHN 20:19–31

The Holy Gospel according to John, the 20th chapter.

[19]When it was evening on that day, the first day of the week,
and the doors of the house where the disciples had met
were locked for fear of the Jews,
Jesus came and stood among them and said,
"Peace be with you."
[20]After he said this, he showed them his hands and his side.
Then the disciples rejoiced when they saw the Lord.
[21]Jesus said to them again,
"Peace be with you.
As the Father has sent me, so I send you."
[22]When he had said this, he breathed on them and said to them,
"Receive the Holy Spirit.
[23]If you forgive the sins of any, they are forgiven them;
if you retain the sins of any, they are retained."

[24]But Thomas (who was called the Twin), one of the twelve,
was not with them when Jesus came.
[25]So the other disciples told him, "We have seen the Lord."
But he said to them,
"Unless I see the mark of the nails in his hands,
and put my finger in the mark of the nails and my hand in his side,
I will not believe."

[26]A week later his disciples were again in the house,
and Thomas was with them.
Although the doors were shut,
Jesus came and stood among them and said,
"Peace be with you."
[27]Then he said to Thomas,
"Put your finger here and see my hands.
Reach out your hand and put it in my side.
Do not doubt but believe."
[28]Thomas answered him,
"My Lord and my God!"
[29]Jesus said to him, "Have you believed because you have seen me?
Blessed are those who have not seen and yet have come to believe."

[30]Now Jesus did many other signs in the presence of his disciples,
which are not written in this book.
[31]But these are written so that you may come to believe that Jesus
        is the Messiah, the Son of God,
and that through believing you may have life in his name.

The Gospel of the Lord.

Third Sunday of Easter

APRIL 26, 1998   APRIL 29, 2001   APRIL 25, 2004

FIRST READING: Acts 9:1–6 [7–20]

A reading from Acts:

¹Meanwhile Saul,
still breathing threats and murder against the disciples of the Lord,
went to the high priest
²and asked him for letters to the synagogues at Damascus,
so that if he found any who belonged to the Way, men or women,
he might bring them bound to Jerusalem.
³Now as he was going along and approaching Damascus,
suddenly a light from heaven flashed around him.
⁴He fell to the ground and heard a voice saying to him,
"Saul, Saul, why do you persecute me?"
⁵He asked, "Who are you, Lord?"
The reply came, "I am Jesus, whom you are persecuting.
⁶But get up and enter the city, and you will be told what you are to do."

[⁷The men who were traveling with him stood speechless
because they heard the voice but saw no one.
⁸Saul got up from the ground,
and though his eyes were open, he could see nothing;
so they led him by the hand and brought him into Damascus.
⁹For three days he was without sight, and neither ate nor drank.

¹⁰Now there was a disciple in Damascus named Ananias.
The Lord said to him in a vision, "Ananias."
He answered, "Here I am, Lord."
¹¹The Lord said to him, "Get up and go to the street called Straight,
and at the house of Judas look for a man of Tarsus named Saul.
At this moment he is praying,
¹²and he has seen in a vision a man named Ananias come in
and lay his hands on him so that he might regain his sight."
¹³But Ananias answered,
"Lord, I have heard from many about this man,
how much evil he has done to your saints in Jerusalem;
¹⁴and here he has authority from the chief priests to bind all who invoke your
        name."
¹⁵But the Lord said to him,

"Go, for he is an instrument whom I have chosen
to bring my name before Gentiles and kings and before the people of Israel;
[16]I myself will show him how much he must suffer for the sake of my name."

[17]So Ananias went and entered the house.
He laid his hands on Saul and said,
"Brother Saul, the Lord Jesus, who appeared to you on your way here,
has sent me so that you may regain your sight
and be filled with the Holy Spirit."
[18]And immediately something like scales fell from his eyes,
and his sight was restored.
Then he got up and was baptized,
[19]and after taking some food, he regained his strength.
For several days he was with the disciples in Damascus,
[20]and immediately he began to proclaim Jesus in the synagogues,
saying, "He is the Son of God."]

The word of the Lord.

PSALMODY: PSALM 30

SECOND READING: REVELATION 5:11–14

A reading from Revelation:

[11]Then I looked, and I heard the voice of many angels surrounding the throne
and the living creatures and the elders;
they numbered myriads of myriads and thousands of thousands,
[12]singing with full voice,
   "Worthy is the Lamb that was slaughtered
   to receive power and wealth and wisdom and might
   and honor and glory and blessing!"
[13]Then I heard every creature in heaven and on earth
and under the earth and in the sea, and all that is in them, singing,
   "To the one seated on the throne and to the Lamb
   be blessing and honor and glory and might
   forever and ever!"
[14]And the four living creatures said, "Amen!"
And the elders fell down and worshiped.

The word of the Lord.

The Holy Gospel according to John, the 21st chapter.

¹After he appeared to his followers in Jerusalem,
Jesus showed himself again to the disciples by the Sea of Tiberias;
and he showed himself in this way.
²Gathered there together were Simon Peter, Thomas called the Twin,
Nathanael of Cana in Galilee, the sons of Zebedee,
and two others of his disciples.
³Simon Peter said to them, "I am going fishing."
They said to him, "We will go with you."
They went out and got into the boat, but that night they caught nothing.

⁴Just after daybreak, Jesus stood on the beach;
but the disciples did not know that it was Jesus.
⁵Jesus said to them, "Children, you have no fish, have you?"
They answered him, "No."
⁶He said to them,
"Cast the net to the right side of the boat, and you will find some."
So they cast it,
and now they were not able to haul it in because there were so many fish.
⁷That disciple whom Jesus loved said to Peter, "It is the Lord!"
When Simon Peter heard that it was the Lord,
he put on some clothes, for he was naked, and jumped into the sea.
⁸But the other disciples came in the boat, dragging the net full of fish,
for they were not far from the land, only about a hundred yards off.

⁹When they had gone ashore, they saw a charcoal fire there,
with fish on it, and bread.
¹⁰Jesus said to them, "Bring some of the fish that you have just caught."
¹¹So Simon Peter went aboard and hauled the net ashore,
full of large fish, a hundred fifty-three of them;
and though there were so many, the net was not torn.
¹²Jesus said to them, "Come and have breakfast."
Now none of the disciples dared to ask him, "Who are you?"
because they knew it was the Lord.
¹³Jesus came and took the bread and gave it to them,
and did the same with the fish.
¹⁴This was now the third time that Jesus appeared to the disciples
after he was raised from the dead.

¹⁵When they had finished breakfast, Jesus said to Simon Peter,
"Simon son of John, do you love me more than these?"
He said to him, "Yes, Lord; you know that I love you."
Jesus said to him, "Feed my lambs."
¹⁶A second time he said to him,
"Simon son of John, do you love me?"

He said to him, "Yes, Lord; you know that I love you."
Jesus said to him, "Tend my sheep."
[17]He said to him the third time, "Simon son of John, do you love me?"
Peter felt hurt because he said to him the third time, "Do you love me?"
And he said to him, "Lord, you know everything;
you know that I love you."
Jesus said to him, "Feed my sheep.
[18]Very truly, I tell you, when you were younger,
you used to fasten your own belt and to go wherever you wished.
But when you grow old, you will stretch out your hands,
and someone else will fasten a belt around you
and take you where you do not wish to go."
[19](He said this to indicate the kind of death by which he would glorify God.)
After this he said to him, "Follow me."

The Gospel of the Lord.

FOURTH SUNDAY OF EASTER

MAY 3, 1998   MAY 6, 2001   MAY 2, 2004

FIRST READING: ACTS 9:36–43

A reading from Acts:

³⁶Now in Joppa there was a disciple whose name was Tabitha,
which in Greek is Dorcas.
She was devoted to good works and acts of charity.
³⁷At that time she became ill and died.
When they had washed her, they laid her in a room upstairs.
³⁸Since Lydda was near Joppa, the disciples, who heard that Peter was there,
sent two men to him with the request,
"Please come to us without delay."

³⁹So Peter got up and went with them;
and when he arrived, they took him to the room upstairs.
All the widows stood beside him,
weeping and showing tunics and other clothing
that Dorcas had made while she was with them.
⁴⁰Peter put all of them outside, and then he knelt down and prayed.
He turned to the body and said, "Tabitha, get up."
Then she opened her eyes, and seeing Peter, she sat up.
⁴¹He gave her his hand and helped her up.
Then calling the saints and widows, he showed her to be alive.

⁴²This became known throughout Joppa,
and many believed in the Lord.
⁴³Meanwhile he stayed in Joppa for some time with a certain Simon, a tanner.

The word of the Lord.

PSALMODY: PSALM 23

SECOND READING: REVELATION 7:9–17

A reading from Revelation:

⁹After this I looked, and there was a great multitude that no one could count,
from every nation, from all tribes and peoples and languages,
standing before the throne and before the Lamb,
robed in white, with palm branches in their hands.

¹⁰They cried out in a loud voice, saying,

> "Salvation belongs to our God who is seated on the throne, and to the
> > Lamb!"

¹¹And all the angels stood around the throne
and around the elders and the four living creatures,
and they fell on their faces before the throne and worshiped God, ¹²singing,

> "Amen! Blessing and glory and wisdom
> and thanksgiving and honor
> and power and might
> be to our God forever and ever! Amen."

¹³Then one of the elders addressed me, saying,
"Who are these, robed in white, and where have they come from?"
¹⁴I said to him, "Sir, you are the one that knows."
Then he said to me,
"These are they who have come out of the great ordeal;
they have washed their robes and made them white in the blood of the Lamb.

> ¹⁵For this reason they are before the throne of God,
> > and worship him day and night within his temple,
> > and the one who is seated on the throne will shelter them.
> ¹⁶They will hunger no more, and thirst no more;
> > the sun will not strike them,
> > nor any scorching heat;
> ¹⁷for the Lamb at the center of the throne will be their shepherd,
> > and he will guide them to springs of the water of life,
> and God will wipe away every tear from their eyes."

The word of the Lord.

GOSPEL: JOHN 10:22–30

The Holy Gospel according to John, the tenth chapter.

²²At that time the festival of the Dedication took place in Jerusalem.
It was winter, ²³and Jesus was walking in the temple,
in the portico of Solomon.
²⁴So the Jews gathered around him and said to him,
"How long will you keep us in suspense?
If you are the Messiah, tell us plainly."
²⁵Jesus answered, "I have told you, and you do not believe.
The works that I do in my Father's name testify to me;
²⁶but you do not believe, because you do not belong to my sheep.
²⁷My sheep hear my voice.
I know them, and they follow me.
²⁸I give them eternal life, and they will never perish.
No one will snatch them out of my hand.
²⁹What my Father has given me is greater than all else,
and no one can snatch it out of the Father's hand.
³⁰The Father and I are one."

The Gospel of the Lord.

FIFTH SUNDAY OF EASTER

MAY 10, 1998   MAY 13, 2001   MAY 9, 2004

FIRST READING: ACTS 11:1–18

A reading from Acts:

[1]Now the apostles and the believers who were in Judea
heard that the Gentiles had also accepted the word of God.
[2]So when Peter went up to Jerusalem,
the circumcised believers criticized him, [3]saying,
"Why did you go to uncircumcised men and eat with them?"
[4]Then Peter began to explain it to them, step by step, saying,
[5]"I was in the city of Joppa praying, and in a trance I saw a vision.
There was something like a large sheet coming down from heaven,
being lowered by its four corners; and it came close to me.
[6]As I looked at it closely I saw four-footed animals,
beasts of prey, reptiles, and birds of the air.
[7]I also heard a voice saying to me, 'Get up, Peter; kill and eat.'
[8]But I replied, 'By no means, Lord;
for nothing profane or unclean has ever entered my mouth.'
[9]But a second time the voice answered from heaven,
'What God has made clean, you must not call profane.'
[10]This happened three times;
then everything was pulled up again to heaven.

[11]"At that very moment three men, sent to me from Caesarea,
arrived at the house where we were.
[12]The Spirit told me to go with them
and not to make a distinction between them and us.
These six brothers also accompanied me,
and we entered the man's house.
[13]He told us how he had seen the angel standing in his house and saying,
'Send to Joppa and bring Simon, who is called Peter;
[14]he will give you a message
by which you and your entire household will be saved.'
[15]And as I began to speak, the Holy Spirit fell upon them
just as it had upon us at the beginning.
[16]And I remembered the word of the Lord, how he had said,
'John baptized with water, but you will be baptized with the Holy Spirit.'
[17]If then God gave them the same gift
that he gave us when we believed in the Lord Jesus Christ,

who was I that I could hinder God?"
¹⁸When they heard this, they were silenced.
And they praised God, saying,
"Then God has given even to the Gentiles the repentance that leads to life."

The word of the Lord.

PSALMODY: PSALM 148

SECOND READING: REVELATION 21:1–6

A reading from Revelation:

¹Then I saw a new heaven and a new earth;
for the first heaven and the first earth had passed away,
and the sea was no more.
²And I saw the holy city, the new Jerusalem,
coming down out of heaven from God,
prepared as a bride adorned for her husband.
³And I heard a loud voice from the throne saying,
        "See, the home of God is among mortals.
        He will dwell with them as their God;
        they will be his peoples,
        and God himself will be with them;
        ⁴he will wipe every tear from their eyes.
        Death will be no more;
        mourning and crying and pain will be no more,
        for the first things have passed away."
⁵And the one who was seated on the throne said,
"See, I am making all things new."
Also he said, "Write this, for these words are trustworthy and true."
⁶Then he said to me, "It is done!
I am the Alpha and the Omega, the beginning and the end.
To the thirsty I will give water as a gift from the spring of the water of life."

The word of the Lord.

The Holy Gospel according to John, the 13th chapter.

³¹When he had gone out, Jesus said,
"Now the Son of Man has been glorified,
and God has been glorified in him.
³²If God has been glorified in him,
God will also glorify him in himself and will glorify him at once.
³³Little children, I am with you only a little longer.
You will look for me; and as I said to the Jews so now I say to you,
'Where I am going, you cannot come.'
³⁴I give you a new commandment, that you love one another.
Just as I have loved you, you also should love one another.
³⁵By this everyone will know that you are my disciples,
if you have love for one another."

The Gospel of the Lord.

Sixth Sunday of Easter

MAY 17, 1998   MAY 20, 2001   MAY 16, 2004

FIRST READING: Acts 16:9–15

A reading from Acts:

⁹During the night Paul had a vision:
there stood a man of Macedonia pleading with him and saying,
"Come over to Macedonia and help us."
¹⁰When he had seen the vision,
we immediately tried to cross over to Macedonia,
being convinced that God had called us to proclaim the good news to them.

¹¹We set sail from Troas and took a straight course to Samothrace,
the following day to Neapolis, ¹²and from there to Philippi,
which is a leading city of the district of Macedonia and a Roman colony.
We remained in this city for some days.
¹³On the sabbath day we went outside the gate by the river,
where we supposed there was a place of prayer;
and we sat down and spoke to the women who had gathered there.
¹⁴A certain woman named Lydia, a worshiper of God, was listening to us;
she was from the city of Thyatira and a dealer in purple cloth.
The Lord opened her heart to listen eagerly to what was said by Paul.
¹⁵When she and her household were baptized, she urged us, saying,
"If you have judged me to be faithful to the Lord,
come and stay at my home."
And she prevailed upon us.

The word of the Lord.

PSALMODY: Psalm 67

SECOND READING: Revelation 21:10, 22—22:5

A reading from Revelation:

¹⁰And in the spirit he carried me away to a great, high mountain
and showed me the holy city Jerusalem
coming down out of heaven from God.

²²I saw no temple in the city,
for its temple is the Lord God the Almighty and the Lamb.
²³And the city has no need of sun or moon to shine on it,
for the glory of God is its light, and its lamp is the Lamb.
²⁴The nations will walk by its light,
and the kings of the earth will bring their glory into it.
²⁵Its gates will never be shut by day—
and there will be no night there.
²⁶People will bring into it the glory and the honor of the nations.
²⁷But nothing unclean will enter it,
nor anyone who practices abomination or falsehood,
but only those who are written in the Lamb's book of life.

²²:¹Then the angel showed me the river of the water of life,
bright as crystal, flowing from the throne of God and of the Lamb
²through the middle of the street of the city.
On either side of the river is the tree of life with its twelve kinds of fruit,
producing its fruit each month;
and the leaves of the tree are for the healing of the nations.
³Nothing accursed will be found there any more.
But the throne of God and of the Lamb will be in it,
and his servants will worship him;
⁴they will see his face,
and his name will be on their foreheads.
⁵And there will be no more night;
they need no light of lamp or sun,
for the Lord God will be their light,
and they will reign forever and ever.

The word of the Lord.

GOSPEL: JOHN 14:23–29

Or John 5:1–9, following

The Holy Gospel according to John, the 14th chapter.

²³Jesus answered Judas (not Iscariot),
"Those who love me will keep my word,
and my Father will love them,
and we will come to them and make our home with them.
²⁴Whoever does not love me does not keep my words;
and the word that you hear is not mine,
but is from the Father who sent me.

²⁵"I have said these things to you while I am still with you.
²⁶But the Advocate, the Holy Spirit,
whom the Father will send in my name, will teach you everything,
and remind you of all that I have said to you.

27Peace I leave with you; my peace I give to you.
I do not give to you as the world gives.
Do not let your hearts be troubled, and do not let them be afraid.
28You heard me say to you,
'I am going away, and I am coming to you.'
If you loved me, you would rejoice that I am going to the Father,
because the Father is greater than I.
29And now I have told you this before it occurs,
so that when it does occur, you may believe."

The Gospel of the Lord.

OR: JOHN 5:1–9

The Holy Gospel according to John, the fifth chapter.

1After this there was a festival of the Jews, and Jesus went up to Jerusalem.
2Now in Jerusalem by the Sheep Gate there is a pool,
called in Hebrew Beth-zatha, which has five porticoes.
3In these lay many invalids—blind, lame, and paralyzed.
5One man was there who had been ill for thirty-eight years.
6When Jesus saw him lying there and knew that he had been there a long time,
he said to him, "Do you want to be made well?"
7The sick man answered him,
"Sir, I have no one to put me into the pool when the water is stirred up;
and while I am making my way, someone else steps down ahead of me."
8Jesus said to him, "Stand up, take your mat and walk."
9At once the man was made well,
and he took up his mat and began to walk.
Now that day was a sabbath.

The Gospel of the Lord.

THE ASCENSION OF OUR LORD

MAY 21, 1998   MAY 24, 2001   MAY 20, 2004

FIRST READING: ACTS 1:1–11

A reading from Acts:

Luke writes:
¹In the first book, Theophilus,
I wrote about all that Jesus did and taught from the beginning
²until the day when he was taken up to heaven,
after giving instructions through the Holy Spirit
to the apostles whom he had chosen.
³After his suffering he presented himself alive to them
by many convincing proofs,
appearing to them during forty days
and speaking about the kingdom of God.
⁴While staying with them, he ordered them not to leave Jerusalem,
but to wait there for the promise of the Father.
"This," he said, "is what you have heard from me;
⁵for John baptized with water,
but you will be baptized with the Holy Spirit not many days from now."

⁶So when they had come together, they asked him,
"Lord, is this the time when you will restore the kingdom to Israel?"
⁷He replied,
"It is not for you to know the times or periods
that the Father has set by his own authority.
⁸But you will receive power when the Holy Spirit has come upon you;
and you will be my witnesses
in Jerusalem, in all Judea and Samaria, and to the ends of the earth."
⁹When he had said this, as they were watching,
he was lifted up, and a cloud took him out of their sight.

¹⁰While he was going and they were gazing up toward heaven,
suddenly two men in white robes stood by them.
¹¹They said, "Men of Galilee,
why do you stand looking up toward heaven?
This Jesus, who has been taken up from you into heaven,
will come in the same way as you saw him go into heaven."

The word of the Lord.

PSALMODY: PSALM 47 or PSALM 93

SECOND READING: Ephesians 1:15–23

A reading from Ephesians:

[15]I have heard of your faith in the Lord Jesus
and your love toward all the saints,
and for this reason [16]I do not cease to give thanks for you
as I remember you in my prayers.
[17]I pray that the God of our Lord Jesus Christ, the Father of glory,
may give you a spirit of wisdom and revelation as you come to know him,
[18]so that, with the eyes of your heart enlightened,
you may know what is the hope to which he has called you,
what are the riches of his glorious inheritance among the saints,
[19]and what is the immeasurable greatness of his power for us who believe,
according to the working of his great power.

[20]God put this power to work in Christ when he raised him from the dead
and seated him at his right hand in the heavenly places,
[21]far above all rule and authority and power and dominion,
and above every name that is named,
not only in this age but also in the age to come.
[22]And he has put all things under his feet
and has made him the head over all things for the church,
[23]which is his body, the fullness of him who fills all in all.

The word of the Lord.

The Holy Gospel according to Luke, the 24th chapter.

44Jesus said to the eleven and those with them,
"These are my words that I spoke to you while I was still with you—
that everything written about me
in the law of Moses, the prophets, and the psalms must be fulfilled."
45Then he opened their minds to understand the scriptures,
46and he said to them,
"Thus it is written, that the Messiah is to suffer
and to rise from the dead on the third day,
47and that repentance and forgiveness of sins
is to be proclaimed in his name to all nations,
beginning from Jerusalem.
48You are witnesses of these things.
49And see, I am sending upon you what my Father promised;
so stay here in the city until you have been clothed with power from on high."

50Then he led them out as far as Bethany,
and, lifting up his hands, he blessed them.
51While he was blessing them, he withdrew from them
and was carried up into heaven.
52And they worshiped him, and returned to Jerusalem with great joy;
53and they were continually in the temple blessing God.

The Gospel of the Lord.

SEVENTH SUNDAY OF EASTER

MAY 24, 1998   MAY 27, 2001   MAY 23, 2004

FIRST READING: ACTS 16:16–34

A reading from Acts:

[16]One day, as we were going to the place of prayer,
we met a slave girl who had a spirit of divination
and brought her owners a great deal of money by fortune-telling.
[17]While she followed Paul and us, she would cry out,
"These men are slaves of the Most High God,
who proclaim to you a way of salvation."
[18]She kept doing this for many days.
But Paul, very much annoyed, turned and said to the spirit,
"I order you in the name of Jesus Christ to come out of her."
And it came out that very hour.

[19]But when her owners saw that their hope of making money was gone,
they seized Paul and Silas
and dragged them into the marketplace before the authorities.
[20]When they had brought them before the magistrates, they said,
"These men are disturbing our city;
they are Jews [21]and are advocating customs
that are not lawful for us as Romans to adopt or observe."
[22]The crowd joined in attacking them,
and the magistrates had them stripped of their clothing
and ordered them to be beaten with rods.
[23]After they had given them a severe flogging,
they threw them into prison and ordered the jailer to keep them securely.
[24]Following these instructions,
he put them in the innermost cell and fastened their feet in the stocks.

[25]About midnight Paul and Silas were praying and singing hymns to God,
and the prisoners were listening to them.
[26]Suddenly there was an earthquake,
so violent that the foundations of the prison were shaken;
and immediately all the doors were opened
and everyone's chains were unfastened.
[27]When the jailer woke up and saw the prison doors wide open,
he drew his sword and was about to kill himself,
since he supposed that the prisoners had escaped.

²⁸But Paul shouted in a loud voice,
"Do not harm yourself, for we are all here."
²⁹The jailer called for lights,
and rushing in, he fell down trembling before Paul and Silas.
³⁰Then he brought them outside and said,
"Sirs, what must I do to be saved?"
³¹They answered, "Believe on the Lord Jesus,
and you will be saved, you and your household."
³²They spoke the word of the Lord to him and to all who were in his house.
³³At the same hour of the night he took them and washed their wounds;
then he and his entire family were baptized without delay.
³⁴He brought them up into the house and set food before them;
and he and his entire household rejoiced that he had become a believer in
     God.

The word of the Lord.

PSALMODY: PSALM 97

SECOND READING: REVELATION 22:12–14, 16–17, 20–21

A reading from Revelation:

¹²"See, I am coming soon;
my reward is with me, to repay according to everyone's work.
¹³I am the Alpha and the Omega,
the first and the last, the beginning and the end."

¹⁴Blessed are those who wash their robes,
so that they will have the right to the tree of life
and may enter the city by the gates.
¹⁶"It is I, Jesus, who sent my angel to you
with this testimony for the churches.
I am the root and the descendant of David, the bright morning star."
     ¹⁷The Spirit and the bride say, "Come."
     And let everyone who hears say, "Come."
     And let everyone who is thirsty come.
     Let anyone who wishes take the water of life as a gift.

²⁰The one who testifies to these things says,
"Surely I am coming soon."
Amen. Come, Lord Jesus!

²¹The grace of the Lord Jesus be with all the saints. Amen.

The word of the Lord.

GOSPEL: JOHN 17:20–26

The Holy Gospel according to John, the 17th chapter.

Jesus prayed:
[20]"I ask not only on behalf of these,
but also on behalf of those who will believe in me through their word,
[21]that they may all be one.
As you, Father, are in me and I am in you,
may they also be in us,
so that the world may believe that you have sent me.
[22]The glory that you have given me I have given them,
so that they may be one, as we are one,
[23]I in them and you in me,
that they may become completely one,
so that the world may know that you have sent me
and have loved them even as you have loved me.
[24]Father, I desire that those also, whom you have given me,
may be with me where I am, to see my glory,
which you have given me
because you loved me before the foundation of the world.

[25]"Righteous Father, the world does not know you,
but I know you;
and these know that you have sent me.
[26]I made your name known to them,
and I will make it known,
so that the love with which you have loved me may be in them,
and I in them."

The Gospel of the Lord.

VIGIL OF PENTECOST

MAY 30, 1998   JUNE 2, 2001   MAY 29, 2004

FIRST READING: EXODUS 19:1–9
Or Acts 2:1–11, following

A reading from Exodus:

¹On the third new moon after the Israelites had gone out of the land of Egypt,
on that very day, they came into the wilderness of Sinai.
²They had journeyed from Rephidim,
entered the wilderness of Sinai, and camped in the wilderness;
Israel camped there in front of the mountain.

³Then Moses went up to God;
the LORD called to him from the mountain, saying,
"Thus you shall say to the house of Jacob, and tell the Israelites:
⁴You have seen what I did to the Egyptians,
and how I bore you on eagles' wings and brought you to myself.
⁵Now therefore, if you obey my voice and keep my covenant,
you shall be my treasured possession out of all the peoples.
Indeed, the whole earth is mine,
⁶but you shall be for me a priestly kingdom and a holy nation.
These are the words that you shall speak to the Israelites."

⁷So Moses came, summoned the elders of the people,
and set before them all these words that the LORD had commanded him.
⁸The people all answered as one:
"Everything that the LORD has spoken we will do."
Moses reported the words of the people to the LORD.
⁹Then the LORD said to Moses,
"I am going to come to you in a dense cloud,
in order that the people may hear when I speak with you
and so trust you ever after."

The word of the Lord.

OR: Acts 2:1–11

A reading from Acts:

[1]When the day of Pentecost had come, they were all together in one place.
[2]And suddenly from heaven there came a sound like the rush of a violent wind,
and it filled the entire house where they were sitting.
[3]Divided tongues, as of fire, appeared among them,
and a tongue rested on each of them.
[4]All of them were filled with the Holy Spirit
and began to speak in other languages, as the Spirit gave them ability.

[5]Now there were devout Jews from every nation under heaven
          living in Jerusalem.
[6]And at this sound the crowd gathered and was bewildered,
because each one heard them speaking in the native language of each.
[7]Amazed and astonished, they asked,
"Are not all these who are speaking Galileans?
[8]And how is it that we hear, each of us, in our own native language?
[9]Parthians, Medes, Elamites,
and residents of Mesopotamia, Judea and Cappadocia, Pontus and Asia,
[10]Phrygia and Pamphylia, Egypt and the parts of Libya belonging to Cyrene,
and visitors from Rome, both Jews and proselytes, [11]Cretans and Arabs—
in our own languages we hear them speaking about God's deeds of power."

The word of the Lord.

PSALMODY: PSALM 33:12–22 or PSALM 130

SECOND READING: ROMANS 8:14–17, 22–27

A reading from Romans:

¹⁴All who are led by the Spirit of God are children of God.
¹⁵For you did not receive a spirit of slavery to fall back into fear,
but you have received a spirit of adoption.
When we cry, "Abba! Father!"
¹⁶it is that very Spirit bearing witness with our spirit
that we are children of God,
¹⁷and if children, then heirs,
heirs of God and joint heirs with Christ—
if, in fact, we suffer with him
so that we may also be glorified with him.

²²We know that the whole creation has been groaning in labor pains until now;
²³and not only the creation,
but we ourselves, who have the first fruits of the Spirit,
groan inwardly while we wait for adoption, the redemption of our bodies.
²⁴For in hope we were saved.
Now hope that is seen is not hope.
For who hopes for what is seen?
²⁵But if we hope for what we do not see, we wait for it with patience.

²⁶Likewise the Spirit helps us in our weakness;
for we do not know how to pray as we ought,
but that very Spirit intercedes with sighs too deep for words.
²⁷And God, who searches the heart,
knows what is the mind of the Spirit,
because the Spirit intercedes for the saints according to the will of God.

The word of the Lord.

GOSPEL: JOHN 7:37–39a

The Holy Gospel according to John, the seventh chapter.

³⁷On the last day of the festival of Booths, the great day,
while Jesus was standing in the temple, he cried out,
"Let anyone who is thirsty come to me,
³⁸and let the one who believes in me drink.
As the scripture has said,
'Out of the believer's heart shall flow rivers of living water.' "
³⁹Now he said this about the Spirit,
which believers in him were to receive.

The Gospel of the Lord.

The Day of Pentecost

MAY 31, 1998   JUNE 3, 2001   MAY 30, 2004

FIRST READING: ACTS 2:1–21

Or Genesis 11:1–9, following

A reading from Acts:

¹When the day of Pentecost had come, they were all together in one place.
²And suddenly from heaven there came a sound like the rush of a violent wind,
and it filled the entire house where they were sitting.
³Divided tongues, as of fire, appeared among them,
and a tongue rested on each of them.
⁴All of them were filled with the Holy Spirit
and began to speak in other languages, as the Spirit gave them ability.

⁵Now there were devout Jews from every nation under heaven living in
  Jerusalem.
⁶And at this sound the crowd gathered and was bewildered,
because each one heard them speaking in the native language of each.
⁷Amazed and astonished, they asked,
"Are not all these who are speaking Galileans?
⁸And how is it that we hear, each of us, in our own native language?
⁹Parthians, Medes, Elamites,
and residents of Mesopotamia, Judea and Cappadocia, Pontus and Asia,
¹⁰Phrygia and Pamphylia, Egypt and the parts of Libya belonging to Cyrene,
and visitors from Rome, both Jews and proselytes, ¹¹Cretans and Arabs—
in our own languages we hear them speaking about God's deeds of power."
¹²All were amazed and perplexed, saying to one another,
"What does this mean?"
¹³But others sneered and said, "They are filled with new wine."

¹⁴But Peter, standing with the eleven, raised his voice and addressed them,
"Men of Judea and all who live in Jerusalem,
let this be known to you, and listen to what I say.
¹⁵Indeed, these are not drunk, as you suppose,
for it is only nine o'clock in the morning.
¹⁶No, this is what was spoken through the prophet Joel:

  ¹⁷'In the last days it will be, God declares,
  that I will pour out my Spirit upon all flesh,
    and your sons and your daughters shall prophesy,

and your young men shall see visions,
    and your old men shall dream dreams.
[18]Even upon my slaves, both men and women,
    in those days I will pour out my Spirit;
    and they shall prophesy.
[19]And I will show portents in the heaven above
    and signs on the earth below,
    blood, and fire, and smoky mist.
[20]The sun shall be turned to darkness
    and the moon to blood,
    before the coming of the Lord's great and glorious day.
[21]Then everyone who calls on the name of the Lord shall be saved.' "

The word of the Lord.

OR: GENESIS 11:1–9

A reading from Genesis:

[1]Now the whole earth had one language and the same words.
[2]And as they migrated from the east,
they came upon a plain in the land of Shinar and settled there.
[3]And they said to one another,
"Come, let us make bricks, and burn them thoroughly."
And they had brick for stone, and bitumen for mortar.
[4]Then they said, "Come, let us build ourselves a city,
and a tower with its top in the heavens,
and let us make a name for ourselves;
otherwise we shall be scattered abroad upon the face of the whole earth."

[5]The LORD came down to see the city and the tower, which mortals had built.
[6]And the LORD said,
"Look, they are one people, and they have all one language;
and this is only the beginning of what they will do;
nothing that they propose to do will now be impossible for them.
[7]Come, let us go down, and confuse their language there,
so that they will not understand one another's speech."
[8]So the LORD scattered them abroad from there over the face of all the earth,
and they left off building the city.
[9]Therefore it was called Babel,
because there the LORD confused the language of all the earth;
and from there the LORD scattered them abroad over the face of all the earth.

The word of the Lord.

PSALMODY: PSALM 104:24–34, 35b   *Psalm 104:25–35, 37* LBW/BCP

SECOND READING: ROMANS 8:14–17
Or Acts 2:1–21, following

A reading from Romans:

[14]For all who are led by the Spirit of God are children of God.
[15]For you did not receive a spirit of slavery to fall back into fear,
but you have received a spirit of adoption.
When we cry, "Abba! Father!"
[16]it is that very Spirit bearing witness with our spirit that we are children of
    God,
[17]and if children, then heirs,
heirs of God and joint heirs with Christ—if, in fact,
we suffer with him so that we may also be glorified with him.

The word of the Lord.

OR: ACTS 2:1–21

A reading from Acts:

[1]When the day of Pentecost had come, they were all together in one place.
[2]And suddenly from heaven there came a sound like the rush of a violent wind,
and it filled the entire house where they were sitting.
[3]Divided tongues, as of fire, appeared among them,
and a tongue rested on each of them.
[4]All of them were filled with the Holy Spirit
and began to speak in other languages, as the Spirit gave them ability.

[5]Now there were devout Jews from every nation under heaven living in
    Jerusalem.
[6]And at this sound the crowd gathered and was bewildered,
because each one heard them speaking in the native language of each.
[7]Amazed and astonished, they asked,
"Are not all these who are speaking Galileans?
[8]And how is it that we hear, each of us, in our own native language?
[9]Parthians, Medes, Elamites,
and residents of Mesopotamia, Judea and Cappadocia, Pontus and Asia,
[10]Phrygia and Pamphylia, Egypt and the parts of Libya belonging to Cyrene,
and visitors from Rome, both Jews and proselytes, [11]Cretans and Arabs—
in our own languages we hear them speaking about God's deeds of power."
[12]All were amazed and perplexed, saying to one another,
"What does this mean?"
[13]But others sneered and said, "They are filled with new wine."

[14]But Peter, standing with the eleven, raised his voice and addressed them,
"Men of Judea and all who live in Jerusalem,
let this be known to you, and listen to what I say.

¹⁵Indeed, these are not drunk, as you suppose,
for it is only nine o'clock in the morning.
¹⁶No, this is what was spoken through the prophet Joel:

> ¹⁷'In the last days it will be, God declares,
> that I will pour out my Spirit upon all flesh,
>   and your sons and your daughters shall prophesy,
> and your young men shall see visions,
>   and your old men shall dream dreams.
> ¹⁸Even upon my slaves, both men and women,
>   in those days I will pour out my Spirit;
>   and they shall prophesy.
> ¹⁹And I will show portents in the heaven above
>   and signs on the earth below,
>   blood, and fire, and smoky mist.
> ²⁰The sun shall be turned to darkness
>   and the moon to blood,
>   before the coming of the Lord's great and glorious day.
> ²¹Then everyone who calls on the name of the Lord shall be saved.' "

The word of the Lord.

The Holy Gospel according to John, the 14th chapter.

⁸Philip said to Jesus,
"Lord, show us the Father, and we will be satisfied."
⁹Jesus said to him, "Have I been with you all this time, Philip,
and you still do not know me?
Whoever has seen me has seen the Father.
How can you say, 'Show us the Father'?
¹⁰Do you not believe that I am in the Father and the Father is in me?
The words that I say to you I do not speak on my own;
but the Father who dwells in me does his works.
¹¹Believe me that I am in the Father and the Father is in me;
but if you do not, then believe me because of the works themselves.
¹²Very truly, I tell you,
the one who believes in me will also do the works that I do and,
in fact, will do greater works than these,
because I am going to the Father.
¹³I will do whatever you ask in my name,
so that the Father may be glorified in the Son.
¹⁴If in my name you ask me for anything, I will do it.

¹⁵"If you love me, you will keep my commandments.
¹⁶And I will ask the Father,
and he will give you another Advocate, to be with you forever.
¹⁷This is the Spirit of truth, whom the world cannot receive,
because it neither sees him nor knows him.
You know him, because he abides with you, and he will be in you."

[²⁵"I have said these things to you while I am still with you.
²⁶But the Advocate, the Holy Spirit, whom the Father will send in my name,
will teach you everything, and remind you of all that I have said to you.
²⁷Peace I leave with you; my peace I give to you.
I do not give to you as the world gives.
Do not let your hearts be troubled, and do not let them be afraid."]

The Gospel of the Lord.

SEASON AFTER PENTECOST

THE HOLY TRINITY
First Sunday after Pentecost

JUNE 7, 1998   JUNE 10, 2001   JUNE 6, 2004

FIRST READING: PROVERBS 8:1–4, 22–31

A reading from Proverbs:

¹Does not wisdom call,
and does not understanding raise her voice?
²On the heights, beside the way,
at the crossroads she takes her stand;
³beside the gates in front of the town,
at the entrance of the portals she cries out:
⁴"To you, O people, I call,
and my cry is to all that live.

²²"The LORD created me at the beginning of his work,
the first of his acts of long ago.
²³Ages ago I was set up,
at the first, before the beginning of the earth.
²⁴When there were no depths I was brought forth,
when there were no springs abounding with water.
²⁵Before the mountains had been shaped,
before the hills, I was brought forth—
²⁶when he had not yet made earth and fields,
or the world's first bits of soil.
²⁷When he established the heavens, I was there,
when he drew a circle on the face of the deep,
²⁸when he made firm the skies above,
when he established the fountains of the deep,
²⁹when he assigned to the sea its limit,
so that the waters might not transgress his command,
when he marked out the foundations of the earth,
³⁰then I was beside him, like a master worker;
and I was daily his delight,
rejoicing before him always,
³¹rejoicing in his inhabited world
and delighting in the human race."

The word of the Lord.

PSALMODY: PSALM 8

SECOND READING: Romans 5:1–5

A reading from Romans:

[1]Therefore, since we are justified by faith,
we have peace with God through our Lord Jesus Christ,
[2]through whom we have obtained access to this grace in which we stand;
and we boast in our hope of sharing the glory of God.
[3]And not only that, but we also boast in our sufferings,
knowing that suffering produces endurance,
[4]and endurance produces character,
and character produces hope,
[5]and hope does not disappoint us,
because God's love has been poured into our hearts
through the Holy Spirit that has been given to us.

The word of the Lord.

GOSPEL: John 16:12–15

The Holy Gospel according to John, the 16th chapter.

[12]"I still have many things to say to you,
but you cannot bear them now.
[13]When the Spirit of truth comes, he will guide you into all the truth;
for he will not speak on his own, but will speak whatever he hears,
and he will declare to you the things that are to come.
[14]He will glorify me, because he will take what is mine and declare it to you.
[15]All that the Father has is mine.
For this reason I said that he will take what is mine and declare it to you."

The Gospel of the Lord.

SUNDAY BETWEEN
MAY 24 AND 28 INCLUSIVE
(if after Trinity Sunday)
PROPER 3

FIRST READING: ISAIAH 55:10–13   *Alternate Reading: Sirach 27:4–7 (p. 404)*

A reading from Isaiah:

10For as the rain and the snow come down from heaven,
    and do not return there until they have watered the earth,
making it bring forth and sprout,
    giving seed to the sower and bread to the eater,
11so shall my word be that goes out from my mouth;
    it shall not return to me empty,
but it shall accomplish that which I purpose,
    and succeed in the thing for which I sent it.

12For you shall go out in joy,
    and be led back in peace;
the mountains and the hills before you
    shall burst into song,
    and all the trees of the field shall clap their hands.
13Instead of the thorn shall come up the cypress;
    instead of the brier shall come up the myrtle;
and it shall be to the LORD for a memorial,
    for an everlasting sign that shall not be cut off.

The word of the Lord.

PSALMODY: PSALM 92:1–4, 12–15

A reading from First Corinthians:

⁵¹Listen, I will tell you a mystery!
We will not all die, but we will all be changed,
⁵²in a moment, in the twinkling of an eye, at the last trumpet.
For the trumpet will sound, and the dead will be raised imperishable,
and we will be changed.
⁵³For this perishable body must put on imperishability,
and this mortal body must put on immortality.
⁵⁴When this perishable body puts on imperishability,
and this mortal body puts on immortality,
then the saying that is written will be fulfilled:
    "Death has been swallowed up in victory."
    ⁵⁵"Where, O death, is your victory?
        Where, O death, is your sting?"
⁵⁶The sting of death is sin, and the power of sin is the law.
⁵⁷But thanks be to God,
who gives us the victory through our Lord Jesus Christ.

⁵⁸Therefore, my beloved, be steadfast, immovable,
always excelling in the work of the Lord,
because you know that in the Lord your labor is not in vain.

The word of the Lord.

The Holy Gospel according to Luke, the sixth chapter.

[39]Jesus also told them a parable:
"Can a blind person guide a blind person?
Will not both fall into a pit?
[40]A disciple is not above the teacher,
but everyone who is fully qualified will be like the teacher.
[41]Why do you see the speck in your neighbor's eye,
but do not notice the log in your own eye?
[42]Or how can you say to your neighbor,
'Friend, let me take out the speck in your eye,'
when you yourself do not see the log in your own eye?
You hypocrite, first take the log out of your own eye,
and then you will see clearly to take the speck out of your neighbor's eye.

[43]"No good tree bears bad fruit,
nor again does a bad tree bear good fruit;
[44]for each tree is known by its own fruit.
Figs are not gathered from thorns,
nor are grapes picked from a bramble bush.
[45]The good person out of the good treasure of the heart produces good,
and the evil person out of evil treasure produces evil;
for it is out of the abundance of the heart that the mouth speaks.

[46]"Why do you call me 'Lord, Lord,' and do not do what I tell you?
[47]I will show you what someone is like who comes to me,
hears my words, and acts on them.
[48]That one is like a man building a house,
who dug deeply and laid the foundation on rock;
when a flood arose, the river burst against that house but could not shake it,
because it had been well built.
[49]But the one who hears and does not act
is like a man who built a house on the ground without a foundation.
When the river burst against it, immediately it fell,
and great was the ruin of that house."

The Gospel of the Lord.

SUNDAY BETWEEN
MAY 29 AND JUNE 4 INCLUSIVE
(if after Trinity Sunday)
PROPER 4

FIRST READING: 1 KINGS 8:22–23, 41–43

A reading from First Kings:

²²Then Solomon stood before the altar of the LORD
in the presence of all the assembly of Israel,
and spread out his hands to heaven.
²³He said, "O LORD, God of Israel,
there is no God like you in heaven above or on earth beneath,
keeping covenant and steadfast love for your servants
who walk before you with all their heart.

⁴¹"Likewise when a foreigner, who is not of your people Israel,
comes from a distant land because of your name—
⁴²for they shall hear of your great name,
your mighty hand, and your outstretched arm—
when a foreigner comes and prays toward this house,
⁴³then hear in heaven your dwelling place,
and do according to all that the foreigner calls to you,
so that all the peoples of the earth may know your name and fear you,
as do your people Israel,
and so that they may know that your name has been invoked on this house
        that I have built."

The word of the Lord.

PSALMODY: PSALM 96:1–9

SECOND READING: GALATIANS 1:1–12

A reading from Galatians:

[1]Paul an apostle—
sent neither by human commission nor from human authorities,
but through Jesus Christ and God the Father, who raised him from the dead—
[2]and all the members of God's family who are with me,
To the churches of Galatia:
[3]Grace to you and peace from God our Father and the Lord Jesus Christ,
[4]who gave himself for our sins to set us free from the present evil age,
according to the will of our God and Father,
[5]to whom be the glory forever and ever. Amen.

[6]I am astonished that you are so quickly deserting the one
who called you in the grace of Christ
and are turning to a different gospel—[7]not that there is another gospel,
but there are some who are confusing you
and want to pervert the gospel of Christ.
[8]But even if we or an angel from heaven should proclaim to you
a gospel contrary to what we proclaimed to you,
let that one be accursed!
[9]As we have said before, so now I repeat,
if anyone proclaims to you a gospel contrary to what you received,
let that one be accursed!

[10]Am I now seeking human approval, or God's approval?
Or am I trying to please people?
If I were still pleasing people, I would not be a servant of Christ.
[11]For I want you to know, brothers and sisters,
that the gospel that was proclaimed by me is not of human origin;
[12]for I did not receive it from a human source, nor was I taught it,
but I received it through a revelation of Jesus Christ.

The word of the Lord.

The Holy Gospel according to Luke, the seventh chapter.

[1]After Jesus had finished all his sayings in the hearing of the people,
he entered Capernaum.
[2]A centurion there had a slave whom he valued highly,
and who was ill and close to death.
[3]When he heard about Jesus, he sent some Jewish elders to him,
asking him to come and heal his slave.
[4]When they came to Jesus, they appealed to him earnestly, saying,
"He is worthy of having you do this for him, [5]for he loves our people,
and it is he who built our synagogue for us."
[6]And Jesus went with them, but when he was not far from the house,
the centurion sent friends to say to him,
"Lord, do not trouble yourself,
for I am not worthy to have you come under my roof;
[7]therefore I did not presume to come to you.
But only speak the word, and let my servant be healed.
[8]For I also am a man set under authority, with soldiers under me;
and I say to one, 'Go,' and he goes,
and to another, 'Come,' and he comes,
and to my slave, 'Do this,' and the slave does it."
[9]When Jesus heard this he was amazed at him,
and turning to the crowd that followed him, he said,
"I tell you, not even in Israel have I found such faith."
[10]When those who had been sent returned to the house,
they found the slave in good health.

The Gospel of the Lord.

SUNDAY BETWEEN
JUNE 5 AND 11 INCLUSIVE
(if after Trinity Sunday)
PROPER 5

FIRST READING: 1 KINGS 17:17–24

A reading from First Kings:

¹⁷After this the son of the woman, the mistress of the house, became ill;
his illness was so severe that there was no breath left in him.
¹⁸She then said to Elijah, "What have you against me, O man of God?
You have come to me to bring my sin to remembrance,
and to cause the death of my son!"
¹⁹But he said to her, "Give me your son."
He took him from her bosom,
carried him up into the upper chamber where he was lodging,
and laid him on his own bed.
²⁰He cried out to the LORD, "O LORD my God,
have you brought calamity even upon the widow with whom I am staying,
by killing her son?"
²¹Then he stretched himself upon the child three times,
and cried out to the LORD,
"O LORD my God, let this child's life come into him again."
²²The LORD listened to the voice of Elijah;
the life of the child came into him again, and he revived.
²³Elijah took the child,
brought him down from the upper chamber into the house,
and gave him to his mother;
then Elijah said, "See, your son is alive."
²⁴So the woman said to Elijah,
"Now I know that you are a man of God,
and that the word of the LORD in your mouth is truth."

The word of the Lord.

PSALMODY: PSALM 30

SECOND READING: GALATIANS 1:11–24

A reading from Galatians:

[11]For I want you to know, brothers and sisters,
that the gospel that was proclaimed by me is not of human origin;
[12]for I did not receive it from a human source, nor was I taught it,
but I received it through a revelation of Jesus Christ.

[13]You have heard, no doubt, of my earlier life in Judaism.
I was violently persecuting the church of God and was trying to destroy it.
[14]I advanced in Judaism beyond many among my people of the same age,
for I was far more zealous for the traditions of my ancestors.
[15]But when God,
who had set me apart before I was born and called me through his grace,
was pleased [16]to reveal his Son to me,
so that I might proclaim him among the Gentiles,
I did not confer with any human being,
[17]nor did I go up to Jerusalem to those who were already apostles before me,
but I went away at once into Arabia, and afterwards I returned to Damascus.
[18]Then after three years I did go up to Jerusalem to visit Cephas
and stayed with him fifteen days;
[19]but I did not see any other apostle except James the Lord's brother.
[20]In what I am writing to you, before God, I do not lie!
[21]Then I went into the regions of Syria and Cilicia,
[22]and I was still unknown by sight to the churches of Judea that are in Christ;
[23]they only heard it said, "The one who formerly was persecuting us
is now proclaiming the faith he once tried to destroy."
[24]And they glorified God because of me.

The word of the Lord.

GOSPEL: LUKE 7:11–17

The Holy Gospel according to Luke, the seventh chapter.

[11]Soon afterwards Jesus went to a town called Nain,
and his disciples and a large crowd went with him.
[12]As he approached the gate of the town,
a man who had died was being carried out.
He was his mother's only son, and she was a widow;
and with her was a large crowd from the town.
[13]When the Lord saw her, he had compassion for her and said to her,
"Do not weep."
[14]Then he came forward and touched the bier, and the bearers stood still.
And he said, "Young man, I say to you, rise!"
[15]The dead man sat up and began to speak,
and Jesus gave him to his mother.
[16]Fear seized all of them; and they glorified God, saying,
"A great prophet has risen among us!" and
"God has looked favorably on his people!"
[17]This word about him spread throughout Judea and all the surrounding
       country.

The Gospel of the Lord.

SUNDAY BETWEEN
JUNE 12 AND 18 INCLUSIVE
(if after Trinity Sunday)

PROPER 6

JUNE 14, 1998   JUNE 17, 2001   JUNE 13, 2004

FIRST READING: 2 SAMUEL 11:26—12:10, 13–15

A reading from Second Samuel:

²⁶When the wife of Uriah heard that her husband was dead,
she made lamentation for him.
²⁷When the mourning was over,
David sent and brought her to his house, and she became his wife,
and bore him a son.

But the thing that David had done displeased the LORD,
¹²:¹and the LORD sent Nathan to David.
He came to him, and said to him,
"There were two men in a certain city,
the one rich and the other poor.
²The rich man had very many flocks and herds;
³but the poor man had nothing but one little ewe lamb,
which he had bought.
He brought it up,
and it grew up with him and with his children;
it used to eat of his meager fare, and drink from his cup,
and lie in his bosom,
and it was like a daughter to him.
⁴Now there came a traveler to the rich man,
and he was loath to take one of his own flock or herd
to prepare for the wayfarer who had come to him,
but he took the poor man's lamb,
and prepared that for the guest who had come to him."

⁵Then David's anger was greatly kindled against the man.
He said to Nathan,
"As the LORD lives, the man who has done this deserves to die;
⁶he shall restore the lamb fourfold,
because he did this thing, and because he had no pity."

⁷Nathan said to David, "You are the man!
Thus says the LORD, the God of Israel:

I anointed you king over Israel,
and I rescued you from the hand of Saul;
⁸I gave you your master's house,
and your master's wives into your bosom,
and gave you the house of Israel and of Judah;
and if that had been too little, I would have added as much more.
⁹Why have you despised the word of the LORD,
to do what is evil in his sight?
You have struck down Uriah the Hittite with the sword,
and have taken his wife to be your wife,
and have killed him with the sword of the Ammonites.
¹⁰Now therefore the sword shall never depart from your house,
for you have despised me,
and have taken the wife of Uriah the Hittite to be your wife."

¹³David said to Nathan,
"I have sinned against the LORD."
Nathan said to David,
"Now the LORD has put away your sin; you shall not die.
¹⁴Nevertheless, because by this deed you have utterly scorned the LORD,
the child that is born to you shall die."
¹⁵Then Nathan went to his house.

The LORD struck the child that Uriah's wife bore to David,
and it became very ill.

The word of the Lord.

PSALMODY: PSALM 32

A reading from Galatians:

[15]We ourselves are Jews by birth and not Gentile sinners;
[16]yet we know that a person is justified not by the works of the law
but through faith in Jesus Christ.
And we have come to believe in Christ Jesus,
so that we might be justified by faith in Christ,
and not by doing the works of the law,
because no one will be justified by the works of the law.
[17]But if, in our effort to be justified in Christ,
we ourselves have been found to be sinners,
is Christ then a servant of sin?
Certainly not!
[18]But if I build up again the very things that I once tore down,
then I demonstrate that I am a transgressor.
[19]For through the law I died to the law,
so that I might live to God.
I have been crucified with Christ;
[20]and it is no longer I who live, but it is Christ who lives in me.
And the life I now live in the flesh I live by faith in the Son of God,
who loved me and gave himself for me.
[21]I do not nullify the grace of God;
for if justification comes through the law, then Christ died for nothing.

The word of the Lord.

GOSPEL: LUKE 7:36—8:3

The Holy Gospel according to Luke, the seventh and eighth chapters.

[36]One of the Pharisees asked Jesus to eat with him,
and he went into the Pharisee's house and took his place at the table.
[37]And a woman in the city, who was a sinner,
having learned that he was eating in the Pharisee's house,
brought an alabaster jar of ointment.
[38]She stood behind him at his feet, weeping,
and began to bathe his feet with her tears and to dry them with her hair.
Then she continued kissing his feet and anointing them with the ointment.
[39]Now when the Pharisee who had invited him saw it,
he said to himself, "If this man were a prophet,
he would have known who and what kind of woman this is who is touching him—
that she is a sinner."

[40]Jesus spoke up and said to him,
"Simon, I have something to say to you."
"Teacher," he replied, "speak."

⁴¹"A certain creditor had two debtors;
one owed five hundred denarii, and the other fifty.
⁴²When they could not pay, he canceled the debts for both of them.
Now which of them will love him more?"
⁴³Simon answered,
"I suppose the one for whom he canceled the greater debt."
And Jesus said to him, "You have judged rightly."
⁴⁴Then turning toward the woman, he said to Simon,
"Do you see this woman?
I entered your house; you gave me no water for my feet,
but she has bathed my feet with her tears and dried them with her hair.
⁴⁵You gave me no kiss,
but from the time I came in she has not stopped kissing my feet.
⁴⁶You did not anoint my head with oil,
but she has anointed my feet with ointment.
⁴⁷Therefore, I tell you, her sins, which were many, have been forgiven;
hence she has shown great love.
But the one to whom little is forgiven, loves little."
⁴⁸Then he said to her, "Your sins are forgiven."
⁴⁹But those who were at the table with him began to say among themselves,
"Who is this who even forgives sins?"
⁵⁰And he said to the woman, "Your faith has saved you; go in peace."

^{8:1}Soon afterwards he went on through cities and villages,
proclaiming and bringing the good news of the kingdom of God.
The twelve were with him,
²as well as some women who had been cured of evil spirits and infirmities:
Mary, called Magdalene, from whom seven demons had gone out,
³and Joanna, the wife of Herod's steward Chuza, and Susanna,
and many others, who provided for them out of their resources.

The Gospel of the Lord.

SUNDAY BETWEEN
JUNE 19 AND 25 INCLUSIVE
(if after Trinity Sunday)

PROPER 7

JUNE 21, 1998   *JUNE 24, 2001*   *JUNE 20, 2004*

FIRST READING: ISAIAH 65:1–9

A reading from Isaiah:

¹I was ready to be sought out by those who did not ask,
 to be found by those who did not seek me.
I said, "Here I am, here I am,"
 to a nation that did not call on my name.
²I held out my hands all day long
 to a rebellious people,
who walk in a way that is not good,
 following their own devices;
³a people who provoke me
 to my face continually,
sacrificing in gardens
 and offering incense on bricks;
⁴who sit inside tombs,
 and spend the night in secret places;
who eat swine's flesh,
 with broth of abominable things in their vessels;
⁵who say, "Keep to yourself,
 do not come near me, for I am too holy for you."
These are a smoke in my nostrils,
 a fire that burns all day long.
⁶See, it is written before me:
 I will not keep silent, but I will repay;
I will indeed repay into their laps
   ⁷their iniquities and their ancestors' iniquities together,
        says the LORD;
because they offered incense on the mountains
 and reviled me on the hills,
I will measure into their laps
 full payment for their actions.
⁸Thus says the LORD:
As the wine is found in the cluster,
 and they say, "Do not destroy it,
 for there is a blessing in it,"

so I will do for my servants' sake,
    and not destroy them all.
⁹I will bring forth descendants from Jacob,
    and from Judah inheritors of my mountains;
my chosen shall inherit it,
    and my servants shall settle there.

The word of the Lord.

PSALMODY: PSALM 22:19–28   *Psalm 22:18–27*, LBW/BCP

SECOND READING: GALATIANS 3:23–29

A reading from Galatians:

[23]Now before faith came,
we were imprisoned and guarded under the law until faith would be revealed.
[24]Therefore the law was our disciplinarian until Christ came,
so that we might be justified by faith.
[25]But now that faith has come,
we are no longer subject to a disciplinarian,
[26]for in Christ Jesus you are all children of God through faith.
[27]As many of you as were baptized into Christ have clothed yourselves with
      Christ.
[28]There is no longer Jew or Greek,
there is no longer slave or free,
there is no longer male and female;
for all of you are one in Christ Jesus.
[29]And if you belong to Christ, then you are Abraham's offspring,
heirs according to the promise.

The word of the Lord.

GOSPEL: LUKE 8:26–39

The Holy Gospel according to Luke, the eighth chapter.

[26]Then Jesus and his disciples arrived at the country of the Gerasenes,
which is opposite Galilee.
[27]As he stepped out on land, a man of the city who had demons met him.
For a long time he had worn no clothes,
and he did not live in a house but in the tombs.
[28]When he saw Jesus, he fell down before him
and shouted at the top of his voice,
"What have you to do with me, Jesus, Son of the Most High God?
I beg you, do not torment me"—
[29]for Jesus had commanded the unclean spirit to come out of the man.
(For many times it had seized him;
he was kept under guard and bound with chains and shackles,
but he would break the bonds and be driven by the demon into the wilds.)
[30]Jesus then asked him, "What is your name?"
He said, "Legion"; for many demons had entered him.
[31]They begged him not to order them to go back into the abyss.

[32]Now there on the hillside a large herd of swine was feeding;
and the demons begged Jesus to let them enter these.
So he gave them permission.
[33]Then the demons came out of the man and entered the swine,
and the herd rushed down the steep bank into the lake and was drowned.

[34]When the swineherds saw what had happened,
they ran off and told it in the city and in the country.
[35]Then people came out to see what had happened,
and when they came to Jesus,
they found the man from whom the demons had gone sitting at the feet of Jesus,
clothed and in his right mind.
And they were afraid.
[36]Those who had seen it
told them how the one who had been possessed by demons had been healed.
[37]Then all the people of the surrounding country of the Gerasenes
asked Jesus to leave them;
for they were seized with great fear.
So he got into the boat and returned.
[38]The man from whom the demons had gone begged that he might be with him;
but Jesus sent him away, saying,
[39]"Return to your home, and declare how much God has done for you."
So he went away,
proclaiming throughout the city how much Jesus had done for him.

The Gospel of the Lord.

PROPER 8

JUNE 28, 1998   JULY 1, 2001   JUNE 27, 2004

FIRST READING: 1 KINGS 19:15–16, 19–21

A reading from First Kings:

[15]Then the LORD said to him,
"Go, return on your way to the wilderness of Damascus;
when you arrive, you shall anoint Hazael as king over Aram.
[16]Also you shall anoint Jehu son of Nimshi as king over Israel;
and you shall anoint Elisha son of Shaphat of Abel-meholah as prophet
        in your place."

[19]So he set out from there, and found Elisha son of Shaphat,
who was plowing.
There were twelve yoke of oxen ahead of him, and he was with the twelfth.
Elijah passed by him and threw his mantle over him.
[20]He left the oxen, ran after Elijah, and said,
"Let me kiss my father and my mother, and then I will follow you."
Then Elijah said to him, "Go back again; for what have I done to you?"
[21]He returned from following him, took the yoke of oxen, and slaughtered
        them;
using the equipment from the oxen, he boiled their flesh,
and gave it to the people, and they ate.
Then he set out and followed Elijah, and became his servant.

The word of the Lord.

PSALMODY: PSALM 16

A reading from Galatians:

[1]For freedom Christ has set us free.
Stand firm, therefore, and do not submit again to a yoke of slavery.
[13]For you were called to freedom, brothers and sisters;
only do not use your freedom as an opportunity for self-indulgence,
but through love become slaves to one another.
[14]For the whole law is summed up in a single commandment,
"You shall love your neighbor as yourself."
[15]If, however, you bite and devour one another,
take care that you are not consumed by one another.

[16]Live by the Spirit, I say, and do not gratify the desires of the flesh.
[17]For what the flesh desires is opposed to the Spirit,
and what the Spirit desires is opposed to the flesh;
for these are opposed to each other,
to prevent you from doing what you want.
[18]But if you are led by the Spirit, you are not subject to the law.
[19]Now the works of the flesh are obvious:
fornication, impurity, licentiousness, [20]idolatry, sorcery,
enmities, strife, jealousy, anger, quarrels, dissensions,
factions, [21]envy, drunkenness, carousing, and things like these.
I am warning you, as I warned you before:
those who do such things will not inherit the kingdom of God.

[22]By contrast, the fruit of the Spirit is love, joy, peace, patience,
kindness, generosity, faithfulness, [23]gentleness, and self-control.
There is no law against such things.
[24]And those who belong to Christ Jesus have crucified the flesh
with its passions and desires.
[25]If we live by the Spirit, let us also be guided by the Spirit.

The word of the Lord.

GOSPEL: LUKE 9:51–62

The Holy Gospel according to Luke, the ninth chapter.

⁵¹When the days drew near for Jesus to be taken up,
he set his face to go to Jerusalem.
⁵²And he sent messengers ahead of him.
On their way they entered a village of the Samaritans to make ready for him;
⁵³but they did not receive him, because his face was set toward Jerusalem.
⁵⁴When his disciples James and John saw it, they said,
"Lord, do you want us to command fire to come down from heaven and consume them?"
⁵⁵But he turned and rebuked them.
⁵⁶Then they went on to another village.

⁵⁷As they were going along the road, someone said to him,
"I will follow you wherever you go."
⁵⁸And Jesus said to him, "Foxes have holes, and birds of the air have nests;
but the Son of Man has nowhere to lay his head."
⁵⁹To another he said, "Follow me."
But he said, "Lord, first let me go and bury my father."
⁶⁰But Jesus said to him, "Let the dead bury their own dead;
but as for you, go and proclaim the kingdom of God."
⁶¹Another said, "I will follow you, Lord;
but let me first say farewell to those at my home."
⁶²Jesus said to him,
"No one who puts a hand to the plow and looks back is fit for the kingdom of God."

The Gospel of the Lord.

SUNDAY BETWEEN JULY 3 AND 9 INCLUSIVE

PROPER 9

JULY 5, 1998 *JULY 8, 2001* *JULY 4, 2004*

FIRST READING: ISAIAH 66:10–14

A reading from Isaiah:

¹⁰Rejoice with Jerusalem, and be glad for her,
    all you who love her;
rejoice with her in joy,
    all you who mourn over her—
¹¹that you may nurse and be satisfied
    from her consoling breast;
that you may drink deeply with delight
    from her glorious bosom.
¹²For thus says the LORD:
I will extend prosperity to her like a river,
    and the wealth of the nations like an overflowing stream;
and you shall nurse and be carried on her arm,
    and dandled on her knees.
¹³As a mother comforts her child,
    so I will comfort you;
    you shall be comforted in Jerusalem.
¹⁴You shall see, and your heart shall rejoice;
    your bodies shall flourish like the grass;
and it shall be known that the hand of the LORD is with his servants,
    and his indignation is against his enemies.

The word of the Lord.

PSALMODY: PSALM 66:1–9

Psalm 66:1–8, LBW/BCP

SECOND READING: GALATIANS 6:[1–6] 7–16

A reading from Galatians:

[¹My friends, if anyone is detected in a transgression,
you who have received the Spirit
should restore such a one in a spirit of gentleness.
Take care that you yourselves are not tempted.
²Bear one another's burdens,
and in this way you will fulfill the law of Christ.
³For if those who are nothing think they are something,
they deceive themselves.
⁴All must test their own work;
then that work, rather than their neighbor's work,
will become a cause for pride.
⁵For all must carry their own loads.
⁶Those who are taught the word must share in all good things with their teacher.]

⁷Do not be deceived; God is not mocked,
for you reap whatever you sow.
⁸If you sow to your own flesh, you will reap corruption from the flesh;
but if you sow to the Spirit, you will reap eternal life from the Spirit.
⁹So let us not grow weary in doing what is right,
for we will reap at harvest time, if we do not give up.
¹⁰So then, whenever we have an opportunity, let us work for the good of all,
and especially for those of the family of faith.

¹¹See what large letters I make when I am writing in my own hand!
¹²It is those who want to make a good showing in the flesh
that try to compel you to be circumcised—
only that they may not be persecuted for the cross of Christ.
¹³Even the circumcised do not themselves obey the law,
but they want you to be circumcised so that they may boast about your flesh.
¹⁴May I never boast of anything except the cross of our Lord Jesus Christ,
by which the world has been crucified to me, and I to the world.
¹⁵For neither circumcision nor uncircumcision is anything;
but a new creation is everything!
¹⁶As for those who will follow this rule—
peace be upon them, and mercy, and upon the Israel of God.

The word of the Lord.

The Holy Gospel according to Luke, the tenth chapter.

[1]After this the Lord appointed seventy others
and sent them on ahead of him in pairs
to every town and place where he himself intended to go.
[2]He said to them,
"The harvest is plentiful, but the laborers are few;
therefore ask the Lord of the harvest to send out laborers into his harvest.
[3]Go on your way.
See, I am sending you out like lambs into the midst of wolves.
[4]Carry no purse, no bag, no sandals; and greet no one on the road.
[5]Whatever house you enter, first say, 'Peace to this house!'
[6]And if anyone is there who shares in peace,
your peace will rest on that person;
but if not, it will return to you.
[7]Remain in the same house, eating and drinking whatever they provide,
for the laborer deserves to be paid.
Do not move about from house to house.
[8]Whenever you enter a town and its people welcome you,
eat what is set before you;
[9]cure the sick who are there, and say to them,
'The kingdom of God has come near to you.'
[10]But whenever you enter a town and they do not welcome you,
go out into its streets and say,
[11]'Even the dust of your town that clings to our feet,
we wipe off in protest against you.
Yet know this: the kingdom of God has come near.' "

[16]"Whoever listens to you listens to me,
and whoever rejects you rejects me,
and whoever rejects me rejects the one who sent me."

[17]The seventy returned with joy, saying,
"Lord, in your name even the demons submit to us!"
[18]He said to them,
"I watched Satan fall from heaven like a flash of lightning.
[19]See, I have given you authority to tread on snakes and scorpions,
and over all the power of the enemy; and nothing will hurt you.
[20]Nevertheless, do not rejoice at this, that the spirits submit to you,
but rejoice that your names are written in heaven."

The Gospel of the Lord.

SUNDAY BETWEEN
JULY 10 AND 16 INCLUSIVE

PROPER 10

JULY 12, 1998   *JULY 15, 2001*   *JULY 11, 2004*

FIRST READING: Deuteronomy 30:9–14

A reading from Deuteronomy:

⁹The LORD your God will make you abundantly prosperous
      in all your undertakings,
in the fruit of your body, in the fruit of your livestock,
and in the fruit of your soil.
For the LORD will again take delight in prospering you,
just as he delighted in prospering your ancestors,
¹⁰when you obey the LORD your God
by observing his commandments and decrees
that are written in this book of the law,
because you turn to the LORD your God
with all your heart and with all your soul.

¹¹Surely, this commandment that I am commanding you today
is not too hard for you, nor is it too far away.
¹²It is not in heaven, that you should say,
"Who will go up to heaven for us,
and get it for us so that we may hear it and observe it?"
¹³Neither is it beyond the sea, that you should say,
"Who will cross to the other side of the sea for us,
and get it for us so that we may hear it and observe it?"
¹⁴No, the word is very near to you;
it is in your mouth and in your heart for you to observe.

The word of the Lord.

PSALMODY: Psalm 25:1–10   *Psalm 25:1–9, LBW/BCP*

SECOND READING: Colossians 1:1–14

A reading from Colossians:

¹Paul, an apostle of Christ Jesus by the will of God, and Timothy our brother,
²To the saints and faithful brothers and sisters in Christ in Colossae:
Grace to you and peace from God our Father.

³In our prayers for you we always thank God,
the Father of our Lord Jesus Christ,
⁴for we have heard of your faith in Christ Jesus
and of the love that you have for all the saints,
⁵because of the hope laid up for you in heaven.
You have heard of this hope before in the word of the truth,
the gospel ⁶that has come to you.
Just as it is bearing fruit and growing in the whole world,
so it has been bearing fruit among yourselves
from the day you heard it and truly comprehended the grace of God.
⁷This you learned from Epaphras, our beloved fellow servant.
He is a faithful minister of Christ on your behalf,
⁸and he has made known to us your love in the Spirit.

⁹For this reason, since the day we heard it,
we have not ceased praying for you
and asking that you may be filled with the knowledge of God's will
in all spiritual wisdom and understanding,
¹⁰so that you may lead lives worthy of the Lord,
fully pleasing to him,
as you bear fruit in every good work
and as you grow in the knowledge of God.
¹¹May you be made strong
with all the strength that comes from his glorious power,
and may you be prepared to endure everything with patience,
while joyfully ¹²giving thanks to the Father,
who has enabled you to share in the inheritance of the saints in the light.
¹³He has rescued us from the power of darkness
and transferred us into the kingdom of his beloved Son,
¹⁴in whom we have redemption, the forgiveness of sins.

The word of the Lord.

The Holy Gospel according to Luke, the tenth chapter.

25Just then a lawyer stood up to test Jesus.
"Teacher," he said, "what must I do to inherit eternal life?"
26He said to him, "What is written in the law? What do you read there?"
27He answered, "You shall love the Lord your God with all your heart,
and with all your soul, and with all your strength, and with all your mind;
and your neighbor as yourself."
28And he said to him, "You have given the right answer;
do this, and you will live."

29But wanting to justify himself, he asked Jesus,
"And who is my neighbor?"
30Jesus replied, "A man was going down from Jerusalem to Jericho,
and fell into the hands of robbers,
who stripped him, beat him, and went away, leaving him half dead.
31Now by chance a priest was going down that road;
and when he saw him, he passed by on the other side.
32So likewise a Levite, when he came to the place and saw him,
passed by on the other side.
33But a Samaritan while traveling came near him;
and when he saw him, he was moved with pity.
34He went to him and bandaged his wounds,
having poured oil and wine on them.
Then he put him on his own animal,
brought him to an inn, and took care of him.
35The next day he took out two denarii, gave them to the innkeeper,
and said, 'Take care of him;
and when I come back, I will repay you whatever more you spend.'

36"Which of these three, do you think,
was a neighbor to the man who fell into the hands of the robbers?"
37He said, "The one who showed him mercy."
Jesus said to him, "Go and do likewise."

The Gospel of the Lord.

PROPER 11

JULY 19, 1998   JULY 22, 2001   JULY 18, 2004

FIRST READING: Genesis 18:1–10a

A reading from Genesis:

¹The Lord appeared to Abraham by the oaks of Mamre,
as he sat at the entrance of his tent in the heat of the day.
²He looked up and saw three men standing near him.
When he saw them, he ran from the tent entrance to meet them,
and bowed down to the ground.
³He said, "My lord, if I find favor with you, do not pass by your servant.
⁴Let a little water be brought, and wash your feet,
and rest yourselves under the tree.
⁵Let me bring a little bread, that you may refresh yourselves,
and after that you may pass on—since you have come to your servant."
So they said, "Do as you have said."
⁶And Abraham hastened into the tent to Sarah, and said,
"Make ready quickly three measures of choice flour, knead it, and make
　　cakes."
⁷Abraham ran to the herd, and took a calf, tender and good,
and gave it to the servant, who hastened to prepare it.
⁸Then he took curds and milk and the calf that he had prepared,
and set it before them;
and he stood by them under the tree while they ate.

⁹They said to him, "Where is your wife Sarah?"
And he said, "There, in the tent."
¹⁰Then one said, "I will surely return to you in due season,
and your wife Sarah shall have a son."

The word of the Lord.

PSALMODY: Psalm 15

SECOND READING: COLOSSIANS 1:15–28

A reading from Colossians:

15He is the image of the invisible God, the firstborn of all creation;
16for in him all things in heaven and on earth were created,
things visible and invisible,
whether thrones or dominions or rulers or powers—
all things have been created through him and for him.
17He himself is before all things, and in him all things hold together.
18He is the head of the body, the church;
he is the beginning, the firstborn from the dead,
so that he might come to have first place in everything.
19For in him all the fullness of God was pleased to dwell,
20and through him God was pleased to reconcile to himself all things,
whether on earth or in heaven, by making peace through the blood of his cross.

21And you who were once estranged and hostile in mind, doing evil deeds,
22he has now reconciled in his fleshly body through death,
so as to present you holy and blameless and irreproachable before him—
23provided that you continue securely established and steadfast in the faith,
without shifting from the hope promised by the gospel that you heard,
which has been proclaimed to every creature under heaven.
I, Paul, became a servant of this gospel.

24I am now rejoicing in my sufferings for your sake,
and in my flesh I am completing what is lacking in Christ's afflictions
for the sake of his body, that is, the church.
25I became its servant according to God's commission
that was given to me for you,
to make the word of God fully known,
26the mystery that has been hidden throughout the ages and generations
but has now been revealed to his saints.
27To them God chose to make known how great among the Gentiles
are the riches of the glory of this mystery,
which is Christ in you, the hope of glory.
28It is he whom we proclaim,
warning everyone and teaching everyone in all wisdom,
so that we may present everyone mature in Christ.

The word of the Lord.

The Holy Gospel according to Luke, the tenth chapter.

[38]Now as Jesus and his disciples went on their way,
he entered a certain village,
where a woman named Martha welcomed him into her home.
[39]She had a sister named Mary,
who sat at the Lord's feet and listened to what he was saying.
[40]But Martha was distracted by her many tasks;
so she came to him and asked,
"Lord, do you not care that my sister has left me to do all the work by myself?
Tell her then to help me."
[41]But the Lord answered her,
"Martha, Martha, you are worried and distracted by many things;
there is need of only one thing.
Mary has chosen the better part,
which will not be taken away from her."

The Gospel of the Lord.

PROPER 12

JULY 26, 1998   JULY 29, 2001   JULY 25, 2004

FIRST READING: GENESIS 18:20–32

A reading from Genesis:

²⁰The LORD said, "How great is the outcry against Sodom and Gomorrah
and how very grave their sin!
²¹I must go down and see whether they have done altogether
according to the outcry that has come to me; and if not, I will know."

²²So the men turned from there, and went toward Sodom,
while Abraham remained standing before the LORD.
²³Then Abraham came near and said,
"Will you indeed sweep away the righteous with the wicked?
²⁴Suppose there are fifty righteous within the city;
will you then sweep away the place
and not forgive it for the fifty righteous who are in it?
²⁵Far be it from you to do such a thing, to slay the righteous with the wicked,
so that the righteous fare as the wicked! Far be that from you!
Shall not the Judge of all the earth do what is just?"
²⁶And the LORD said, "If I find at Sodom fifty righteous in the city,
I will forgive the whole place for their sake."
²⁷Abraham answered, "Let me take it upon myself to speak to the Lord,
I who am but dust and ashes.
²⁸Suppose five of the fifty righteous are lacking?
Will you destroy the whole city for lack of five?"
And he said, "I will not destroy it if I find forty-five there."
²⁹Again he spoke to him, "Suppose forty are found there."
He answered, "For the sake of forty I will not do it."
³⁰Then he said, "Oh do not let the Lord be angry if I speak.
Suppose thirty are found there."
He answered, "I will not do it, if I find thirty there."
³¹He said, "Let me take it upon myself to speak to the Lord.
Suppose twenty are found there."
He answered, "For the sake of twenty I will not destroy it."
³²Then he said, "Oh do not let the Lord be angry if I speak just once more.
Suppose ten are found there."
He answered, "For the sake of ten I will not destroy it."

The word of the Lord.

PSALMODY: PSALM 138

SECOND READING: COLOSSIANS 2:6–15 [16–19]

A reading from Colossians:

⁶As you therefore have received Christ Jesus the Lord,
continue to live your lives in him, ⁷rooted and built up in him
and established in the faith, just as you were taught,
abounding in thanksgiving.

⁸See to it that no one takes you captive through philosophy and empty deceit,
according to human tradition, according to the elemental spirits of the universe,
and not according to Christ.
⁹For in him the whole fullness of deity dwells bodily,
¹⁰and you have come to fullness in him,
who is the head of every ruler and authority.
¹¹In him also you were circumcised with a spiritual circumcision,
by putting off the body of the flesh in the circumcision of Christ;
¹²when you were buried with him in baptism,
you were also raised with him through faith in the power of God,
who raised him from the dead.
¹³And when you were dead in trespasses and the uncircumcision of your flesh,
God made you alive together with him,
when he forgave us all our trespasses,
¹⁴erasing the record that stood against us with its legal demands.
He set this aside, nailing it to the cross.
¹⁵He disarmed the rulers and authorities and made a public example of them,
triumphing over them in it.

[¹⁶Therefore do not let anyone condemn you
in matters of food and drink or of observing festivals, new moons, or sabbaths.
¹⁷These are only a shadow of what is to come,
but the substance belongs to Christ.
¹⁸Do not let anyone disqualify you,
insisting on self-abasement and worship of angels,
dwelling on visions, puffed up without cause by a human way of thinking,
¹⁹and not holding fast to the head, from whom the whole body,
nourished and held together by its ligaments and sinews,
grows with a growth that is from God.]

The word of the Lord.

GOSPEL: LUKE 11:1–13

The Holy Gospel according to Luke, the eleventh chapter.

[1]Jesus was praying in a certain place,
and after he had finished, one of his disciples said to him,
"Lord, teach us to pray, as John taught his disciples."
[2]He said to them, "When you pray, say:
    Father, hallowed be your name.
        Your kingdom come.
        [3]Give us each day our daily bread.
        [4]And forgive us our sins,
            for we ourselves forgive everyone indebted to us.
        And do not bring us to the time of trial."

[5]And he said to them, "Suppose one of you has a friend,
and you go to him at midnight and say to him,
'Friend, lend me three loaves of bread;
[6]for a friend of mine has arrived, and I have nothing to set before him.'
[7]And he answers from within,
'Do not bother me; the door has already been locked,
and my children are with me in bed;
I cannot get up and give you anything.'
[8]I tell you, even though he will not get up and give him anything
because he is his friend,
at least because of his persistence he will get up and give him whatever
        he needs.

[9]"So I say to you, Ask, and it will be given you;
search, and you will find;
knock, and the door will be opened for you.
[10]For everyone who asks receives, and everyone who searches finds,
and for everyone who knocks, the door will be opened.
[11]Is there anyone among you who, if your child asks for a fish,
will give a snake instead of a fish?
[12]Or if the child asks for an egg, will give a scorpion?
[13]If you then, who are evil, know how to give good gifts to your children,
how much more will the heavenly Father
give the Holy Spirit to those who ask him!"

The Gospel of the Lord.

SUNDAY BETWEEN
JULY 31 AND AUGUST 6 INCLUSIVE

PROPER 13

AUGUST 2, 1998   AUGUST 5, 2001   AUGUST 1, 2004

FIRST READING: ECCLESIASTES 1:2, 12–14; 2:18–23

A reading from Ecclesiastes:

> ²Vanity of vanities, says the Teacher,
> vanity of vanities! All is vanity.

¹²I, the Teacher, when king over Israel in Jerusalem,
¹³applied my mind to seek and to search out by wisdom all that is done under
heaven;
it is an unhappy business that God has given to human beings to be busy with.
¹⁴I saw all the deeds that are done under the sun;
and see, all is vanity and a chasing after wind.

²:¹⁸I hated all my toil in which I had toiled under the sun,
seeing that I must leave it to those who come after me—
¹⁹and who knows whether they will be wise or foolish?
Yet they will be master of all for which I toiled
and used my wisdom under the sun.
This also is vanity.
²⁰So I turned and gave my heart up to despair
concerning all the toil of my labors under the sun,
²¹because sometimes one who has toiled with wisdom and knowledge and skill
must leave all to be enjoyed by another who did not toil for it.
This also is vanity and a great evil.
²²What do mortals get from all the toil and strain with which they toil under
the sun?
²³For all their days are full of pain, and their work is a vexation;
even at night their minds do not rest.
This also is vanity.

The word of the Lord.

PSALMODY: PSALM 49:1–12

Psalm 49:1–11, LBW/BCP

SECOND READING: COLOSSIANS 3:1–11

A reading from Colossians:

¹So if you have been raised with Christ, seek the things that are above,
where Christ is, seated at the right hand of God.
²Set your minds on things that are above, not on things that are on earth,
³for you have died, and your life is hidden with Christ in God.
⁴When Christ who is your life is revealed,
then you also will be revealed with him in glory.

⁵Put to death, therefore, whatever in you is earthly:
fornication, impurity, passion, evil desire, and greed (which is idolatry).
⁶On account of these
the wrath of God is coming on those who are disobedient.
⁷These are the ways you also once followed, when you were living that life.
⁸But now you must get rid of all such things—
anger, wrath, malice, slander, and abusive language from your mouth.
⁹Do not lie to one another,
seeing that you have stripped off the old self with its practices
¹⁰and have clothed yourselves with the new self,
which is being renewed in knowledge according to the image of its creator.
¹¹In that renewal there is no longer Greek and Jew,
circumcised and uncircumcised,
barbarian, Scythian, slave and free;
but Christ is all and in all!

The word of the Lord.

The Holy Gospel according to Luke, the twelfth chapter.

¹³Someone in the crowd said to Jesus,
"Teacher, tell my brother to divide the family inheritance with me."
¹⁴But he said to him,
"Friend, who set me to be a judge or arbitrator over you?"
¹⁵And he said to them, "Take care!
Be on your guard against all kinds of greed;
for one's life does not consist in the abundance of possessions."
¹⁶Then he told them a parable:
"The land of a rich man produced abundantly.
¹⁷And he thought to himself,
'What should I do, for I have no place to store my crops?'
¹⁸Then he said, 'I will do this:
I will pull down my barns and build larger ones,
and there I will store all my grain and my goods.
¹⁹And I will say to my soul,
'Soul, you have ample goods laid up for many years;
relax, eat, drink, be merry.'
²⁰But God said to him, 'You fool!
This very night your life is being demanded of you.
And the things you have prepared, whose will they be?'
²¹So it is with those who store up treasures for themselves
but are not rich toward God."

The Gospel of the Lord.

SUNDAY BETWEEN
AUGUST 7 AND 13 INCLUSIVE

PROPER 14

AUGUST 9, 1998   *AUGUST 12, 2001*   *AUGUST 8, 2004*

FIRST READING: GENESIS 15:1–6

A reading from Genesis:

¹After these things the word of the LORD came to Abram in a vision,
"Do not be afraid, Abram, I am your shield;
your reward shall be very great."
²But Abram said, "O Lord GOD, what will you give me,
for I continue childless,
and the heir of my house is Eliezer of Damascus?"
³And Abram said, "You have given me no offspring,
and so a slave born in my house is to be my heir."
⁴But the word of the LORD came to him,
"This man shall not be your heir;
no one but your very own issue shall be your heir."
⁵He brought him outside and said,
"Look toward heaven and count the stars,
if you are able to count them."
Then he said to him, "So shall your descendants be."
⁶And he believed the LORD;
and the LORD reckoned it to him as righteousness.

The word of the Lord.

PSALMODY: PSALM 33:12–22

SECOND READING: Hebrews 11:1–3, 8–16

A reading from Hebrews:

¹Now faith is the assurance of things hoped for,
the conviction of things not seen.
²Indeed, by faith our ancestors received approval.
³By faith we understand that the worlds were prepared by the word of God,
so that what is seen was made from things that are not visible.

⁸By faith Abraham obeyed
when he was called to set out for a place that he was to receive as an inheri-
        tance;
and he set out, not knowing where he was going.
⁹By faith he stayed for a time in the land he had been promised,
as in a foreign land, living in tents, as did Isaac and Jacob,
who were heirs with him of the same promise.
¹⁰For he looked forward to the city that has foundations,
whose architect and builder is God.
¹¹By faith he received power of procreation,
even though he was too old—and Sarah herself was barren—
because he considered him faithful who had promised.
¹²Therefore from one person, and this one as good as dead,
descendants were born, "as many as the stars of heaven
and as the innumerable grains of sand by the seashore."

¹³All of these died in faith without having received the promises,
but from a distance they saw and greeted them.
They confessed that they were strangers and foreigners on the earth,
¹⁴for people who speak in this way make it clear that they are seeking a home-
        land.
¹⁵If they had been thinking of the land that they had left behind,
they would have had opportunity to return.
¹⁶But as it is, they desire a better country, that is, a heavenly one.
Therefore God is not ashamed to be called their God;
indeed, he has prepared a city for them.

The word of the Lord.

The Holy Gospel according to Luke, the twelfth chapter.

Jesus said:
[32]"Do not be afraid, little flock,
for it is your Father's good pleasure to give you the kingdom.
[33]Sell your possessions, and give alms.
Make purses for yourselves that do not wear out,
an unfailing treasure in heaven,
where no thief comes near and no moth destroys.
[34]For where your treasure is, there your heart will be also.

[35]"Be dressed for action and have your lamps lit;
[36]be like those who are waiting for their master to return from the wedding
        banquet,
so that they may open the door for him as soon as he comes and knocks.
[37]Blessed are those slaves whom the master finds alert when he comes;
truly I tell you, he will fasten his belt and have them sit down to eat,
and he will come and serve them.
[38]If he comes during the middle of the night, or near dawn,
and finds them so, blessed are those slaves.

[39]"But know this:
if the owner of the house had known at what hour the thief was coming,
he would not have let his house be broken into.
[40]You also must be ready,
for the Son of Man is coming at an unexpected hour."

The Gospel of the Lord.

SUNDAY BETWEEN
AUGUST 14 AND 20 INCLUSIVE

PROPER 15

AUGUST 16, 1998   AUGUST 19, 2001   AUGUST 15, 2004

FIRST READING: JEREMIAH 23:23–29

A reading from Jeremiah:

²³Am I a God near by, says the LORD, and not a God far off?
²⁴Who can hide in secret places so that I cannot see them? says the LORD.
Do I not fill heaven and earth? says the LORD.
²⁵I have heard what the prophets have said
who prophesy lies in my name, saying,
"I have dreamed, I have dreamed!"
²⁶How long?
Will the hearts of the prophets ever turn back—those who prophesy lies,
and who prophesy the deceit of their own heart?
²⁷They plan to make my people forget my name by their dreams that they tell
        one another,
just as their ancestors forgot my name for Baal.
²⁸Let the prophet who has a dream tell the dream,
but let the one who has my word speak my word faithfully.
What has straw in common with wheat? says the LORD.
²⁹Is not my word like fire, says the LORD,
and like a hammer that breaks a rock in pieces?

The word of the Lord.

PSALMODY: PSALM 82

A reading from Hebrews:

29By faith the people passed through the Red Sea as if it were dry land,
but when the Egyptians attempted to do so they were drowned.
30By faith the walls of Jericho fell after they had been encircled for seven days.
31By faith Rahab the prostitute did not perish with those who were disobedient,
because she had received the spies in peace.

32And what more should I say?
For time would fail me to tell of Gideon, Barak, Samson, Jephthah,
of David and Samuel and the prophets—
33who through faith conquered kingdoms, administered justice,
obtained promises, shut the mouths of lions,
34quenched raging fire, escaped the edge of the sword,
won strength out of weakness,
became mighty in war, put foreign armies to flight.
35Women received their dead by resurrection.
Others were tortured, refusing to accept release,
in order to obtain a better resurrection.
36Others suffered mocking and flogging, and even chains and imprisonment.
37They were stoned to death, they were sawn in two,
they were killed by the sword;
they went about in skins of sheep and goats, destitute, persecuted, tor-
    mented—
38of whom the world was not worthy.
They wandered in deserts and mountains,
and in caves and holes in the ground.

39Yet all these, though they were commended for their faith,
did not receive what was promised,
40since God had provided something better so that they would not,
apart from us, be made perfect.

12:1Therefore, since we are surrounded by so great a cloud of witnesses,
let us also lay aside every weight and the sin that clings so closely,
and let us run with perseverance the race that is set before us,
2looking to Jesus the pioneer and perfecter of our faith,
who for the sake of the joy that was set before him endured the cross,
disregarding its shame,
and has taken his seat at the right hand of the throne of God.

The word of the Lord.

The Holy Gospel according to Luke, the twelfth chapter.

Jesus said:
[49]"I came to bring fire to the earth, and how I wish it were already kindled!
[50]I have a baptism with which to be baptized,
and what stress I am under until it is completed!
[51]Do you think that I have come to bring peace to the earth?
No, I tell you, but rather division!
[52]From now on five in one household will be divided,
three against two and two against three; [53]they will be divided:
>   father against son
>   and son against father,
>   mother against daughter
>   and daughter against mother,
>   mother-in-law against her daughter-in-law
>   and daughter-in-law against mother-in-law."

[54]He also said to the crowds, "When you see a cloud rising in the west,
you immediately say, 'It is going to rain'; and so it happens.
[55]And when you see the south wind blowing, you say,
'There will be scorching heat'; and it happens.
[56]You hypocrites!
You know how to interpret the appearance of earth and sky,
but why do you not know how to interpret the present time?"

The Gospel of the Lord.

SUNDAY BETWEEN
AUGUST 21 AND 27 INCLUSIVE

PROPER 16

AUGUST 23, 1998   AUGUST 26, 2001   AUGUST 22, 2004

FIRST READING: ISAIAH 58:9b–14

A reading from Isaiah:

9bIf you remove the yoke from among you,
   the pointing of the finger, the speaking of evil,
10if you offer your food to the hungry
   and satisfy the needs of the afflicted,
then your light shall rise in the darkness
   and your gloom be like the noonday.
11The LORD will guide you continually,
   and satisfy your needs in parched places,
   and make your bones strong;
and you shall be like a watered garden,
   like a spring of water,
   whose waters never fail.
12Your ancient ruins shall be rebuilt;
   you shall raise up the foundations of many generations;
you shall be called the repairer of the breach,
   the restorer of streets to live in.

13If you refrain from trampling the sabbath,
   from pursuing your own interests on my holy day;
if you call the sabbath a delight
   and the holy day of the LORD honorable;
if you honor it, not going your own ways,
   serving your own interests, or pursuing your own affairs;
14then you shall take delight in the LORD,
   and I will make you ride upon the heights of the earth;
I will feed you with the heritage of your ancestor Jacob,
   for the mouth of the LORD has spoken.

The word of the Lord.

PSALMODY: PSALM 103:1–8

A reading from Hebrews:

[18]You have not come to something that can be touched,
a blazing fire, and darkness, and gloom,
and a tempest, [19]and the sound of a trumpet,
and a voice whose words made the hearers beg
that not another word be spoken to them.
[20](For they could not endure the order that was given,
"If even an animal touches the mountain, it shall be stoned to death."
[21]Indeed, so terrifying was the sight that Moses said, "I tremble with fear.")
[22]But you have come to Mount Zion and to the city of the living God,
the heavenly Jerusalem,
and to innumerable angels in festal gathering,
[23]and to the assembly of the firstborn who are enrolled in heaven,
and to God the judge of all,
and to the spirits of the righteous made perfect,
[24]and to Jesus, the mediator of a new covenant,
and to the sprinkled blood that speaks a better word than the blood of Abel.

[25]See that you do not refuse the one who is speaking;
for if they did not escape when they refused the one who warned them on
    earth,
how much less will we escape if we reject the one who warns from heaven!
[26]At that time his voice shook the earth;
but now he has promised,
"Yet once more I will shake not only the earth but also the heaven."
[27]This phrase, "Yet once more,"
indicates the removal of what is shaken—that is, created things—
so that what cannot be shaken may remain.
[28]Therefore, since we are receiving a kingdom that cannot be shaken,
let us give thanks,
by which we offer to God an acceptable worship with reverence and awe;
[29]for indeed our God is a consuming fire.

The word of the Lord.

GOSPEL: LUKE 13:10–17

The Holy Gospel according to Luke, the 13th chapter.

[10]Now Jesus was teaching in one of the synagogues on the sabbath.
[11]And just then there appeared a woman
with a spirit that had crippled her for eighteen years.
She was bent over and was quite unable to stand up straight.
[12]When Jesus saw her, he called her over and said,
"Woman, you are set free from your ailment."
[13]When he laid his hands on her,
immediately she stood up straight and began praising God.
[14]But the leader of the synagogue,
indignant because Jesus had cured on the sabbath,
kept saying to the crowd,
"There are six days on which work ought to be done;
come on those days and be cured, and not on the sabbath day."
[15]But the Lord answered him and said, "You hypocrites!
Does not each of you on the sabbath untie his ox or his donkey from the
        manger,
and lead it away to give it water?
[16]And ought not this woman,
a daughter of Abraham whom Satan bound for eighteen long years,
be set free from this bondage on the sabbath day?"
[17]When he said this, all his opponents were put to shame;
and the entire crowd was rejoicing at all the wonderful things that he was
        doing.

The Gospel of the Lord.

SUNDAY BETWEEN
AUGUST 28 AND SEPTEMBER 3
INCLUSIVE

PROPER 17

AUGUST 30, 1998　　*SEPTEMBER 2, 2001*　　*AUGUST 29, 2004*

FIRST READING: PROVERBS 25:6–7　　　*Alternate Reading: Sirach 10:12–18 (p. 405)*

A reading from Proverbs:

⁶Do not put yourself forward in the king's presence
　　or stand in the place of the great;
⁷for it is better to be told, "Come up here,"
　　than to be put lower in the presence of a noble.

The word of the Lord.

PSALMODY: PSALM 112

SECOND READING: HEBREWS 13:1–8, 15–16

A reading from Hebrews:

¹Let mutual love continue.
²Do not neglect to show hospitality to strangers,
for by doing that some have entertained angels without knowing it.
³Remember those who are in prison, as though you were in prison with them;
those who are being tortured, as though you yourselves were being tortured.
⁴Let marriage be held in honor by all,
and let the marriage bed be kept undefiled;
for God will judge fornicators and adulterers.
⁵Keep your lives free from the love of money,
and be content with what you have;
for he has said, "I will never leave you or forsake you."
⁶So we can say with confidence,
    "The Lord is my helper;
        I will not be afraid.
    What can anyone do to me?"

⁷Remember your leaders, those who spoke the word of God to you;
consider the outcome of their way of life, and imitate their faith.
⁸Jesus Christ is the same yesterday and today and forever.
¹⁵Through him, then, let us continually offer a sacrifice of praise to God,
that is, the fruit of lips that confess his name.
¹⁶Do not neglect to do good and to share what you have,
for such sacrifices are pleasing to God.

The word of the Lord.

The Holy Gospel according to Luke, the 14th chapter.

¹On one occasion when Jesus was going to the house of a leader of the
       Pharisees
to eat a meal on the sabbath,
they were watching him closely.
⁷When he noticed how the guests chose the places of honor,
he told them a parable.
⁸"When you are invited by someone to a wedding banquet,
do not sit down at the place of honor,
in case someone more distinguished than you has been invited by your host;
⁹and the host who invited both of you may come and say to you,
'Give this person your place,'
and then in disgrace you would start to take the lowest place.
¹⁰But when you are invited, go and sit down at the lowest place,
so that when your host comes, he may say to you,
'Friend, move up higher';
then you will be honored in the presence of all who sit at the table with you.
¹¹For all who exalt themselves will be humbled,
and those who humble themselves will be exalted."

¹²He said also to the one who had invited him,
"When you give a luncheon or a dinner,
do not invite your friends or your brothers or your relatives or rich neighbors,
in case they may invite you in return, and you would be repaid.
¹³But when you give a banquet,
invite the poor, the crippled, the lame, and the blind.
¹⁴And you will be blessed,
because they cannot repay you,
for you will be repaid at the resurrection of the righteous."

The Gospel of the Lord.

PROPER 18

SEPTEMBER 6, 1998   *SEPTEMBER 9, 2001*   *SEPTEMBER 5, 2004*

FIRST READING: Deuteronomy 30:15–20

A reading from Deuteronomy:

15See, I have set before you today
life and prosperity,
death and adversity.

16If you obey the commandments of the Lord your God
that I am commanding you today,
by loving the Lord your God,
walking in his ways,
and observing his commandments, decrees, and ordinances,
then you shall live and become numerous,
and the Lord your God will bless you
in the land that you are entering to possess.

17But if your heart turns away and you do not hear,
but are led astray to bow down to other gods and serve them,
18I declare to you today that you shall perish;
you shall not live long in the land
that you are crossing the Jordan to enter and possess.

19I call heaven and earth to witness against you today
that I have set before you life and death, blessings and curses.
Choose life so that you and your descendants may live,
20loving the Lord your God, obeying him, and holding fast to him;
for that means life to you and length of days,
so that you may live in the land that the Lord swore to give to your ancestors,
to Abraham, to Isaac, and to Jacob.

The word of the Lord.

PSALMODY: Psalm 1

A reading from Philemon:

[1]Paul, a prisoner of Christ Jesus, and Timothy our brother,
To Philemon our dear friend and co-worker,
[2]to Apphia our sister, to Archippus our fellow soldier,
and to the church in your house:

[3]Grace to you and peace from God our Father and the Lord Jesus Christ.
[4]When I remember you in my prayers,
I always thank my God [5]because I hear of your love for all the saints
and your faith toward the Lord Jesus.
[6]I pray that the sharing of your faith may become effective
when you perceive all the good that we may do for Christ.
[7]I have indeed received much joy and encouragement from your love,
because the hearts of the saints have been refreshed through you, my brother.

[8]For this reason, though I am bold enough in Christ
to command you to do your duty,
[9]yet I would rather appeal to you on the basis of love—
and I, Paul, do this as an old man,
and now also as a prisoner of Christ Jesus.
[10]I am appealing to you for my child, Onesimus,
whose father I have become during my imprisonment.
[11]Formerly he was useless to you,
but now he is indeed useful both to you and to me.
[12]I am sending him, that is, my own heart, back to you.
[13]I wanted to keep him with me,
so that he might be of service to me in your place
during my imprisonment for the gospel;
[14]but I preferred to do nothing without your consent,
in order that your good deed might be voluntary and not something forced.
[15]Perhaps this is the reason he was separated from you for a while,
so that you might have him back forever,
[16]no longer as a slave but more than a slave,
a beloved brother—especially to me but how much more to you,
both in the flesh and in the Lord.

[17]So if you consider me your partner,
welcome him as you would welcome me.
[18]If he has wronged you in any way, or owes you anything,
charge that to my account.
[19]I, Paul, am writing this with my own hand: I will repay it.
I say nothing about your owing me even your own self.
[20]Yes, brother, let me have this benefit from you in the Lord!
Refresh my heart in Christ.
[21]Confident of your obedience, I am writing to you,
knowing that you will do even more than I say.

The word of the Lord.

GOSPEL: LUKE 14:25–33

The Holy Gospel according to Luke, the 14th chapter.

[25]Now large crowds were traveling with Jesus;
and he turned and said to them,
[26]"Whoever comes to me and does not hate father and mother,
wife and children, brothers and sisters,
yes, and even life itself, cannot be my disciple.
[27]Whoever does not carry the cross and follow me cannot be my disciple.
[28]For which of you, intending to build a tower,
does not first sit down and estimate the cost,
to see whether he has enough to complete it?
[29]Otherwise, when he has laid a foundation and is not able to finish,
all who see it will begin to ridicule him, [30]saying,
'This fellow began to build and was not able to finish.'
[31]Or what king, going out to wage war against another king,
will not sit down first and consider whether he is able with ten thousand
to oppose the one who comes against him with twenty thousand?
[32]If he cannot, then, while the other is still far away,
he sends a delegation and asks for the terms of peace.
[33]So therefore, none of you can become my disciple
if you do not give up all your possessions.

The Gospel of the Lord.

SUNDAY BETWEEN
SEPTEMBER 11 AND 17 INCLUSIVE

PROPER 19

SEPTEMBER 13, 1998   SEPTEMBER 16, 2001   SEPTEMBER 12, 2004

FIRST READING: Exodus 32:7–14

A reading from Exodus:

⁷The Lord said to Moses, "Go down at once!
Your people, whom you brought up out of the land of Egypt,
have acted perversely;
⁸they have been quick to turn aside from the way that I commanded them;
they have cast for themselves an image of a calf,
and have worshiped it and sacrificed to it, and said,
'These are your gods, O Israel, who brought you up out of the land of Egypt!' "
⁹The Lord said to Moses,
"I have seen this people, how stiff-necked they are.
¹⁰Now let me alone,
so that my wrath may burn hot against them and I may consume them;
and of you I will make a great nation."

¹¹But Moses implored the Lord his God, and said,
"O Lord, why does your wrath burn hot against your people,
whom you brought out of the land of Egypt with great power and with a
     mighty hand?
¹²Why should the Egyptians say,
'It was with evil intent that he brought them out to kill them in the mountains,
and to consume them from the face of the earth'?
Turn from your fierce wrath;
change your mind and do not bring disaster on your people.
¹³Remember Abraham, Isaac, and Israel, your servants,
how you swore to them by your own self, saying to them,
'I will multiply your descendants like the stars of heaven,
and all this land that I have promised I will give to your descendants,
and they shall inherit it forever.' "
¹⁴And the Lord changed his mind
about the disaster that he planned to bring on his people.

The word of the Lord.

PSALMODY: Psalm 51:1–10

Psalm 51:1–11, LBW/BCP

SECOND READING: 1 TIMOTHY 1:12–17

A reading from First Timothy:

[12]I am grateful to Christ Jesus our Lord, who has strengthened me,
because he judged me faithful and appointed me to his service,
[13]even though I was formerly a blasphemer, a persecutor,
      and a man of violence.
But I received mercy because I had acted ignorantly in unbelief,
[14]and the grace of our Lord overflowed for me
with the faith and love that are in Christ Jesus.
[15]The saying is sure and worthy of full acceptance,
that Christ Jesus came into the world to save sinners—
of whom I am the foremost.
[16]But for that very reason I received mercy,
so that in me, as the foremost,
Jesus Christ might display the utmost patience,
making me an example to those who would come to believe in him for
      eternal life.
[17]To the King of the ages, immortal, invisible, the only God,
be honor and glory forever and ever. Amen.

The word of the Lord.

GOSPEL: LUKE 15:1–10

The Holy Gospel according to Luke, the 15th chapter.

[1]Now all the tax collectors and sinners were coming near to listen to Jesus.
[2]And the Pharisees and the scribes were grumbling and saying,
"This fellow welcomes sinners and eats with them."

[3]So he told them this parable:
[4]"Which one of you, having a hundred sheep and losing one of them,
does not leave the ninety-nine in the wilderness
and go after the one that is lost until he finds it?
[5]When he has found it, he lays it on his shoulders and rejoices.
[6]And when he comes home, he calls together his friends and neighbors,
saying to them, 'Rejoice with me,
for I have found my sheep that was lost.'
[7]Just so, I tell you, there will be more joy in heaven over one sinner who
repents
than over ninety-nine righteous persons who need no repentance.

[8]"Or what woman having ten silver coins, if she loses one of them,
does not light a lamp, sweep the house,
and search carefully until she finds it?
[9]When she has found it, she calls together her friends and neighbors, saying,
'Rejoice with me, for I have found the coin that I had lost.'
[10]Just so, I tell you,
there is joy in the presence of the angels of God over one sinner who repents."

The Gospel of the Lord.

S U N D A Y B E T W E E N
S E P T E M B E R 18 A N D 24 I N C L U S I V E

PROPER 20

SEPTEMBER 20, 1998   *SEPTEMBER 23, 2001*   *SEPTEMBER 19, 2004*

FIRST READING: AMOS 8:4–7

A reading from Amos:

⁴Hear this, you that trample on the needy,
    and bring to ruin the poor of the land,
⁵saying, "When will the new moon be over
    so that we may sell grain;
and the sabbath,
    so that we may offer wheat for sale?
We will make the ephah small and the shekel great,
    and practice deceit with false balances,
⁶buying the poor for silver
    and the needy for a pair of sandals,
    and selling the sweepings of the wheat."

⁷The LORD has sworn by the pride of Jacob:
Surely I will never forget any of their deeds.

The word of the Lord.

PSALMODY: PSALM 113

SECOND READING: 1 TIMOTHY 2:1–7

A reading from First Timothy:

[1]First of all, then, I urge that supplications, prayers, intercessions,
    and thanksgivings
be made for everyone,
[2]for kings and all who are in high positions,
so that we may lead a quiet and peaceable life in all godliness and dignity.
[3]This is right and is acceptable in the sight of God our Savior,
[4]who desires everyone to be saved and to come to the knowledge of the truth.
[5]For

    there is one God;

        there is also one mediator between God and humankind,
    Christ Jesus, himself human,
        [6]who gave himself a ransom for all
—this was attested at the right time.
[7]For this I was appointed a herald and an apostle
(I am telling the truth, I am not lying),
a teacher of the Gentiles in faith and truth.

The word of the Lord.

GOSPEL: LUKE 16:1–13

The Holy Gospel according to Luke, the 16th chapter.

[1]Then Jesus said to the disciples,
"There was a rich man who had a manager,
and charges were brought to him that this man was squandering his property.
[2]So he summoned him and said to him,
'What is this that I hear about you?
Give me an accounting of your management,
because you cannot be my manager any longer.'
[3]Then the manager said to himself,
'What will I do, now that my master is taking the position away from me?
I am not strong enough to dig, and I am ashamed to beg.
[4]I have decided what to do so that, when I am dismissed as manager,
people may welcome me into their homes.'
[5]So, summoning his master's debtors one by one, he asked the first,
'How much do you owe my master?'
[6]He answered, 'A hundred jugs of olive oil.'
He said to him, 'Take your bill, sit down quickly, and make it fifty.'
[7]Then he asked another, 'And how much do you owe?'
He replied, 'A hundred containers of wheat.'
He said to him, 'Take your bill and make it eighty.'
[8]And his master commended the dishonest manager because he had acted
shrewdly;
for the children of this age are more shrewd in dealing with their own
generation
than are the children of light.
[9]And I tell you, make friends for yourselves by means of dishonest wealth
so that when it is gone, they may welcome you into the eternal homes.

[10]"Whoever is faithful in a very little is faithful also in much;
and whoever is dishonest in a very little is dishonest also in much.
[11]If then you have not been faithful with the dishonest wealth,
who will entrust to you the true riches?
[12]And if you have not been faithful with what belongs to another,
who will give you what is your own?
[13]No slave can serve two masters;
for a slave will either hate the one and love the other,
or be devoted to the one and despise the other.
You cannot serve God and wealth."

The Gospel of the Lord.

SUNDAY BETWEEN
SEPTEMBER 25 AND OCTOBER 1
INCLUSIVE

PROPER 21

SEPTEMBER 27, 1998   *SEPTEMBER 30, 2001*   *SEPTEMBER 26, 2004*

FIRST READING: Amos 6:1a, 4–7

A reading from Amos:

¹Alas for those who are at ease in Zion,
and for those who feel secure on Mount Samaria,
⁴Alas for those who lie on beds of ivory,
and lounge on their couches,
and eat lambs from the flock,
and calves from the stall;
⁵who sing idle songs to the sound of the harp,
and like David improvise on instruments of music;
⁶who drink wine from bowls,
and anoint themselves with the finest oils,
but are not grieved over the ruin of Joseph!
⁷Therefore they shall now be the first to go into exile,
and the revelry of the loungers shall pass away.

The word of the Lord.

PSALMODY: Psalm 146

SECOND READING: 1 TIMOTHY 6:6–19

A reading from First Timothy:

⁶Of course, there is great gain in godliness combined with contentment;
⁷for we brought nothing into the world,
so that we can take nothing out of it;
⁸but if we have food and clothing, we will be content with these.
⁹But those who want to be rich fall into temptation
and are trapped by many senseless and harmful desires
that plunge people into ruin and destruction.
¹⁰For the love of money is a root of all kinds of evil,
and in their eagerness to be rich
some have wandered away from the faith
and pierced themselves with many pains.

¹¹But as for you, man of God, shun all this;
pursue righteousness, godliness, faith, love, endurance, gentleness.
¹²Fight the good fight of the faith;
take hold of the eternal life, to which you were called
and for which you made the good confession in the presence of many
witnesses.
¹³In the presence of God, who gives life to all things,
and of Christ Jesus,
who in his testimony before Pontius Pilate made the good confession,
I charge you ¹⁴to keep the commandment without spot or blame
until the manifestation of our Lord Jesus Christ,
¹⁵which he will bring about at the right time—
he who is the blessed and only Sovereign,
the King of kings and Lord of lords.
¹⁶It is he alone who has immortality and dwells in unapproachable light,
whom no one has ever seen or can see;
to him be honor and eternal dominion. Amen.

¹⁷As for those who in the present age are rich,
command them not to be haughty,
or to set their hopes on the uncertainty of riches,
but rather on God who richly provides us with everything for our enjoyment.
¹⁸They are to do good, to be rich in good works,
generous, and ready to share,
¹⁹thus storing up for themselves the treasure of a good foundation for the
future,
so that they may take hold of the life that really is life.

The word of the Lord.

GOSPEL: LUKE 16:19–31

The Holy Gospel according to Luke, the 16th chapter.

Jesus said:
¹⁹"There was a rich man who was dressed in purple and fine linen
and who feasted sumptuously every day.
²⁰And at his gate lay a poor man named Lazarus, covered with sores,
²¹who longed to satisfy his hunger with what fell from the rich man's table;
even the dogs would come and lick his sores.
²²The poor man died and was carried away by the angels to be with Abraham.
The rich man also died and was buried.
²³In Hades, where he was being tormented,
he looked up and saw Abraham far away with Lazarus by his side.
²⁴He called out, 'Father Abraham, have mercy on me,
and send Lazarus to dip the tip of his finger in water and cool my tongue;
for I am in agony in these flames.'
²⁵But Abraham said,
'Child, remember that during your lifetime you received your good things,
and Lazarus in like manner evil things;
but now he is comforted here, and you are in agony.
²⁶Besides all this, between you and us a great chasm has been fixed,
so that those who might want to pass from here to you cannot do so,
and no one can cross from there to us.'
²⁷He said, 'Then, father, I beg you to send him to my father's house—
²⁸for I have five brothers—that he may warn them,
so that they will not also come into this place of torment.'
²⁹Abraham replied, 'They have Moses and the prophets;
they should listen to them.'
³⁰He said, 'No, father Abraham;
but if someone goes to them from the dead, they will repent.'
³¹He said to him, 'If they do not listen to Moses and the prophets,
neither will they be convinced even if someone rises from the dead.' "

The Gospel of the Lord.

S U N D A Y   B E T W E E N
O C T O B E R   2   A N D   8   I N C L U S I V E
PROPER 22

OCTOBER 4, 1998   *OCTOBER 7, 2001*   *OCTOBER 3, 2004*

FIRST READING: HABAKKUK 1:1–4; 2:1–4

A reading from Habakkuk:

¹The oracle that the prophet Habakkuk saw.

²O LORD, how long shall I cry for help,
    and you will not listen?
Or cry to you "Violence!"
    and you will not save?
³Why do you make me see wrong-doing
    and look at trouble?
Destruction and violence are before me;
    strife and contention arise.
⁴So the law becomes slack
    and justice never prevails.
The wicked surround the righteous—
    therefore judgment comes forth perverted.
²:¹I will stand at my watchpost,
    and station myself on the rampart;
I will keep watch to see what he will say to me,
    and what he will answer concerning my complaint.

²Then the LORD answered me and said:
Write the vision;
    make it plain on tablets,
    so that a runner may read it.
³For there is still a vision for the appointed time;
    it speaks of the end, and does not lie.
If it seems to tarry, wait for it;
    it will surely come, it will not delay.
⁴Look at the proud!
    Their spirit is not right in them,
    but the righteous live by their faith.

The word of the Lord.

PSALMODY: PSALM 37:1–9   *Psalm 37:1–10*, LBW/BCP

SECOND READING: 2 TIMOTHY 1:1–14

A reading from Second Timothy:

¹Paul, an apostle of Christ Jesus by the will of God,
for the sake of the promise of life that is in Christ Jesus,
²To Timothy, my beloved child:
Grace, mercy, and peace from God the Father and Christ Jesus our Lord.

³I am grateful to God—
whom I worship with a clear conscience,
as my ancestors did—
when I remember you constantly in my prayers night and day.
⁴Recalling your tears, I long to see you so that I may be filled with joy.
⁵I am reminded of your sincere faith,
a faith that lived first in your grandmother Lois
and your mother Eunice and now,
I am sure, lives in you.
⁶For this reason I remind you to rekindle the gift of God that is within you
through the laying on of my hands;
⁷for God did not give us a spirit of cowardice,
but rather a spirit of power and of love and of self-discipline.

⁸Do not be ashamed, then, of the testimony about our Lord
or of me his prisoner,
but join with me in suffering for the gospel,
relying on the power of God,
⁹who saved us and called us with a holy calling,
not according to our works but according to his own purpose and grace.
This grace was given to us in Christ Jesus before the ages began,
¹⁰but it has now been revealed through the appearing of our Savior Christ
        Jesus,
who abolished death and brought life and immortality to light through the
        gospel.
¹¹For this gospel I was appointed a herald and an apostle and a teacher,
¹²and for this reason I suffer as I do.
But I am not ashamed, for I know the one in whom I have put my trust,
and I am sure that he is able to guard until that day what I have entrusted to
        him.
¹³Hold to the standard of sound teaching that you have heard from me,
in the faith and love that are in Christ Jesus.
¹⁴Guard the good treasure entrusted to you,
with the help of the Holy Spirit living in us.

The word of the Lord.

GOSPEL: LUKE 17:5–10

The Holy Gospel according to Luke, the 17th chapter.

[5]The apostles said to the Lord, "Increase our faith!"
[6]The Lord replied, "If you had faith the size of a mustard seed,
you could say to this mulberry tree,
'Be uprooted and planted in the sea,'
and it would obey you.

[7]"Who among you would say to your slave
who has just come in from plowing or tending sheep in the field,
'Come here at once and take your place at the table'?
[8]Would you not rather say to him,
'Prepare supper for me, put on your apron and serve me while I eat and drink;
later you may eat and drink'?
[9]Do you thank the slave for doing what was commanded?
[10]So you also, when you have done all that you were ordered to do, say,
'We are worthless slaves;
we have done only what we ought to have done!' "

The Gospel of the Lord.

PROPER 23

OCTOBER 11, 1998   OCTOBER 14, 2001   OCTOBER 10, 2004

FIRST READING: 2 KINGS 5:1–3, 7–15c

A reading from Second Kings:

¹Naaman, commander of the army of the king of Aram,
was a great man and in high favor with his master,
because by him the LORD had given victory to Aram.
The man, though a mighty warrior, suffered from leprosy.
²Now the Arameans on one of their raids
had taken a young girl captive from the land of Israel,
and she served Naaman's wife.
³She said to her mistress,
"If only my lord were with the prophet who is in Samaria!
He would cure him of his leprosy."

⁷When the king of Israel read the letter, he tore his clothes and said,
"Am I God, to give death or life,
that this man sends word to me to cure a man of his leprosy?
Just look and see how he is trying to pick a quarrel with me."

⁸But when Elisha the man of God
heard that the king of Israel had torn his clothes,
he sent a message to the king, "Why have you torn your clothes?
Let him come to me, that he may learn that there is a prophet in Israel."
⁹So Naaman came with his horses and chariots,
and halted at the entrance of Elisha's house.
¹⁰Elisha sent a messenger to him, saying,
"Go, wash in the Jordan seven times,
and your flesh shall be restored and you shall be clean."
¹¹But Naaman became angry and went away, saying,
"I thought that for me he would surely come out,
and stand and call on the name of the LORD his God,
and would wave his hand over the spot, and cure the leprosy!
¹²Are not Abana and Pharpar, the rivers of Damascus,
better than all the waters of Israel?
Could I not wash in them, and be clean?"
He turned and went away in a rage.

[13]But his servants approached and said to him,
"Father, if the prophet had commanded you to do something difficult,
would you not have done it?
How much more, when all he said to you was, 'Wash, and be clean'?"
[14]So he went down and immersed himself seven times in the Jordan,
according to the word of the man of God;
his flesh was restored like the flesh of a young boy, and he was clean.

[15]Then he returned to the man of God, he and all his company;
he came and stood before him and said,
"Now I know that there is no God in all the earth except in Israel."

The word of the Lord.

PSALMODY: PSALM 111

A reading from Second Timothy:

[8]Remember Jesus Christ, raised from the dead, a descendant of David—
that is my gospel, [9]for which I suffer hardship,
even to the point of being chained like a criminal.
But the word of God is not chained.
[10]Therefore I endure everything for the sake of the elect,
so that they may also obtain the salvation that is in Christ Jesus,
with eternal glory.
[11]The saying is sure:
> If we have died with him, we will also live with him;
> [12]if we endure, we will also reign with him;
> if we deny him, he will also deny us;
> [13]if we are faithless, he remains faithful—
> for he cannot deny himself.

[14]Remind them of this,
and warn them before God that they are to avoid wrangling over words,
which does no good but only ruins those who are listening.
[15]Do your best to present yourself to God as one approved by him,
a worker who has no need to be ashamed,
rightly explaining the word of truth.

The word of the Lord.

GOSPEL: LUKE 17:11–19

The Holy Gospel according to Luke, the 17th chapter.

[11]On the way to Jerusalem
Jesus was going through the region between Samaria and Galilee.
[12]As he entered a village, ten lepers approached him.
Keeping their distance, [13]they called out, saying,
"Jesus, Master, have mercy on us!"
[14]When he saw them, he said to them,
"Go and show yourselves to the priests."
And as they went, they were made clean.
[15]Then one of them, when he saw that he was healed,
turned back, praising God with a loud voice.
[16]He prostrated himself at Jesus' feet and thanked him.
And he was a Samaritan.
[17]Then Jesus asked, "Were not ten made clean?
But the other nine, where are they?
[18]Was none of them found to return and give praise to God except this foreigner?"
[19]Then he said to him, "Get up and go on your way;
your faith has made you well."

The Gospel of the Lord.

SUNDAY BETWEEN
OCTOBER 16 AND 22 INCLUSIVE

PROPER 24

OCTOBER 18, 1998   *OCTOBER 21, 2001*   *OCTOBER 17, 2004*

FIRST READING: GENESIS 32:22–31

A reading from Genesis:

²²The same night Jacob got up and took his two wives,
          his two maids, and his eleven children,
and crossed the ford of the Jabbok.
²³He took them and sent them across the stream,
and likewise everything that he had.
²⁴Jacob was left alone; and a man wrestled with him until daybreak.
²⁵When the man saw that he did not prevail against Jacob,
he struck him on the hip socket;
and Jacob's hip was put out of joint as he wrestled with him.
²⁶Then he said, "Let me go, for the day is breaking."
But Jacob said, "I will not let you go, unless you bless me."
²⁷So he said to him, "What is your name?"
And he said, "Jacob."
²⁸Then the man said, "You shall no longer be called Jacob, but Israel,
for you have striven with God and with humans, and have prevailed."
²⁹Then Jacob asked him, "Please tell me your name."
But he said, "Why is it that you ask my name?"
And there he blessed him.
³⁰So Jacob called the place Peniel, saying,
"For I have seen God face to face, and yet my life is preserved."
³¹The sun rose upon him as he passed Penuel, limping because of his hip.

The word of the Lord.

PSALMODY: PSALM 121

SECOND READING: 2 Timothy 3:14—4:5

A reading from Second Timothy:

14But as for you, continue in what you have learned and firmly believed,
knowing from whom you learned it,
15and how from childhood you have known the sacred writings
that are able to instruct you for salvation through faith in Christ Jesus.
16All scripture is inspired by God and is useful for teaching, for reproof,
for correction, and for training in righteousness,
17so that everyone who belongs to God may be proficient,
equipped for every good work.

4:1In the presence of God and of Christ Jesus,
who is to judge the living and the dead,
and in view of his appearing and his kingdom,
I solemnly urge you:
2proclaim the message;
be persistent whether the time is favorable or unfavorable;
convince, rebuke, and encourage,
with the utmost patience in teaching.
3For the time is coming when people will not put up with sound doctrine,
but having itching ears,
they will accumulate for themselves teachers to suit their own desires,
4and will turn away from listening to the truth and wander away to myths.
5As for you, always be sober, endure suffering,
do the work of an evangelist, carry out your ministry fully.

The word of the Lord.

The Holy Gospel according to Luke, the 18th chapter.

¹Then Jesus told them a parable about their need to pray always
and not to lose heart.
²He said, "In a certain city there was a judge who neither feared God
nor had respect for people.
³In that city there was a widow who kept coming to him and saying,
'Grant me justice against my opponent.'
⁴For a while he refused; but later he said to himself,
'Though I have no fear of God and no respect for anyone,
⁵yet because this widow keeps bothering me,
I will grant her justice,
so that she may not wear me out by continually coming.' "

⁶And the Lord said, "Listen to what the unjust judge says.
⁷And will not God grant justice to his chosen ones who cry to him
    day and night?
Will he delay long in helping them?
⁸I tell you, he will quickly grant justice to them.
And yet, when the Son of Man comes, will he find faith on earth?"

The Gospel of the Lord.

SUNDAY BETWEEN
OCTOBER 23 AND 29 INCLUSIVE
PROPER 25

OCTOBER 25, 1998   OCTOBER 28, 2001   OCTOBER 24, 2004

FIRST READING: JEREMIAH 14:7–10, 19–22   *Alternate Reading: Sirach 35:12–17 (p. 406)*

A reading from Jeremiah:

⁷Although our iniquities testify against us,
    act, O LORD, for your name's sake;
our apostasies indeed are many,
    and we have sinned against you.
⁸O hope of Israel,
    its savior in time of trouble,
why should you be like a stranger in the land,
    like a traveler turning aside for the night?
⁹Why should you be like someone confused,
    like a mighty warrior who cannot give help?
Yet you, O LORD, are in the midst of us,
    and we are called by your name;
    do not forsake us!

¹⁰Thus says the LORD concerning this people:
Truly they have loved to wander,
    they have not restrained their feet;
therefore the LORD does not accept them,
    now he will remember their iniquity
    and punish their sins.

¹⁹Have you completely rejected Judah?
    Does your heart loathe Zion?
Why have you struck us down
    so that there is no healing for us?
We look for peace, but find no good;
    for a time of healing, but there is terror instead.
²⁰We acknowledge our wickedness, O LORD,
    the iniquity of our ancestors,
    for we have sinned against you.
²¹Do not spurn us, for your name's sake;
    do not dishonor your glorious throne;
    remember and do not break your covenant with us.

²²Can any idols of the nations bring rain?
　　Or can the heavens give showers?
Is it not you, O Lord our God?
　　We set our hope on you,
　　for it is you who do all this.

The word of the Lord.

PSALMODY: PSALM 84:1–7

Psalm 84:1–6, LBW/BCP

SECOND READING: 2 TIMOTHY 4:6–8, 16–18

A reading from Second Timothy:

^{6}As for me, I am already being poured out as a libation,
and the time of my departure has come.
^{7}I have fought the good fight, I have finished the race, I have kept the faith.
^{8}From now on there is reserved for me the crown of righteousness,
which the Lord, the righteous judge, will give me on that day,
and not only to me
but also to all who have longed for his appearing.

^{16}At my first defense no one came to my support, but all deserted me.
May it not be counted against them!
^{17}But the Lord stood by me and gave me strength,
so that through me the message might be fully proclaimed
and all the Gentiles might hear it.
So I was rescued from the lion's mouth.
^{18}The Lord will rescue me from every evil attack
and save me for his heavenly kingdom.
To him be the glory forever and ever. Amen.

The word of the Lord.

GOSPEL: LUKE 18:9–14

The Holy Gospel according to Luke, the 18th chapter.

^{9}Jesus also told this parable to some who trusted in themselves that they were
righteous
and regarded others with contempt:
^{10}"Two men went up to the temple to pray,
one a Pharisee and the other a tax collector.
^{11}The Pharisee, standing by himself, was praying thus,
'God, I thank you that I am not like other people:
thieves, rogues, adulterers, or even like this tax collector.
^{12}I fast twice a week; I give a tenth of all my income.'
^{13}But the tax collector, standing far off, would not even look up to heaven,
but was beating his breast and saying,
'God, be merciful to me, a sinner!'
^{14}I tell you, this man went down to his home justified rather than the other;
for all who exalt themselves will be humbled,
but all who humble themselves will be exalted."

The Gospel of the Lord.

PROPER 26

NOVEMBER 1, 1998   *NOVEMBER 4, 2001*   *OCTOBER 31, 2004*

FIRST READING: Isaiah 1:10–18

A reading from Isaiah:

¹⁰Hear the word of the Lord,
    you rulers of Sodom!
Listen to the teaching of our God,
    you people of Gomorrah!
¹¹What to me is the multitude of your sacrifices?
    says the Lord;
I have had enough of burnt offerings of rams
    and the fat of fed beasts;
I do not delight in the blood of bulls,
    or of lambs, or of goats.

¹²When you come to appear before me,
    who asked this from your hand?
    Trample my courts no more;
¹³bringing offerings is futile;
    incense is an abomination to me.
New moon and sabbath and calling of convocation
    I cannot endure solemn assemblies with iniquity.
¹⁴Your new moons and your appointed festivals
    my soul hates;
they have become a burden to me,
    I am weary of bearing them.
¹⁵When you stretch out your hands,
    I will hide my eyes from you;
even though you make many prayers,
    I will not listen;
    your hands are full of blood.
¹⁶Wash yourselves; make yourselves clean;
    remove the evil of your doings
    from before my eyes;
cease to do evil,
    ¹⁷learn to do good;

seek justice,
> rescue the oppressed,
defend the orphan,
> plead for the widow.

[18]Come now, let us argue it out,
> says the LORD:
though your sins are like scarlet,
> they shall be like snow;
though they are red like crimson,
> they shall become like wool.

The word of the Lord.

PSALMODY: PSALM 32:1–7

Psalm 32:1–8, LBW/BCP

SECOND READING: 2 THESSALONIANS 1:1–4, 11–12

A reading from Second Thessalonians:

¹Paul, Silvanus, and Timothy,
To the church of the Thessalonians in God our Father and the Lord Jesus Christ:
²Grace to you and peace from God our Father and the Lord Jesus Christ.

³We must always give thanks to God for you,
brothers and sisters, as is right,
because your faith is growing abundantly,
and the love of everyone of you for one another is increasing.
⁴Therefore we ourselves boast of you among the churches of God
for your steadfastness and faith
during all your persecutions and the afflictions that you are enduring.
¹¹To this end we always pray for you,
asking that our God will make you worthy of his call
and will fulfill by his power every good resolve and work of faith,
¹²so that the name of our Lord Jesus may be glorified in you,
and you in him,
according to the grace of our God and the Lord Jesus Christ.

The word of the Lord.

GOSPEL: LUKE 19:1–10

The Holy Gospel according to Luke, the 19th chapter.

¹Jesus entered Jericho and was passing through it.
²A man was there named Zacchaeus;
he was a chief tax collector and was rich.
³He was trying to see who Jesus was,
but on account of the crowd he could not, because he was short in stature.
⁴So he ran ahead and climbed a sycamore tree to see him,
because he was going to pass that way.
⁵When Jesus came to the place, he looked up and said to him,
"Zacchaeus, hurry and come down;
for I must stay at your house today."
⁶So he hurried down and was happy to welcome him.
⁷All who saw it began to grumble and said,
"He has gone to be the guest of one who is a sinner."
⁸Zacchaeus stood there and said to the Lord,
"Look, half of my possessions, Lord, I will give to the poor;
and if I have defrauded anyone of anything,
I will pay back four times as much."
⁹Then Jesus said to him, "Today salvation has come to this house,
because he too is a son of Abraham.
¹⁰For the Son of Man came to seek out and to save the lost."

The Gospel of the Lord.

FIRST READING: JOB 19:23–27a

A reading from Job:

²³"O that my words were written down!
    O that they were inscribed in a book!
²⁴O that with an iron pen and with lead
    they were engraved on a rock forever!
²⁵For I know that my Redeemer lives,
    and that at the last he will stand upon the earth;
²⁶and after my skin has been thus destroyed,
    then in my flesh I shall see God,
²⁷whom I shall see on my side,
    and my eyes shall behold, and not another."

The word of the Lord.

PSALMODY: PSALM 17:1–9

SECOND READING: 2 Thessalonians 2:1–5, 13–17

A reading from Second Thessalonians:

[1]As to the coming of our Lord Jesus Christ
and our being gathered together to him,
we beg you, brothers and sisters,
[2]not to be quickly shaken in mind or alarmed,
either by spirit or by word or by letter, as though from us,
to the effect that the day of the Lord is already here.
[3]Let no one deceive you in any way;
for that day will not come unless the rebellion comes first
and the lawless one is revealed, the one destined for destruction.
[4]He opposes and exalts himself above every so-called god or object of worship,
so that he takes his seat in the temple of God,
declaring himself to be God.
[5]Do you not remember that I told you these things when I was still with you?

[13]But we must always give thanks to God for you,
brothers and sisters beloved by the Lord,
because God chose you as the first fruits for salvation
through sanctification by the Spirit and through belief in the truth.
[14]For this purpose he called you through our proclamation of the good news,
so that you may obtain the glory of our Lord Jesus Christ.
[15]So then, brothers and sisters, stand firm
and hold fast to the traditions that you were taught by us,
either by word of mouth or by our letter.

[16]Now may our Lord Jesus Christ himself and God our Father,
who loved us and through grace gave us eternal comfort and good hope,
[17]comfort your hearts and strengthen them in every good work and word.

The word of the Lord.

The Holy Gospel according to Luke, the 20th chapter.

²⁷Some Sadducees, those who say there is no resurrection,
came to Jesus ²⁸and asked him a question,
"Teacher, Moses wrote for us that if a man's brother dies,
leaving a wife but no children,
the man shall marry the widow and raise up children for his brother.
²⁹Now there were seven brothers; the first married, and died childless;
³⁰then the second ³¹and the third married her,
and so in the same way all seven died childless.
³²Finally the woman also died.
³³In the resurrection, therefore, whose wife will the woman be?
For the seven had married her."

³⁴Jesus said to them,
"Those who belong to this age marry and are given in marriage;
³⁵but those who are considered worthy of a place in that age
and in the resurrection from the dead
neither marry nor are given in marriage.
³⁶Indeed they cannot die anymore,
because they are like angels and are children of God,
being children of the resurrection.
³⁷And the fact that the dead are raised Moses himself showed,
in the story about the bush,
where he speaks of the Lord as the God of Abraham,
the God of Isaac, and the God of Jacob.
³⁸Now he is God not of the dead,
but of the living;
for to him all of them are alive."

The Gospel of the Lord.

Sunday between November 13 and 19 inclusive

PROPER 28

NOVEMBER 15, 1998 *NOVEMBER 18, 2001* *NOVEMBER 14, 2004*

FIRST READING: MALACHI 4:1–2a

A reading from Malachi:

1See, the day is coming, burning like an oven,
when all the arrogant and all evildoers will be stubble;
the day that comes shall burn them up, says the LORD of hosts,
so that it will leave them neither root nor branch.
2But for you who revere my name
the sun of righteousness shall rise,
with healing in its wings.

The word of the Lord.

PSALMODY: PSALM 98

A reading from Second Thessalonians:

6Now we command you, beloved, in the name of our Lord Jesus Christ,
to keep away from believers who are living in idleness
and not according to the tradition that they received from us.
7For you yourselves know how you ought to imitate us;
we were not idle when we were with you,
8and we did not eat anyone's bread without paying for it;
but with toil and labor we worked night and day,
so that we might not burden any of you.
9This was not because we do not have that right,
but in order to give you an example to imitate.
10For even when we were with you, we gave you this command:
Anyone unwilling to work should not eat.
11For we hear that some of you are living in idleness,
mere busybodies, not doing any work.
12Now such persons we command and exhort in the Lord Jesus Christ
to do their work quietly and to earn their own living.
13Brothers and sisters, do not be weary in doing what is right.

The word of the Lord.

The Holy Gospel according to Luke, the 21st chapter.

5When some were speaking about the temple,
how it was adorned with beautiful stones and gifts dedicated to God,
Jesus said, 6"As for these things that you see,
the days will come when not one stone will be left upon another;
all will be thrown down."

7They asked him, "Teacher, when will this be,
and what will be the sign that this is about to take place?"
8And he said, "Beware that you are not led astray;
for many will come in my name and say, 'I am he!'
and, 'The time is near!'
Do not go after them.

9"When you hear of wars and insurrections, do not be terrified;
for these things must take place first,
but the end will not follow immediately."
10Then he said to them,
"Nation will rise against nation, and kingdom against kingdom;
11there will be great earthquakes, and in various places famines and plagues;
and there will be dreadful portents and great signs from heaven.

12"But before all this occurs, they will arrest you and persecute you;
they will hand you over to synagogues and prisons,
and you will be brought before kings and governors because of my name.
13This will give you an opportunity to testify.
14So make up your minds not to prepare your defense in advance;
15for I will give you words and a wisdom
that none of your opponents will be able to withstand or contradict.
16You will be betrayed even by parents and brothers, by relatives and friends;
and they will put some of you to death.
17You will be hated by all because of my name.
18But not a hair of your head will perish.
19By your endurance you will gain your souls."

The Gospel of the Lord.

CHRIST THE KING

Last Sunday after Pentecost[†]

PROPER 29

NOVEMBER 22, 1998   *NOVEMBER 25, 2001*   *NOVEMBER 21, 2004*

FIRST READING: JEREMIAH 23:1–6

A reading from Jeremiah:

[1]Woe to the shepherds who destroy and scatter the sheep of my pasture!
says the LORD.
[2]Therefore thus says the LORD, the God of Israel,
concerning the shepherds who shepherd my people:
It is you who have scattered my flock,
and have driven them away,
and you have not attended to them.
So I will attend to you for your evil doings, says the LORD.

[3]Then I myself will gather the remnant of my flock
out of all the lands where I have driven them,
and I will bring them back to their fold,
and they shall be fruitful and multiply.
[4]I will raise up shepherds over them who will shepherd them,
and they shall not fear any longer, or be dismayed,
nor shall any be missing, says the LORD.

[5]The days are surely coming, says the LORD,
when I will raise up for David a righteous Branch,
and he shall reign as king and deal wisely,
and shall execute justice and righteousness in the land.
[6]In his days Judah will be saved and Israel will live in safety.
And this is the name by which he will be called:
"The LORD is our righteousness."

The word of the Lord.

PSALMODY: PSALM 46

[†]*Sunday between November 20 and 26 inclusive*

SECOND READING: Colossians 1:11–20

A reading from Colossians:

[11]May you be made strong
with all the strength that comes from his glorious power,
and may you be prepared to endure everything with patience,
while joyfully [12]giving thanks to the Father,
who has enabled you to share in the inheritance of the saints in the light.
[13]He has rescued us from the power of darkness
and transferred us into the kingdom of his beloved Son,
[14]in whom we have redemption, the forgiveness of sins.

[15]He is the image of the invisible God, the firstborn of all creation;
[16]for in him all things in heaven and on earth were created,
things visible and invisible,
whether thrones or dominions or rulers or powers—
all things have been created through him and for him.
[17]He himself is before all things, and in him all things hold together.
[18]He is the head of the body, the church;
he is the beginning, the firstborn from the dead,
so that he might come to have first place in everything.
[19]For in him all the fullness of God was pleased to dwell,
[20]and through him God was pleased to reconcile to himself all things,
whether on earth or in heaven,
by making peace through the blood of his cross.

The word of the Lord.

The Holy Gospel according to Luke, the 23rd chapter.

[33]When they came to the place that is called The Skull,
they crucified Jesus there with the criminals,
one on his right and one on his left.
[[34]Then Jesus said, "Father, forgive them;
for they do not know what they are doing."]
And they cast lots to divide his clothing.
[35]And the people stood by, watching;
but the leaders scoffed at him, saying,
"He saved others;
let him save himself if he is the Messiah of God, his chosen one!"
[36]The soldiers also mocked him,
coming up and offering him sour wine, [37]and saying,
"If you are the King of the Jews, save yourself!"
[38]There was also an inscription over him,
"This is the King of the Jews."

[39]One of the criminals who were hanged there kept deriding him
and saying, "Are you not the Messiah?
Save yourself and us!"
[40]But the other rebuked him, saying, "Do you not fear God,
since you are under the same sentence of condemnation?
[41]And we indeed have been condemned justly,
for we are getting what we deserve for our deeds,
but this man has done nothing wrong."
[42]Then he said,
"Jesus, remember me when you come into your kingdom."
[43]He replied, "Truly I tell you, today you will be with me in Paradise."

The Gospel of the Lord.

LESSER FESTIVALS
AND OCCASIONS

St. Andrew, Apostle

NOVEMBER 30

FIRST READING: Ezekiel 3:16–21

A reading from Ezekiel:

¹⁶At the end of seven days, the word of the LORD came to me:
¹⁷Mortal, I have made you a sentinel for the house of Israel;
whenever you hear a word from my mouth,
you shall give them warning from me.
¹⁸If I say to the wicked, "You shall surely die,"
and you give them no warning,
or speak to warn the wicked from their wicked way, in order to save their life,
those wicked persons shall die for their iniquity;
but their blood I will require at your hand.
¹⁹But if you warn the wicked,
and they do not turn from their wickedness, or from their wicked way,
they shall die for their iniquity; but you will have saved your life.

²⁰Again, if the righteous turn from their righteousness and commit iniquity,
and I lay a stumbling block before them, they shall die;
because you have not warned them, they shall die for their sin,
and their righteous deeds that they have done shall not be remembered;
but their blood I will require at your hand.
²¹If, however, you warn the righteous not to sin, and they do not sin,
they shall surely live, because they took warning;
and you will have saved your life.

The word of the Lord.

PSALMODY: Psalm 19:1–6

SECOND READING: Romans 10:10–18

A reading from Romans:

¹⁰One believes with the heart and so is justified,
and one confesses with the mouth and so is saved.
¹¹The scripture says,
"No one who believes in him will be put to shame."

[12]For there is no distinction between Jew and Greek;
the same Lord is Lord of all and is generous to all who call on him.
[13]For, "Everyone who calls on the name of the Lord shall be saved."

[14]But how are they to call on one in whom they have not believed?
And how are they to believe in one of whom they have never heard?
And how are they to hear without someone to proclaim him?
[15]And how are they to proclaim him unless they are sent?
As it is written,
"How beautiful are the feet of those who bring good news!"
[16]But not all have obeyed the good news; for Isaiah says,
"Lord, who has believed our message?"
[17]So faith comes from what is heard,
and what is heard comes through the word of Christ.
[18]But I ask, have they not heard? Indeed they have; for
    "Their voice has gone out to all the earth,
        and their words to the ends of the world."

The word of the Lord.

GOSPEL: JOHN 1:35–42

The Holy Gospel according to John, the first chapter.

[35]The next day John again was standing with two of his disciples,
[36]and as he watched Jesus walk by, he exclaimed,
"Look, here is the Lamb of God!"
[37]The two disciples heard him say this, and they followed Jesus.
[38]When Jesus turned and saw them following, he said to them,
"What are you looking for?"
They said to him,
"Rabbi" (which translated means Teacher),
"where are you staying?"
[39]He said to them, "Come and see."

They came and saw where he was staying,
and they remained with him that day.
It was about four o'clock in the afternoon.
[40]One of the two who heard John speak and followed him
was Andrew, Simon Peter's brother.
[41]He first found his brother Simon and said to him,
"We have found the Messiah" (which is translated Anointed).
[42]He brought Simon to Jesus, who looked at him and said,
"You are Simon son of John.
You are to be called Cephas" (which is translated Peter).

The Gospel of the Lord.

ST. THOMAS, APOSTLE

DECEMBER 21

FIRST READING: JUDGES 6:36–40

A reading from Judges:

³⁶Gideon said to God,
"In order to see whether you will deliver Israel by my hand, as you have said,
³⁷I am going to lay a fleece of wool on the threshing floor;
if there is dew on the fleece alone, and it is dry on all the ground,
then I shall know that you will deliver Israel by my hand, as you have said."
³⁸And it was so.
When he rose early next morning and squeezed the fleece,
he wrung enough dew from the fleece to fill a bowl with water.

³⁹Then Gideon said to God, "Do not let your anger burn against me,
let me speak one more time;
let me, please, make trial with the fleece just once more;
let it be dry only on the fleece, and on all the ground let there be dew."
⁴⁰And God did so that night.
It was dry on the fleece only, and on all the ground there was dew.

The word of the Lord.

PSALMODY: PSALM 136:1–4, 23–26

SECOND READING: EPHESIANS 4:11–16

A reading from Ephesians:

¹¹The gifts he gave were that some would be apostles,
some prophets, some evangelists, some pastors and teachers,
¹²to equip the saints for the work of ministry,
for building up the body of Christ,
¹³until all of us come to the unity of the faith
and of the knowledge of the Son of God,
to maturity, to the measure of the full stature of Christ.

¹⁴We must no longer be children,
tossed to and fro and blown about by every wind of doctrine,
by people's trickery, by their craftiness in deceitful scheming.

[15]But speaking the truth in love,
we must grow up in every way into him who is the head, into Christ,
[16]from whom the whole body,
joined and knit together by every ligament with which it is equipped,
as each part is working properly,
promotes the body's growth in building itself up in love.

The word of the Lord.

GOSPEL: JOHN 14:1–7

The Holy Gospel according to John, the 14th chapter.

Jesus said to the disciples:
[1]"Do not let your hearts be troubled.
Believe in God, believe also in me.
[2]In my Father's house there are many dwelling places.
If it were not so, would I have told you that I go to prepare a place for you?
[3]And if I go and prepare a place for you,
I will come again and will take you to myself,
so that where I am, there you may be also.
[4]And you know the way to the place where I am going."

[5]Thomas said to him, "Lord, we do not know where you are going.
How can we know the way?"
[6]Jesus said to him, "I am the way, and the truth, and the life.
No one comes to the Father except through me.
[7]If you know me, you will know my Father also.
From now on you do know him and have seen him."

The Gospel of the Lord.

St. Stephen, Deacon and Martyr

DECEMBER 26

FIRST READING: 2 CHRONICLES 24:17–22

A reading from Second Chronicles:

¹⁷Now after the death of Jehoiada the officials of Judah came
and did obeisance to the king;
then the king listened to them.
¹⁸They abandoned the house of the LORD, the God of their ancestors,
and served the sacred poles and the idols.
And wrath came upon Judah and Jerusalem for this guilt of theirs.
¹⁹Yet he sent prophets among them to bring them back to the LORD;
they testified against them, but they would not listen.

²⁰Then the spirit of God took possession of Zechariah
son of the priest Jehoiada;
he stood above the people and said to them,
"Thus says God:
Why do you transgress the commandments of the LORD,
so that you cannot prosper?
Because you have forsaken the LORD, he has also forsaken you."
²¹But they conspired against him,
and by command of the king
they stoned him to death in the court of the house of the LORD.
²²King Joash did not remember the kindness that Jehoiada,
Zechariah's father, had shown him, but killed his son.
As he was dying, he said, "May the LORD see and avenge!"

The word of the Lord.

PSALMODY: PSALM 17:1–9, 15   *Psalm 17:1–9, 16* LBW/BCP

SECOND READING: ACTS 6:8—7:2a, 51–60

A reading from Acts:

⁸Stephen, full of grace and power,
did great wonders and signs among the people.
⁹Then some of those who belonged to the synagogue of the Freedmen
(as it was called),

Cyrenians, Alexandrians, and others of those from Cilicia and Asia,
stood up and argued with Stephen.
¹⁰But they could not withstand the wisdom and the Spirit with which he spoke.
¹¹Then they secretly instigated some men to say,
"We have heard him speak blasphemous words against Moses and God."

¹²They stirred up the people as well as the elders and the scribes;
then they suddenly confronted him, seized him,
and brought him before the council.
¹³They set up false witnesses who said,
"This man never stops saying things against this holy place and the law;
¹⁴for we have heard him say that this Jesus of Nazareth will destroy this place
and will change the customs that Moses handed on to us."
¹⁵And all who sat in the council looked intently at him,
and they saw that his face was like the face of an angel.
⁷:¹Then the high priest asked him,
"Are these things so?"
²And Stephen replied: "Brothers and fathers, listen to me.

⁵¹"You stiff-necked people, uncircumcised in heart and ears,
you are forever opposing the Holy Spirit, just as your ancestors used to do.
⁵²Which of the prophets did your ancestors not persecute?
They killed those who foretold the coming of the Righteous One,
and now you have become his betrayers and murderers.
⁵³You are the ones that received the law as ordained by angels,
and yet you have not kept it."

⁵⁴When they heard these things, they became enraged
and ground their teeth at Stephen.
⁵⁵But filled with the Holy Spirit,
he gazed into heaven and saw the glory of God
and Jesus standing at the right hand of God.
⁵⁶"Look," he said,
"I see the heavens opened
and the Son of Man standing at the right hand of God!"

⁵⁷But they covered their ears,
and with a loud shout all rushed together against him.
⁵⁸Then they dragged him out of the city and began to stone him;
and the witnesses laid their coats at the feet of a young man named Saul.
⁵⁹While they were stoning Stephen, he prayed,
"Lord Jesus, receive my spirit."
⁶⁰Then he knelt down and cried out in a loud voice,
"Lord, do not hold this sin against them."
When he had said this, he died.

The word of the Lord.

GOSPEL: MATTHEW 23:34–39

The Holy Gospel according to Matthew, the 23rd chapter.

Jesus said:
[34]"Therefore I send you prophets, sages, and scribes,
some of whom you will kill and crucify,
and some you will flog in your synagogues and pursue from town to town,
[35]so that upon you may come all the righteous blood shed on earth,
from the blood of righteous Abel to the blood of Zechariah son of Barachiah,
whom you murdered between the sanctuary and the altar.
[36]Truly I tell you, all this will come upon this generation.

[37]"Jerusalem, Jerusalem,
the city that kills the prophets and stones those who are sent to it!
How often have I desired to gather your children together
as a hen gathers her brood under her wings,
and you were not willing!
[38]See, your house is left to you, desolate.
[39]For I tell you, you will not see me again until you say,
'Blessed is the one who comes in the name of the Lord.' "

The Gospel of the Lord.

St. John, Apostle and Evangelist

DECEMBER 27

FIRST READING: GENESIS 1:1–5, 26–31

A reading from Genesis:

¹In the beginning when God created the heavens and the earth,
²the earth was a formless void
and darkness covered the face of the deep,
while a wind from God swept over the face of the waters.
³Then God said, "Let there be light"; and there was light.
⁴And God saw that the light was good;
and God separated the light from the darkness.
⁵God called the light Day, and the darkness he called Night.
And there was evening and there was morning, the first day.

²⁶Then God said,
"Let us make humankind in our image, according to our likeness;
and let them have dominion over the fish of the sea,
and over the birds of the air, and over the cattle,
and over all the wild animals of the earth,
and over every creeping thing that creeps upon the earth."

²⁷So God created humankind in his image,
in the image of God he created them;
male and female he created them.
²⁸God blessed them, and God said to them,
"Be fruitful and multiply, and fill the earth and subdue it;
and have dominion over the fish of the sea
and over the birds of the air
and over every living thing that moves upon the earth."

²⁹God said,
"See, I have given you every plant yielding seed that is upon the face
of all the earth,
and every tree with seed in its fruit;
you shall have them for food.
³⁰And to every beast of the earth, and to every bird of the air,
and to everything that creeps on the earth,
everything that has the breath of life,
I have given every green plant for food."

And it was so.

[31]God saw everything that he had made,
and indeed, it was very good.
And there was evening and there was morning, the sixth day.

The word of the Lord.

PSALMODY: Psalm 116:12–19

Psalm 116:10–17 LBW/BCP

SECOND READING: 1 John 1:1—2:2

A reading from First John:

[1]We declare to you what was from the beginning,
what we have heard, what we have seen with our eyes,
what we have looked at and touched with our hands,
concerning the word of life—
[2]this life was revealed, and we have seen it and testify to it,
and declare to you the eternal life that was with the Father
and was revealed to us—
[3]we declare to you what we have seen and heard
so that you also may have fellowship with us;
and truly our fellowship is with the Father and with his Son Jesus Christ.
[4]We are writing these things so that our joy may be complete.

[5]This is the message we have heard from him and proclaim to you,
that God is light and in him there is no darkness at all.
[6]If we say that we have fellowship with him while we are walking in darkness,
we lie and do not do what is true;
[7]but if we walk in the light as he himself is in the light,
we have fellowship with one another,
and the blood of Jesus his Son cleanses us from all sin.
[8]If we say that we have no sin, we deceive ourselves,
and the truth is not in us.
[9]If we confess our sins,
he who is faithful and just will forgive us our sins
and cleanse us from all unrighteousness.
[10]If we say that we have not sinned, we make him a liar,
and his word is not in us.

[2:1]My little children,
I am writing these things to you so that you may not sin.
But if anyone does sin, we have an advocate with the Father,
Jesus Christ the righteous;
[2]and he is the atoning sacrifice for our sins,
and not for ours only but also for the sins of the whole world.

The word of the Lord.

The Holy Gospel according to John, the 21st chapter.

²⁰Peter turned and saw the disciple whom Jesus loved following them;
he was the one who had reclined next to Jesus at the supper and had said,
"Lord, who is it that is going to betray you?"
²¹When Peter saw him, he said to Jesus,
"Lord, what about him?"
²²Jesus said to him,
"If it is my will that he remain until I come, what is that to you?
Follow me!"
²³So the rumor spread in the community that this disciple would not die.
Yet Jesus did not say to him that he would not die, but,
"If it is my will that he remain until I come, what is that to you?"

²⁴This is the disciple who is testifying to these things
and has written them, and we know that his testimony is true.
²⁵But there are also many other things that Jesus did;
if every one of them were written down,
I suppose that the world itself could not contain the books that would be
      written.

The Gospel of the Lord.

THE HOLY INNOCENTS, MARTYRS

DECEMBER 28

FIRST READING: JEREMIAH 31:15–17

A reading from Jeremiah:

¹⁵Thus says the LORD:
A voice is heard in Ramah,
    lamentation and bitter weeping.
Rachel is weeping for her children;
    she refuses to be comforted for her children,
    because they are no more.
¹⁶Thus says the LORD:
Keep your voice from weeping,
    and your eyes from tears;
for there is a reward for your work,
                says the LORD:
    they shall come back from the land of the enemy;
¹⁷there is hope for your future,
              says the LORD:
    your children shall come back to their own country.

The word of the Lord.

PSALMODY: PSALM 124

SECOND READING: 1 PETER 4:12–19

A reading from First Peter:

¹²Beloved, do not be surprised at the fiery ordeal
that is taking place among you to test you,
as though something strange were happening to you.
¹³But rejoice insofar as you are sharing Christ's sufferings,
so that you may also be glad and shout for joy when his glory is revealed.
¹⁴If you are reviled for the name of Christ, you are blessed,
because the spirit of glory, which is the Spirit of God, is resting on you.
¹⁵But let none of you suffer as a murderer, a thief,
a criminal, or even as a mischief maker.

[16]Yet if any of you suffers as a Christian, do not consider it a disgrace,
but glorify God because you bear this name.
[17]For the time has come for judgment to begin with the household of God;
if it begins with us,
what will be the end for those who do not obey the gospel of God?
[18]And

> "If it is hard for the righteous to be saved,
>   what will become of the ungodly and the sinners?"

[19]Therefore, let those suffering in accordance with God's will
entrust themselves to a faithful Creator, while continuing to do good.

The word of the Lord.

GOSPEL: MATTHEW 2:13–18

The Holy Gospel according to Matthew, the second chapter.

[13]Now after the wise men had left,
an angel of the Lord appeared to Joseph in a dream and said,
"Get up, take the child and his mother, and flee to Egypt,
and remain there until I tell you;
for Herod is about to search for the child, to destroy him."
[14]Then Joseph got up, took the child and his mother by night,
and went to Egypt,
[15]and remained there until the death of Herod.
This was to fulfill what had been spoken by the Lord through the prophet,
"Out of Egypt I have called my son."

[16]When Herod saw that he had been tricked by the wise men,
he was infuriated,
and he sent and killed all the children in and around Bethlehem
who were two years old or under,
according to the time that he had learned from the wise men.
[17]Then was fulfilled what had been spoken through the prophet Jeremiah:

> [18]"A voice was heard in Ramah,
>   wailing and loud lamentation,
> Rachel weeping for her children;
>   she refused to be consoled, because they are no more."

The Gospel of the Lord.

The Name of Jesus

JANUARY 1

FIRST READING: NUMBERS 6:22–27

A reading from Numbers:

²²The LORD spoke to Moses, saying:
²³Speak to Aaron and his sons, saying,
Thus you shall bless the Israelites:
You shall say to them,
    ²⁴The LORD bless you and keep you;
    ²⁵the LORD make his face to shine upon you, and be gracious to you;
    ²⁶the LORD lift up his countenance upon you, and give you peace.

²⁷So they shall put my name on the Israelites, and I will bless them.

The word of the Lord.

PSALMODY: PSALM 8

SECOND READING: GALATIANS 4:4–7
Or Philippians 2:5–11, following

A reading from Galatians:

⁴When the fullness of time had come,
God sent his Son, born of a woman, born under the law,
⁵in order to redeem those who were under the law,
so that we might receive adoption as children.
⁶And because you are children,
God has sent the Spirit of his Son into our hearts,
crying, "Abba! Father!"
⁷So you are no longer a slave but a child,
and if a child then also an heir, through God.

The word of the Lord.

OR: PHILIPPIANS 2:5–11

A reading from Philippians:

⁵Let the same mind be in you that was in Christ Jesus,
⁶who, though he was in the form of God,
did not regard equality with God
as something to be exploited,
⁷but emptied himself,
taking the form of a slave,
being born in human likeness.
And being found in human form,
⁸he humbled himself
and became obedient to the point of death—
even death on a cross.
⁹Therefore God also highly exalted him
and gave him the name that is above every name,
¹⁰so that at the name of Jesus every knee should bend,
in heaven and on earth and under the earth,
¹¹and every tongue should confess
that Jesus Christ is Lord,
to the glory of God the Father.

The word of the Lord.

GOSPEL: LUKE 2:15–21

The Holy Gospel according to Luke, the second chapter.

¹⁵When the angels had left them and gone into heaven,
the shepherds said to one another,
"Let us go now to Bethlehem
and see this thing that has taken place,
which the Lord has made known to us."
¹⁶So they went with haste and found Mary and Joseph,
and the child lying in the manger.
¹⁷When they saw this,
they made known what had been told them about this child;
¹⁸and all who heard it were amazed at what the shepherds told them.
¹⁹But Mary treasured all these words and pondered them in her heart.
²⁰The shepherds returned,
glorifying and praising God for all they had heard and seen,
as it had been told them.

²¹After eight days had passed, it was time to circumcise the child;
and he was called Jesus,
the name given by the angel before he was conceived in the womb.

The Gospel of the Lord.

The Confession of St. Peter

JANUARY 18

FIRST READING: ACTS 4:8–13

A reading from Acts:

⁸Peter, filled with the Holy Spirit, said to the authorities,
"Rulers of the people and elders,
⁹if we are questioned today
because of a good deed done to someone who was sick
and are asked how this man has been healed,
¹⁰let it be known to all of you, and to all the people of Israel,
that this man is standing before you in good health
by the name of Jesus Christ of Nazareth,
whom you crucified, whom God raised from the dead.
¹¹This Jesus is
'the stone that was rejected by you, the builders;
it has become the cornerstone.'
¹²There is salvation in no one else,
for there is no other name under heaven given among mortals
by which we must be saved."

¹³Now when they saw the boldness of Peter and John
and realized that they were uneducated and ordinary men,
they were amazed and recognized them as companions of Jesus.

The word of the Lord.

PSALMODY: PSALM 18:1–6, 16–19   *Psalm 18:1–7, 17–20*   LBW/BCP

SECOND READING: 1 Corinthians 10:1–5

A reading from First Corinthians:

¹I do not want you to be unaware, brothers and sisters,
that our ancestors were all under the cloud,
and all passed through the sea,
²and all were baptized into Moses in the cloud and in the sea,
³and all ate the same spiritual food,
⁴and all drank the same spiritual drink.
For they drank from the spiritual rock that followed them,
and the rock was Christ.
⁵Nevertheless, God was not pleased with most of them,
and they were struck down in the wilderness.

The word of the Lord.

GOSPEL: Matthew 16:13–19

The Holy Gospel according to Matthew, the 16th chapter.

¹³Now when Jesus came into the district of Caesarea Philippi,
he asked his disciples, "Who do people say that the Son of Man is?"
¹⁴And they said,
"Some say John the Baptist, but others Elijah,
and still others Jeremiah or one of the prophets."
¹⁵He said to them, "But who do you say that I am?"
¹⁶Simon Peter answered,
"You are the Messiah, the Son of the living God."

¹⁷And Jesus answered him,
"Blessed are you, Simon son of Jonah!
For flesh and blood has not revealed this to you,
but my Father in heaven.
¹⁸And I tell you, you are Peter,
and on this rock I will build my church,
and the gates of Hades will not prevail against it.
¹⁹I will give you the keys of the kingdom of heaven,
and whatever you bind on earth will be bound in heaven,
and whatever you loose on earth will be loosed in heaven."

The Gospel of the Lord.

THE CONVERSION OF ST. PAUL

JANUARY 25

FIRST READING: ACTS 9:1–22

A reading from Acts:

¹Saul, still breathing threats and murder against the disciples of the Lord,
went to the high priest
²and asked him for letters to the synagogues at Damascus,
so that if he found any who belonged to the Way, men or women,
he might bring them bound to Jerusalem.

³Now as he was going along and approaching Damascus,
suddenly a light from heaven flashed around him.
⁴He fell to the ground and heard a voice saying to him,
"Saul, Saul, why do you persecute me?"
⁵He asked, "Who are you, Lord?"
The reply came, "I am Jesus, whom you are persecuting.
⁶But get up and enter the city,
and you will be told what you are to do."
⁷The men who were traveling with him stood speechless
because they heard the voice but saw no one.
⁸Saul got up from the ground,
and though his eyes were open, he could see nothing;
so they led him by the hand and brought him into Damascus.
⁹For three days he was without sight, and neither ate nor drank.

¹⁰Now there was a disciple in Damascus named Ananias.
The Lord said to him in a vision, "Ananias."
He answered, "Here I am, Lord."
¹¹The Lord said to him,
"Get up and go to the street called Straight,
and at the house of Judas look for a man of Tarsus named Saul.
At this moment he is praying,
¹²and he has seen in a vision a man named Ananias come in
and lay his hands on him so that he might regain his sight."
¹³But Ananias answered,
"Lord, I have heard from many about this man,
how much evil he has done to your saints in Jerusalem;
¹⁴and here he has authority from the chief priests
to bind all who invoke your name."

[15]But the Lord said to him,
"Go, for he is an instrument whom I have chosen
to bring my name before Gentiles and kings and before the people of Israel;
[16]I myself will show him how much he must suffer for the sake of my name."

[17]So Ananias went and entered the house.
He laid his hands on Saul and said,
"Brother Saul, the Lord Jesus, who appeared to you on your way here,
has sent me so that you may regain your sight
and be filled with the Holy Spirit."
[18]And immediately something like scales fell from his eyes,
and his sight was restored.
Then he got up and was baptized,
[19]and after taking some food, he regained his strength.

For several days he was with the disciples in Damascus,
[20]and immediately he began to proclaim Jesus in the synagogues, saying,
"He is the Son of God."
[21]All who heard him were amazed and said,
"Is not this the man who made havoc in Jerusalem
among those who invoked this name?
And has he not come here
for the purpose of bringing them bound before the chief priests?"
[22]Saul became increasingly more powerful
and confounded the Jews who lived in Damascus
by proving that Jesus was the Messiah.

The word of the Lord.

PSALMODY: PSALM 67

SECOND READING: GALATIANS 1:11–24

A reading from Galatians:

[11]I want you to know, brothers and sisters,
that the gospel that was proclaimed by me is not of human origin;
[12]for I did not receive it from a human source,
nor was I taught it,
but I received it through a revelation of Jesus Christ.

[13]You have heard, no doubt, of my earlier life in Judaism.
I was violently persecuting the church of God and was trying to destroy it.
[14]I advanced in Judaism beyond many among my people of the same age,
for I was far more zealous for the traditions of my ancestors.

[15]But when God, who had set me apart before I was born
and called me through his grace,

was pleased ¹⁶to reveal his Son to me,
so that I might proclaim him among the Gentiles,
I did not confer with any human being,
¹⁷nor did I go up to Jerusalem to those who were already apostles before me,
but I went away at once into Arabia,
and afterwards I returned to Damascus.
¹⁸Then after three years I did go up to Jerusalem to visit Cephas
and stayed with him fifteen days;
¹⁹but I did not see any other apostle except James the Lord's brother.
²⁰In what I am writing to you, before God, I do not lie!
²¹Then I went into the regions of Syria and Cilicia,
²²and I was still unknown by sight to the churches of Judea that are in Christ;
²³they only heard it said,
"The one who formerly was persecuting us
is now proclaiming the faith he once tried to destroy."
²⁴And they glorified God because of me.

The word of the Lord.

GOSPEL: LUKE 21:10–19

The Holy Gospel according to Luke, the 21st chapter.

¹⁰Jesus said to the disciples,
"Nation will rise against nation, and kingdom against kingdom;
¹¹there will be great earthquakes,
and in various places famines and plagues;
and there will be dreadful portents and great signs from heaven.

¹²"But before all this occurs, they will arrest you and persecute you;
they will hand you over to synagogues and prisons,
and you will be brought before kings and governors because of my name.
¹³This will give you an opportunity to testify.
¹⁴So make up your minds not to prepare your defense in advance;
¹⁵for I will give you words and a wisdom
that none of your opponents will be able to withstand or contradict.
¹⁶You will be betrayed even by parents and brothers,
by relatives and friends;
and they will put some of you to death.
¹⁷You will be hated by all because of my name.
¹⁸But not a hair of your head will perish.
¹⁹By your endurance you will gain your souls."

The Gospel of the Lord.

THE PRESENTATION OF OUR LORD

FEBRUARY 2

FIRST READING: MALACHI 3:1–4

A reading from Malachi:

¹See, I am sending my messenger to prepare the way before me,
and the Lord whom you seek will suddenly come to his temple.
The messenger of the covenant in whom you delight—
indeed, he is coming, says the LORD of hosts.
²But who can endure the day of his coming,
and who can stand when he appears?

For he is like a refiner's fire and like fullers' soap;
³he will sit as a refiner and purifier of silver,
and he will purify the descendants of Levi
and refine them like gold and silver,
until they present offerings to the LORD in righteousness.
⁴Then the offering of Judah and Jerusalem will be pleasing to the LORD
as in the days of old and as in former years.

The word of the Lord.

PSALMODY: PSALM 84 or PSALM 24:7–10

SECOND READING: HEBREWS 2:14–18

A reading from Hebrews:

¹⁴Since, therefore, the children share flesh and blood,
Jesus himself likewise shared the same things,
so that through death he might destroy the one who has the power of death,
that is, the devil,
¹⁵and free those who all their lives were held in slavery by the fear of death.

[16]For it is clear that he did not come to help angels,
but the descendants of Abraham.
[17]Therefore he had to become like his brothers and sisters in every respect,
so that he might be a merciful and faithful high priest in the service of God,
to make a sacrifice of atonement for the sins of the people.
[18]Because he himself was tested by what he suffered,
he is able to help those who are being tested.

The word of the Lord.

GOSPEL: LUKE 2:22–40

The Holy Gospel according to Luke, the second chapter.

[22]When the time came for their purification according to the law of Moses,
Mary and Joseph brought Jesus up to Jerusalem to present him to the Lord
[23](as it is written in the law of the Lord,
"Every firstborn male shall be designated as holy to the Lord"),
[24]and they offered a sacrifice according to what is stated in the law of the Lord,
"a pair of turtledoves or two young pigeons."

[25]Now there was a man in Jerusalem whose name was Simeon;
this man was righteous and devout,
looking forward to the consolation of Israel,
and the Holy Spirit rested on him.
[26]It had been revealed to him by the Holy Spirit
that he would not see death before he had seen the Lord's Messiah.
[27]Guided by the Spirit, Simeon came into the temple;
and when the parents brought in the child Jesus,
to do for him what was customary under the law,
[28]Simeon took him in his arms and praised God, saying,
  [29]"Master, now you are dismissing your servant in peace,
        according to your word;
  [30]for my eyes have seen your salvation,
        [31]which you have prepared in the presence of all peoples,
  [32]a light for revelation to the Gentiles
        and for glory to your people Israel."
[33]And the child's father and mother were amazed at what was being said
        about him.

[34]Then Simeon blessed them and said to his mother Mary,
"This child is destined for the falling and the rising of many in Israel,
and to be a sign that will be opposed
[35]so that the inner thoughts of many will be revealed—
and a sword will pierce your own soul too."

³⁶There was also a prophet,
Anna the daughter of Phanuel, of the tribe of Asher.
She was of a great age,
having lived with her husband seven years after her marriage,
³⁷then as a widow to the age of eighty-four.
She never left the temple
but worshiped there with fasting and prayer night and day.
³⁸At that moment she came, and began to praise God
and to speak about the child to all who were looking for the redemption of
       Jerusalem.

³⁹When they had finished everything required by the law of the Lord,
they returned to Galilee, to their own town of Nazareth.
⁴⁰The child grew and became strong, filled with wisdom;
and the favor of God was upon him.

The Gospel of the Lord.

ST. MATTHIAS, APOSTLE

FEBRUARY 24

FIRST READING: ISAIAH 66:1–2

A reading from Isaiah:

¹Thus says the LORD:
Heaven is my throne
    and the earth is my footstool;
what is the house that you would build for me,
    and what is my resting place?
²All these things my hand has made,
    and so all these things are mine,
                    says the LORD.
But this is the one to whom I will look,
    to the humble and contrite in spirit,
    who trembles at my word.

The word of the Lord.

PSALMODY: PSALM 56

SECOND READING: ACTS 1:15–26

A reading from Acts:

¹⁵In those days Peter stood up among the believers
(together the crowd numbered about one hundred twenty persons)
and said,
¹⁶"Friends, the scripture had to be fulfilled,
which the Holy Spirit through David foretold concerning Judas,
who became a guide for those who arrested Jesus—
¹⁷for he was numbered among us and was allotted his share in this ministry."
¹⁸(Now this man acquired a field with the reward of his wickedness;
and falling headlong, he burst open in the middle
and all his bowels gushed out.
¹⁹This became known to all the residents of Jerusalem,
so that the field was called in their language Hakeldama,
that is, Field of Blood.)

²⁰"For it is written in the book of Psalms,
  'Let his homestead become desolate,
      and let there be no one to live in it';
and
      'Let another take his position of overseer.'

²¹"So one of the men who have accompanied us
during all the time that the Lord Jesus went in and out among us,
²²beginning from the baptism of John
until the day when he was taken up from us—
one of these must become a witness with us to his resurrection."
²³So they proposed two,
Joseph called Barsabbas, who was also known as Justus, and Matthias.
²⁴Then they prayed and said,
"Lord, you know everyone's heart.
Show us which one of these two you have chosen
²⁵to take the place in this ministry and apostleship
from which Judas turned aside to go to his own place."
²⁶And they cast lots for them, and the lot fell on Matthias;
and he was added to the eleven apostles.

The word of the Lord.

GOSPEL: LUKE 6:12–16

The Holy Gospel according to Luke, the sixth chapter.

¹²During those days Jesus went out to the mountain to pray;
and he spent the night in prayer to God.
¹³And when day came, he called his disciples and chose twelve of them,
whom he also named apostles:
¹⁴Simon, whom he named Peter, and his brother Andrew,
and James, and John, and Philip, and Bartholomew,
¹⁵and Matthew, and Thomas, and James son of Alphaeus,
and Simon, who was called the Zealot,
¹⁶and Judas son of James, and Judas Iscariot, who became a traitor.

The Gospel of the Lord.

THE ANNUNCIATION OF OUR LORD

MARCH 25

FIRST READING: ISAIAH 7:10–14

A reading from Isaiah:

¹⁰The LORD spoke to Ahaz, saying,
¹¹Ask a sign of the LORD your God;
let it be deep as Sheol or high as heaven.
¹²But Ahaz said, I will not ask,
and I will not put the LORD to the test.
¹³Then Isaiah said:
"Hear then, O house of David!
Is it too little for you to weary mortals, that you weary my God also?
¹⁴Therefore the Lord himself will give you a sign.
Look, the young woman is with child and shall bear a son,
and shall name him Immanuel."

The word of the Lord.

PSALMODY: PSALM 45 or PSALM 40:5–10 *Psalm 40:5–11* LBW/BCP

SECOND READING: HEBREWS 10:4–10

A reading from Hebrews:

⁴It is impossible for the blood of bulls and goats to take away sins.
⁵Consequently, when Christ came into the world, he said,
    "Sacrifices and offerings you have not desired,
        but a body you have prepared for me;
    ⁶in burnt offerings and sin offerings
        you have taken no pleasure.
    ⁷Then I said, 'See, God, I have come to do your will, O God'
        (in the scroll of the book it is written of me)."
⁸When he said above,
"You have neither desired nor taken pleasure in sacrifices
and offerings and burnt offerings and sin offerings"
(these are offered according to the law),
⁹then he added, "See, I have come to do your will."

He abolishes the first in order to establish the second.
¹⁰And it is by God's will that we have been sanctified
through the offering of the body of Jesus Christ once for all.

The word of the Lord.

GOSPEL: LUKE 1:26–38

The Holy Gospel according to Luke, the first chapter.

²⁶In the sixth month the angel Gabriel was sent by God
to a town in Galilee called Nazareth,
²⁷to a virgin engaged to a man whose name was Joseph, of the house of David.
The virgin's name was Mary.
²⁸And he came to her and said,
"Greetings, favored one! The Lord is with you."
²⁹But she was much perplexed by his words
and pondered what sort of greeting this might be.

³⁰The angel said to her,
"Do not be afraid, Mary, for you have found favor with God.
³¹And now, you will conceive in your womb and bear a son,
and you will name him Jesus.
³²He will be great, and will be called the Son of the Most High,
and the Lord God will give to him the throne of his ancestor David.
³³He will reign over the house of Jacob forever,
and of his kingdom there will be no end."
³⁴Mary said to the angel,
"How can this be, since I am a virgin?"
³⁵The angel said to her,
"The Holy Spirit will come upon you,
and the power of the Most High will overshadow you;
therefore the child to be born will be holy;
he will be called Son of God.
³⁶And now, your relative Elizabeth in her old age has also conceived a son;
and this is the sixth month for her who was said to be barren.
³⁷For nothing will be impossible with God."

³⁸Then Mary said, "Here am I, the servant of the Lord;
let it be with me according to your word."

Then the angel departed from her.

The Gospel of the Lord.

ST. MARK, EVANGELIST

APRIL 25

FIRST READING: Isaiah 52:7–10

A reading from Isaiah:

⁷How beautiful upon the mountains
    are the feet of the messenger who announces peace,
who brings good news,
    who announces salvation,
    who says to Zion, "Your God reigns."
⁸Listen! Your sentinels lift up their voices,
    together they sing for joy;
for in plain sight they see
    the return of the LORD to Zion.
⁹Break forth together into singing,
    you ruins of Jerusalem;
for the LORD has comforted his people,
    he has redeemed Jerusalem.
¹⁰The LORD has bared his holy arm
    before the eyes of all the nations;
and all the ends of the earth shall see
    the salvation of our God.

The word of the Lord.

PSALMODY: Psalm 57

SECOND READING: 2 Timothy 4:6–11, 18

A reading from Second Timothy:

Paul writes:
⁶As for me, I am already being poured out as a libation,
and the time of my departure has come.
⁷I have fought the good fight,
I have finished the race,
I have kept the faith.
⁸From now on there is reserved for me the crown of righteousness,
which the Lord, the righteous judge, will give me on that day,
and not only to me
but also to all who have longed for his appearing.

⁹Do your best to come to me soon,
¹⁰for Demas, in love with this present world,

has deserted me and gone to Thessalonica;
Crescens has gone to Galatia, Titus to Dalmatia.
[11]Only Luke is with me.
Get Mark and bring him with you,
for he is useful in my ministry.

[18]The Lord will rescue me from every evil attack
and save me for his heavenly kingdom.
To him be the glory forever and ever. Amen.

The word of the Lord.

GOSPEL: MARK 1:1–15

The Holy Gospel according to Mark, the first chapter.

[1]The beginning of the good news of Jesus Christ, the Son of God.
[2]As it is written in the prophet Isaiah,
     "See, I am sending my messenger ahead of you,
         who will prepare your way;
     [3]the voice of one crying out in the wilderness:
         'Prepare the way of the Lord,
         make his paths straight,' "
[4]John the baptizer appeared in the wilderness,
proclaiming a baptism of repentance for the forgiveness of sins.
[5]And people from the whole Judean countryside
and all the people of Jerusalem were going out to him,
and were baptized by him in the river Jordan, confessing their sins.
[6]Now John was clothed with camel's hair, with a leather belt around his waist,
and he ate locusts and wild honey.
[7]He proclaimed, "The one who is more powerful than I is coming after me;
I am not worthy to stoop down and untie the thong of his sandals.
[8]I have baptized you with water;
but he will baptize you with the Holy Spirit."

[9]In those days Jesus came from Nazareth of Galilee
and was baptized by John in the Jordan.
[10]And just as he was coming up out of the water,
he saw the heavens torn apart and the Spirit descending like a dove on him.
[11]And a voice came from heaven,
"You are my Son, the Beloved; with you I am well pleased."

[12]And the Spirit immediately drove him out into the wilderness.
[13]He was in the wilderness forty days, tempted by Satan;
and he was with the wild beasts; and the angels waited on him.

[14]Now after John was arrested, Jesus came to Galilee,
proclaiming the good news of God, [15]and saying,
"The time is fulfilled, and the kingdom of God has come near;
repent, and believe in the good news."

The Gospel of the Lord.

St. Philip and St. James, Apostles

MAY 1

FIRST READING: Isaiah 30:18–21

A reading from Isaiah:

> [18]The Lord waits to be gracious to you;
> therefore he will rise up to show mercy to you.
> For the Lord is a God of justice;
> blessed are all those who wait for him.

> [19]Truly, O people in Zion, inhabitants of Jerusalem,
> you shall weep no more.
> He will surely be gracious to you at the sound of your cry;
> when he hears it, he will answer you.
> [20]Though the Lord may give you the bread of adversity
> and the water of affliction,
> yet your Teacher will not hide himself any more,
> but your eyes shall see your Teacher.
> [21]And when you turn to the right or when you turn to the left,
> your ears shall hear a word behind you, saying,
> "This is the way; walk in it."

The word of the Lord.

PSALMODY: Psalm 44:1–3, 20–26

SECOND READING: 2 Corinthians 4:1–6

A reading from Second Corinthians:

> [1]Since it is by God's mercy that we are engaged in this ministry,
> we do not lose heart.
> [2]We have renounced the shameful things that one hides;
> we refuse to practice cunning or to falsify God's word;
> but by the open statement of the truth
> we commend ourselves to the conscience of everyone in the sight of God.
> [3]And even if our gospel is veiled,
> it is veiled to those who are perishing.
> [4]In their case the god of this world has blinded the minds of the unbelievers,

to keep them from seeing the light of the gospel of the glory of Christ,
who is the image of God.

⁵For we do not proclaim ourselves;
we proclaim Jesus Christ as Lord
and ourselves as your slaves for Jesus' sake.
⁶For it is the God who said, "Let light shine out of darkness,"
who has shone in our hearts
to give the light of the knowledge of the glory of God
in the face of Jesus Christ.

The word of the Lord.

GOSPEL: JOHN 14:8–14

The Holy Gospel according to John, the 14th chapter.

⁸Philip said to Jesus,
"Lord, show us the Father, and we will be satisfied."
⁹Jesus said to him,
"Have I been with you all this time, Philip,
and you still do not know me?
Whoever has seen me has seen the Father.
How can you say, 'Show us the Father'?
¹⁰Do you not believe that I am in the Father and the Father is in me?
The words that I say to you I do not speak on my own;
but the Father who dwells in me does his works.
¹¹Believe me that I am in the Father and the Father is in me;
but if you do not, then believe me because of the works themselves.

¹²"Very truly, I tell you,
the one who believes in me will also do the works that I do and,
in fact, will do greater works than these,
because I am going to the Father.
¹³I will do whatever you ask in my name,
so that the Father may be glorified in the Son.
¹⁴If in my name you ask me for anything, I will do it."

The Gospel of the Lord.

The Visitation

MAY 31

FIRST READING: 1 SAMUEL 2:1–10

A reading from First Samuel:

¹Hannah prayed and said,

"My heart exults in the LORD;
    my strength is exalted in my God.
My mouth derides my enemies,
    because I rejoice in my victory.

²"There is no Holy One like the LORD,
    no one besides you;
    there is no Rock like our God.
³Talk no more so very proudly,
    let not arrogance come from your mouth;
for the LORD is a God of knowledge,
    and by him actions are weighed.
⁴The bows of the mighty are broken,
    but the feeble gird on strength.
⁵Those who were full have hired themselves out for bread,
    but those who were hungry are fat with spoil.
The barren has borne seven,
    but she who has many children is forlorn.
⁶The LORD kills and brings to life;
    he brings down to Sheol and raises up.
⁷The LORD makes poor and makes rich;
    he brings low, he also exalts.
⁸He raises up the poor from the dust;
    he lifts the needy from the ash heap,
to make them sit with princes
    and inherit a seat of honor.
For the pillars of the earth are the LORD's,
    and on them he has set the world.

⁹"He will guard the feet of his faithful ones,
    but the wicked shall be cut off in darkness;
    for not by might does one prevail.

10The LORD! His adversaries shall be shattered;
    the Most High will thunder in heaven.
The LORD will judge the ends of the earth;
    he will give strength to his king,
       and exalt the power of his anointed."

The word of the Lord.

PSALMODY: PSALM 113

SECOND READING: ROMANS 12:9–16b

A reading from Romans:

9Let love be genuine;
hate what is evil, hold fast to what is good;
10love one another with mutual affection;
outdo one another in showing honor.
11Do not lag in zeal, be ardent in spirit, serve the Lord.
12Rejoice in hope, be patient in suffering, persevere in prayer.
13Contribute to the needs of the saints;
extend hospitality to strangers.

14Bless those who persecute you; bless and do not curse them.
15Rejoice with those who rejoice, weep with those who weep.
16Live in harmony with one another;
do not be haughty, but associate with the lowly.

The word of the Lord.

The Holy Gospel according to Luke, the first chapter.

³⁹In those days Mary set out
and went with haste to a Judean town in the hill country,
⁴⁰where she entered the house of Zechariah and greeted Elizabeth.
⁴¹When Elizabeth heard Mary's greeting, the child leaped in her womb.
And Elizabeth was filled with the Holy Spirit
⁴²and exclaimed with a loud cry,
"Blessed are you among women, and blessed is the fruit of your womb.
⁴³And why has this happened to me,
that the mother of my Lord comes to me?
⁴⁴For as soon as I heard the sound of your greeting,
the child in my womb leaped for joy.
⁴⁵And blessed is she who believed
that there would be a fulfillment of what was spoken to her by the Lord."

⁴⁶And Mary said,
    "My soul magnifies the Lord,
        ⁴⁷and my spirit rejoices in God my Savior,
    ⁴⁸for he has looked with favor on the lowliness of his servant.
        Surely, from now on all generations will call me blessed;
    ⁴⁹for the Mighty One has done great things for me,
        and holy is his name.
    ⁵⁰His mercy is for those who fear him
        from generation to generation.
    ⁵¹He has shown strength with his arm;
        he has scattered the proud in the thoughts of their hearts.
    ⁵²He has brought down the powerful from their thrones,
        and lifted up the lowly;
    ⁵³he has filled the hungry with good things,
        and sent the rich away empty.
    ⁵⁴He has helped his servant Israel,
        in remembrance of his mercy,
    ⁵⁵according to the promise he made to our ancestors,
        to Abraham and to his descendants forever."

⁵⁶And Mary remained with her about three months
and then returned to her home.

⁵⁷Now the time came for Elizabeth to give birth,
and she bore a son.

The Gospel of the Lord.

St. Barnabas, Apostle

JUNE 11

FIRST READING: Isaiah 42:5–12

A reading from Isaiah:

⁵Thus says God, the Lord,
   who created the heavens and stretched them out,
   who spread out the earth and what comes from it,
who gives breath to the people upon it
   and spirit to those who walk in it:
⁶I am the Lord, I have called you in righteousness,
   I have taken you by the hand and kept you;
I have given you as a covenant to the people,
   a light to the nations,
   ⁷to open the eyes that are blind,
to bring out the prisoners from the dungeon,
   from the prison those who sit in darkness.
⁸I am the Lord, that is my name;
   my glory I give to no other,
   nor my praise to idols.
⁹See, the former things have come to pass,
   and new things I now declare;
before they spring forth,
   I tell you of them.

¹⁰Sing to the Lord a new song,
   his praise from the end of the earth!
Let the sea roar and all that fills it,
   the coastlands and their inhabitants.
¹¹Let the desert and its towns lift up their voice,
   the villages that Kedar inhabits;
let the inhabitants of Sela sing for joy,
   let them shout from the tops of the mountains.
¹²Let them give glory to the Lord,
   and declare his praise in the coastlands.

The word of the Lord.

PSALMODY: Psalm 112

A reading from Acts:

¹⁹Now those who were scattered
because of the persecution that took place over Stephen
traveled as far as Phoenicia, Cyprus, and Antioch,
and they spoke the word to no one except Jews.
²⁰But among them were some men of Cyprus and Cyrene who,
on coming to Antioch, spoke to the Hellenists also,
proclaiming the Lord Jesus.
²¹The hand of the Lord was with them,
and a great number became believers and turned to the Lord.
²²News of this came to the ears of the church in Jerusalem,
and they sent Barnabas to Antioch.

²³When he came and saw the grace of God, he rejoiced,
and he exhorted them all to remain faithful to the Lord with steadfast devotion;
²⁴for he was a good man, full of the Holy Spirit and of faith.
And a great many people were brought to the Lord.
²⁵Then Barnabas went to Tarsus to look for Saul,
²⁶and when he had found him, he brought him to Antioch.
So it was that for an entire year
they met with the church and taught a great many people,
and it was in Antioch that the disciples were first called "Christians."

²⁷At that time prophets came down from Jerusalem to Antioch.
²⁸One of them named Agabus stood up and predicted by the Spirit
that there would be a severe famine over all the world;
and this took place during the reign of Claudius.
²⁹The disciples determined that according to their ability,
each would send relief to the believers living in Judea;
³⁰this they did, sending it to the elders by Barnabas and Saul.

¹³:¹Now in the church at Antioch there were prophets and teachers:
Barnabas, Simeon who was called Niger,
Lucius of Cyrene, Manaen a member of the court of Herod the ruler, and Saul.
²While they were worshiping the Lord and fasting,
the Holy Spirit said,
"Set apart for me Barnabas and Saul for the work to which I have called them."
³Then after fasting and praying
they laid their hands on them and sent them off.

The word of the Lord.

The Holy Gospel according to Matthew, the tenth chapter.

Jesus said to the twelve:
[7]"As you go, proclaim the good news,
'The kingdom of heaven has come near.'
[8]Cure the sick, raise the dead, cleanse the lepers, cast out demons.
You received without payment; give without payment.
[9]Take no gold, or silver, or copper in your belts,
[10]no bag for your journey, or two tunics, or sandals, or a staff;
for laborers deserve their food.

[11]"Whatever town or village you enter, find out who in it is worthy,
and stay there until you leave.
[12]As you enter the house, greet it.
[13]If the house is worthy, let your peace come upon it;
but if it is not worthy, let your peace return to you.
[14]If anyone will not welcome you or listen to your words,
shake off the dust from your feet as you leave that house or town.
[15]Truly I tell you,
it will be more tolerable for the land of Sodom and Gomorrah
          on the day of judgment
than for that town.

[16]"See, I am sending you out like sheep into the midst of wolves;
so be wise as serpents and innocent as doves."

The Gospel of the Lord.

The Nativity of
St. John the Baptist

JUNE 24

FIRST READING: MALACHI 3:1–4

A reading from Malachi:

¹See, I am sending my messenger to prepare the way before me,
and the Lord whom you seek will suddenly come to his temple.
The messenger of the covenant in whom you delight—
indeed, he is coming, says the LORD of hosts.
²But who can endure the day of his coming,
and who can stand when he appears?

For he is like a refiner's fire and like fullers' soap;
³he will sit as a refiner and purifier of silver,
and he will purify the descendants of Levi
and refine them like gold and silver,
until they present offerings to the LORD in righteousness.
⁴Then the offering of Judah and Jerusalem will be pleasing to the LORD
as in the days of old and as in former years.

The word of the Lord.

PSALMODY: PSALM 141

SECOND READING: ACTS 13:13–26

A reading from Acts:

¹³Paul and his companions set sail from Paphos
and came to Perga in Pamphylia.
John, however, left them and returned to Jerusalem;
¹⁴but they went on from Perga and came to Antioch in Pisidia.
And on the sabbath day they went into the synagogue and sat down.
¹⁵After the reading of the law and the prophets,
the officials of the synagogue sent them a message, saying,
"Brothers, if you have any word of exhortation for the people, give it."

¹⁶So Paul stood up and with a gesture began to speak:
"You Israelites, and others who fear God, listen.

[17]The God of this people Israel chose our ancestors
and made the people great during their stay in the land of Egypt,
and with uplifted arm he led them out of it.
[18]For about forty years he put up with them in the wilderness.
[19]After he had destroyed seven nations in the land of Canaan,
he gave them their land as an inheritance
[20]for about four hundred fifty years.
After that he gave them judges until the time of the prophet Samuel.
[21]Then they asked for a king;
and God gave them Saul son of Kish, a man of the tribe of Benjamin,
who reigned for forty years.
[22]When he had removed him, he made David their king.
In his testimony about him he said,
'I have found David, son of Jesse, to be a man after my heart,
who will carry out all my wishes.'
[23]Of this man's posterity God has brought to Israel a Savior,
Jesus, as he promised;
[24]before his coming John had already proclaimed a baptism of repentance
to all the people of Israel.
[25]And as John was finishing his work, he said,
'What do you suppose that I am? I am not he.
No, but one is coming after me;
I am not worthy to untie the thong of the sandals on his feet.'

[26]"My brothers, you descendants of Abraham's family,
and others who fear God,
to us the message of this salvation has been sent."

The word of the Lord.

GOSPEL: LUKE 1:57–67 [68–80]

The Holy Gospel according to Luke, the first chapter.

[57]Now the time came for Elizabeth to give birth, and she bore a son.
[58]Her neighbors and relatives heard that the Lord had shown his great mercy
to her,
and they rejoiced with her.

[59]On the eighth day they came to circumcise the child,
and they were going to name him Zechariah after his father.
[60]But his mother said, "No; he is to be called John."
[61]They said to her, "None of your relatives has this name."
[62]Then they began motioning to his father
to find out what name he wanted to give him.
[63]He asked for a writing tablet and wrote,
"His name is John."
And all of them were amazed.

⁶⁴Immediately his mouth was opened and his tongue freed,
and he began to speak, praising God.
⁶⁵Fear came over all their neighbors,
and all these things were talked about
throughout the entire hill country of Judea.
⁶⁶All who heard them pondered them and said,
"What then will this child become?"
For, indeed, the hand of the Lord was with him.

⁶⁷Then his father Zechariah was filled with the Holy Spirit
and spoke this prophecy:
  [⁶⁸"Blessed be the Lord God of Israel,
      for he has looked favorably on his people and redeemed them.
  ⁶⁹He has raised up a mighty savior for us
      in the house of his servant David,
  ⁷⁰as he spoke through the mouth of his holy prophets from of old,
      ⁷¹that we would be saved from our enemies and from the hand of all
          who hate us.
  ⁷²Thus he has shown the mercy promised to our ancestors,
      and has remembered his holy covenant,
  ⁷³the oath that he swore to our ancestor Abraham,
      to grant us ⁷⁴that we, being rescued from the hands of our enemies,
  might serve him without fear, ⁷⁵in holiness and righteousness
      before him all our days.

  ⁷⁶"And you, child, will be called the prophet of the Most High;
      for you will go before the Lord to prepare his ways,
  ⁷⁷to give knowledge of salvation to his people
      by the forgiveness of their sins.
  ⁷⁸By the tender mercy of our God,
      the dawn from on high will break upon us,
  ⁷⁹to give light to those who sit in darkness and in the shadow of death,
      to guide our feet into the way of peace."

⁸⁰The child grew and became strong in spirit,
and he was in the wilderness until the day he appeared publicly to Israel.]

The Gospel of the Lord.

St. Peter and St. Paul, Apostles

JUNE 29

FIRST READING: Ezekiel 34:11–16

A reading from Ezekiel:

¹¹Thus says the Lord God:
I myself will search for my sheep, and will seek them out.
¹²As shepherds seek out their flocks
when they are among their scattered sheep,
so I will seek out my sheep.
I will rescue them from all the places to which they have been scattered
on a day of clouds and thick darkness.
¹³I will bring them out from the peoples and gather them from the countries,
and will bring them into their own land;
and I will feed them on the mountains of Israel,
by the watercourses, and in all the inhabited parts of the land.
¹⁴I will feed them with good pasture,
and the mountain heights of Israel shall be their pasture;
there they shall lie down in good grazing land,
and they shall feed on rich pasture on the mountains of Israel.
¹⁵I myself will be the shepherd of my sheep,
and I will make them lie down, says the Lord God.
¹⁶I will seek the lost, and I will bring back the strayed,
and I will bind up the injured, and I will strengthen the weak,
but the fat and the strong I will destroy.
I will feed them with justice.

The word of the Lord.

PSALMODY: Psalm 87:1–3, 5–7   *Psalm 87:1–2, 4–6*   LBW/BCP

A reading from First Corinthians:

¹⁶Do you not know that you are God's temple
and that God's Spirit dwells in you?
¹⁷If anyone destroys God's temple, God will destroy that person.
For God's temple is holy, and you are that temple.

¹⁸Do not deceive yourselves.
If you think that you are wise in this age,
you should become fools so that you may become wise.
¹⁹For the wisdom of this world is foolishness with God.
For it is written,
    "He catches the wise in their craftiness,"
²⁰and again,
    "The Lord knows the thoughts of the wise,
        that they are futile."
²¹So let no one boast about human leaders.
For all things are yours,
²²whether Paul or Apollos or Cephas
or the world or life or death or the present or the future—
all belong to you,
²³and you belong to Christ,
and Christ belongs to God.

The word of the Lord.

The Holy Gospel according to Mark, the eighth chapter.

27Jesus went on with his disciples to the villages of Caesarea Philippi;
and on the way he asked his disciples,
"Who do people say that I am?"
28And they answered him,
"John the Baptist; and others, Elijah;
and still others, one of the prophets."
29He asked them, "But who do you say that I am?"
Peter answered him, "You are the Messiah."
30And he sternly ordered them not to tell anyone about him.

31Then he began to teach them
that the Son of Man must undergo great suffering,
and be rejected by the elders, the chief priests, and the scribes,
and be killed, and after three days rise again.
32He said all this quite openly.
And Peter took him aside and began to rebuke him.
33But turning and looking at his disciples, he rebuked Peter and said,
"Get behind me, Satan!
For you are setting your mind not on divine things but on human things."

34He called the crowd with his disciples, and said to them,
"If any want to become my followers,
let them deny themselves and take up their cross and follow me.
35For those who want to save their life will lose it,
and those who lose their life for my sake, and for the sake of the gospel,
will save it."

The Gospel of the Lord.

ST. MARY MAGDALENE

JULY 22

FIRST READING: RUTH 1:6–18

Or Exodus 2:1–10, following

A reading from Ruth:

⁶Naomi started to return with her daughters-in-law Orpah and Ruth
      from the country of Moab,
for she had heard in the country of Moab
that the Lᴏʀᴅ had considered his people
and given them food.
⁷So she set out from the place where she had been living,
she and her two daughters-in-law,
and they went on their way to go back to the land of Judah.
⁸But Naomi said to her two daughters-in-law,
"Go back each of you to your mother's house.
May the Lᴏʀᴅ deal kindly with you,
as you have dealt with the dead and with me.
⁹The Lᴏʀᴅ grant that you may find security,
each of you in the house of your husband."
Then she kissed them, and they wept aloud.

¹⁰They said to her, "No, we will return with you to your people."
¹¹But Naomi said,
"Turn back, my daughters, why will you go with me?
Do I still have sons in my womb that they may become your husbands?
¹²Turn back, my daughters, go your way,
for I am too old to have a husband.
Even if I thought there was hope for me,
even if I should have a husband tonight and bear sons,
¹³would you then wait until they were grown?
Would you then refrain from marrying?
No, my daughters, it has been far more bitter for me than for you,
because the hand of the Lᴏʀᴅ has turned against me."

¹⁴Then they wept aloud again.
Orpah kissed her mother-in-law, but Ruth clung to her.

¹⁵So she said,
"See, your sister-in-law has gone back to her people and to her gods;
return after your sister-in-law."
¹⁶But Ruth said,
    "Do not press me to leave you
        or to turn back from following you!
    Where you go, I will go;
        where you lodge, I will lodge;
    your people shall be my people,
        and your God my God.
    ¹⁷Where you die, I will die—
        there will I be buried.
    May the LORD do thus and so to me,
        and more as well,
    if even death parts me from you!"
¹⁸When Naomi saw that she was determined to go with her,
she said no more to her.

The word of the Lord.

OR: EXODUS 2:1–10

A reading from Exodus:

¹Now a man from the house of Levi went and married a Levite woman.
²The woman conceived and bore a son;
and when she saw that he was a fine baby, she hid him three months.
³When she could hide him no longer she got a papyrus basket for him,
and plastered it with bitumen and pitch;
she put the child in it and placed it among the reeds on the bank of the river.
⁴His sister stood at a distance, to see what would happen to him.

⁵The daughter of Pharaoh came down to bathe at the river,
while her attendants walked beside the river.
She saw the basket among the reeds and sent her maid to bring it.
⁶When she opened it, she saw the child.
He was crying, and she took pity on him.
"This must be one of the Hebrews' children," she said.
⁷Then his sister said to Pharaoh's daughter,
"Shall I go and get you a nurse from the Hebrew women
to nurse the child for you?"
⁸Pharaoh's daughter said to her, "Yes."
So the girl went and called the child's mother.
⁹Pharaoh's daughter said to her,
"Take this child and nurse it for me, and I will give you your wages."
So the woman took the child and nursed it.

[10]When the child grew up, she brought him to Pharaoh's daughter,
and she took him as her son.
She named him Moses, "because," she said,
"I drew him out of the water."

The word of the Lord.

PSALMODY: PSALM 73:23–28   *Psalm 73:23–29*   LBW/BCP

SECOND READING: ACTS 13:26–33a

A reading from Acts:

[26]"My brothers, you descendants of Abraham's family,
and others who fear God,
to us the message of this salvation has been sent.
[27]Because the residents of Jerusalem and their leaders did not recognize him
or understand the words of the prophets that are read every sabbath,
they fulfilled those words by condemning him.
[28]Even though they found no cause for a sentence of death,
they asked Pilate to have him killed.
[29]When they had carried out everything that was written about him,
they took him down from the tree and laid him in a tomb.

[30]"But God raised him from the dead;
[31]and for many days he appeared to those who came up with him
from Galilee to Jerusalem,
and they are now his witnesses to the people.
[32]And we bring you the good news that what God promised to our ancestors
[33]he has fulfilled for us, their children, by raising Jesus."

The word of the Lord.

The Holy Gospel according to John, the 20th chapter.

[1]Early on the first day of the week, while it was still dark,
Mary Magdalene came to the tomb
and saw that the stone had been removed from the tomb.
[2]So she ran and went to Simon Peter and the other disciple,
the one whom Jesus loved, and said to them,
"They have taken the Lord out of the tomb,
and we do not know where they have laid him."

[11]Mary stood weeping outside the tomb.
As she wept, she bent over to look into the tomb;
[12]and she saw two angels in white,
sitting where the body of Jesus had been lying,
one at the head and the other at the feet.
[13]They said to her, "Woman, why are you weeping?"
She said to them,
"They have taken away my Lord, and I do not know where they have laid him."
[14]When she had said this, she turned around and saw Jesus standing there,
but she did not know that it was Jesus.
[15]Jesus said to her,
"Woman, why are you weeping? Whom are you looking for?"
Supposing him to be the gardener, she said to him,
"Sir, if you have carried him away, tell me where you have laid him,
and I will take him away."

[16]Jesus said to her, "Mary!"
She turned and said to him in Hebrew,
"Rabbouni!" (which means Teacher).
[17]Jesus said to her,
"Do not hold on to me, because I have not yet ascended to the Father.
But go to my brothers and say to them,
'I am ascending to my Father and your Father, to my God and your God.' "
[18]Mary Magdalene went and announced to the disciples,
"I have seen the Lord";
and she told them that he had said these things to her.

The Gospel of the Lord.

St. James the Elder, Apostle

JULY 25

FIRST READING: 1 KINGS 19:9–18

A reading from First Kings:

⁹At Horeb, the mount of God,
Elijah came to a cave, and spent the night there.
Then the word of the LORD came to him, saying,
"What are you doing here, Elijah?"
¹⁰He answered, "I have been very zealous for the LORD, the God of hosts;
for the Israelites have forsaken your covenant, thrown down your altars,
and killed your prophets with the sword.
I alone am left, and they are seeking my life, to take it away."
¹¹He said, "Go out and stand on the mountain before the LORD,
for the LORD is about to pass by."

Now there was a great wind, so strong that it was splitting mountains
and breaking rocks in pieces before the LORD,
but the LORD was not in the wind;
and after the wind an earthquake,
but the LORD was not in the earthquake;
¹²and after the earthquake a fire,
but the LORD was not in the fire;
and after the fire a sound of sheer silence.
¹³When Elijah heard it, he wrapped his face in his mantle
and went out and stood at the entrance of the cave.

Then there came a voice to him that said,
"What are you doing here, Elijah?"
¹⁴He answered,
"I have been very zealous for the LORD, the God of hosts;
for the Israelites have forsaken your covenant, thrown down your altars,
and killed your prophets with the sword.
I alone am left, and they are seeking my life, to take it away."
¹⁵Then the LORD said to him,
"Go, return on your way to the wilderness of Damascus;
when you arrive, you shall anoint Hazael as king over Aram.
¹⁶Also you shall anoint Jehu son of Nimshi as king over Israel;
and you shall anoint Elisha son of Shaphat of Abel-meholah
as prophet in your place.

¹⁷Whoever escapes from the sword of Hazael, Jehu shall kill;
and whoever escapes from the sword of Jehu, Elisha shall kill.
¹⁸Yet I will leave seven thousand in Israel,
all the knees that have not bowed to Baal,
and every mouth that has not kissed him."

The word of the Lord.

PSALMODY: PSALM 7:1–10   *Psalm 7:1–11*   LBW/BCP

SECOND READING: ACTS 11:27—12:3a

A reading from Acts:

²⁷At that time when Barnabas and Saul were in Antioch,
prophets came down from Jerusalem to Antioch.
²⁸One of them named Agabus stood up and predicted by the Spirit
that there would be a severe famine over all the world;
and this took place during the reign of Claudius.
²⁹The disciples determined that according to their ability,
each would send relief to the believers living in Judea;
this they did, sending it to the elders by Barnabas and Saul.

¹²:¹About that time
King Herod laid violent hands upon some who belonged to the church.
²He had James, the brother of John, killed with the sword.
³After he saw that it pleased the Jews, he proceeded to arrest Peter also.

The word of the Lord.

GOSPEL: MARK 10:35–45

The Holy Gospel according to Mark, the tenth chapter.

[35]James and John, the sons of Zebedee, came forward to Jesus and said to him,
 "Teacher, we want you to do for us whatever we ask of you."
[36]And he said to them, "What is it you want me to do for you?"
[37]And they said to him,
"Grant us to sit, one at your right hand and one at your left, in your glory."
[38]But Jesus said to them,
"You do not know what you are asking.
Are you able to drink the cup that I drink,
or be baptized with the baptism that I am baptized with?"
[39]They replied, "We are able."
Then Jesus said to them,
"The cup that I drink you will drink;
and with the baptism with which I am baptized, you will be baptized;
[40]but to sit at my right hand or at my left is not mine to grant,
but it is for those for whom it has been prepared."

[41]When the ten heard this, they began to be angry with James and John.
[42]So Jesus called them and said to them,
"You know that among the Gentiles
those whom they recognize as their rulers lord it over them,
and their great ones are tyrants over them.
[43]But it is not so among you;
but whoever wishes to become great among you must be your servant,
[44]and whoever wishes to be first among you must be slave of all.
[45]For the Son of Man came not to be served but to serve,
and to give his life a ransom for many."

The Gospel of the Lord.

MARY, MOTHER OF OUR LORD

AUGUST 15

FIRST READING: ISAIAH 61:7–11

A reading from Isaiah:

⁷Because their shame was double,
  and dishonor was proclaimed as their lot,
therefore they shall possess a double portion;
  everlasting joy shall be theirs.

⁸For I the LORD love justice,
  I hate robbery and wrongdoing;
I will faithfully give them their recompense,
  and I will make an everlasting covenant with them.
⁹Their descendants shall be known among the nations,
  and their offspring among the peoples;
all who see them shall acknowledge
  that they are a people whom the LORD has blessed.
¹⁰I will greatly rejoice in the LORD,
  my whole being shall exult in my God;
for he has clothed me with the garments of salvation,
  he has covered me with the robe of righteousness,
as a bridegroom decks himself with a garland,
  and as a bride adorns herself with her jewels.
¹¹For as the earth brings forth its shoots,
  and as a garden causes what is sown in it to spring up,
so the Lord GOD will cause righteousness and praise
  to spring up before all the nations.

The word of the Lord.

PSALMODY: PSALM 45:10–15   *Psalm 45:11–16* LBW/BCP

SECOND READING: GALATIANS 4:4–7

A reading from Galatians:

⁴When the fullness of time had come,
God sent his Son, born of a woman, born under the law,
⁵in order to redeem those who were under the law,

so that we might receive adoption as children.
[6]And because you are children,
God has sent the Spirit of his Son into our hearts,
crying, "Abba! Father!"
[7]So you are no longer a slave but a child,
and if a child then also an heir, through God.

The word of the Lord.

GOSPEL: LUKE 1:46–55

The Holy Gospel according to Luke, the first chapter.

[46]Mary said,

"My soul magnifies the Lord,
    [47]and my spirit rejoices in God my Savior,
[48]for he has looked with favor on the lowliness of his servant.
    Surely, from now on all generations will call me blessed;
[49]for the Mighty One has done great things for me,
    and holy is his name.
[50]His mercy is for those who fear him
    from generation to generation.
[51]He has shown strength with his arm;
    he has scattered the proud in the thoughts of their hearts.
[52]He has brought down the powerful from their thrones,
    and lifted up the lowly;
[53]he has filled the hungry with good things,
    and sent the rich away empty.
[54]He has helped his servant Israel,
    in remembrance of his mercy,
[55]according to the promise he made to our ancestors,
    to Abraham and to his descendants forever."

The Gospel of the Lord.

St. Bartholomew, Apostle

AUGUST 24

FIRST READING: Exodus 19:1–6

A reading from Exodus:

¹On the third new moon after the Israelites had gone out of the land of Egypt,
on that very day, they came into the wilderness of Sinai.
²They had journeyed from Rephidim, entered the wilderness of Sinai,
and camped in the wilderness;
Israel camped there in front of the mountain.
³Then Moses went up to God;
the Lord called to him from the mountain, saying,
"Thus you shall say to the house of Jacob, and tell the Israelites:
⁴You have seen what I did to the Egyptians,
and how I bore you on eagles' wings and brought you to myself.
⁵Now therefore, if you obey my voice and keep my covenant,
you shall be my treasured possession out of all the peoples.
Indeed, the whole earth is mine,
⁶but you shall be for me a priestly kingdom and a holy nation.
These are the words that you shall speak to the Israelites."

The word of the Lord.

PSALMODY: Psalm 12

SECOND READING: 1 Corinthians 12:27–31a

A reading from First Corinthians:

²⁷Now you are the body of Christ and individually members of it.
²⁸And God has appointed in the church first apostles,
second prophets, third teachers;
then deeds of power, then gifts of healing,
forms of assistance, forms of leadership, various kinds of tongues.
²⁹Are all apostles? Are all prophets? Are all teachers?
Do all work miracles? Do all possess gifts of healing?
³⁰Do all speak in tongues? Do all interpret?
³¹But strive for the greater gifts.

The word of the Lord.

GOSPEL: JOHN 1:43–51

The Holy Gospel according to John, the first chapter.

[43]The next day Jesus decided to go to Galilee.
He found Philip and said to him, "Follow me."
[44]Now Philip was from Bethsaida, the city of Andrew and Peter.
[45]Philip found Nathanael and said to him,
"We have found him
about whom Moses in the law and also the prophets wrote,
Jesus son of Joseph from Nazareth."
[46]Nathanael said to him, "Can anything good come out of Nazareth?"
Philip said to him, "Come and see."

[47]When Jesus saw Nathanael coming toward him, he said of him,
"Here is truly an Israelite in whom there is no deceit!"
[48]Nathanael asked him, "Where did you get to know me?"
Jesus answered, "I saw you under the fig tree before Philip called you."
[49]Nathanael replied,
"Rabbi, you are the Son of God! You are the King of Israel!"
[50]Jesus answered,
"Do you believe because I told you that I saw you under the fig tree?
You will see greater things than these."
[51]And he said to him,
"Very truly, I tell you, you will see heaven opened
and the angels of God ascending and descending upon the Son of Man."

The Gospel of the Lord.

HOLY CROSS DAY

SEPTEMBER 14

FIRST READING: NUMBERS 21:4b–9

A reading from Numbers:

From Mount Hor the Israelites set out,
⁴ᵇbut the people became impatient on the way.
⁵The people spoke against God and against Moses,
"Why have you brought us up out of Egypt to die in the wilderness?
For there is no food and no water, and we detest this miserable food."
⁶Then the LORD sent poisonous serpents among the people,
and they bit the people, so that many Israelites died.

⁷The people came to Moses and said,
"We have sinned by speaking against the LORD and against you;
pray to the LORD to take away the serpents from us."
So Moses prayed for the people.
⁸And the LORD said to Moses,
"Make a poisonous serpent, and set it on a pole;
and everyone who is bitten shall look at it and live."
⁹So Moses made a serpent of bronze, and put it upon a pole;
and whenever a serpent bit someone,
that person would look at the serpent of bronze and live.

The word of the Lord.

PSALMODY: PSALM 98:1–4 or PSALM 78:1–2, 34–38   *Psalm 98:1–5*   LBW/BCP

SECOND READING: 1 CORINTHIANS 1:18–24

A reading from First Corinthians:

¹⁸The message about the cross is foolishness to those who are perishing,
but to us who are being saved it is the power of God.
¹⁹For it is written,
    "I will destroy the wisdom of the wise,
        and the discernment of the discerning I will thwart."
²⁰Where is the one who is wise?
Where is the scribe?

Where is the debater of this age?
Has not God made foolish the wisdom of the world?

²¹For since, in the wisdom of God,
the world did not know God through wisdom,
God decided, through the foolishness of our proclamation,
to save those who believe.
²²For Jews demand signs and Greeks desire wisdom,
²³but we proclaim Christ crucified,
a stumbling block to Jews and foolishness to Gentiles,
²⁴but to those who are the called, both Jews and Greeks,
Christ the power of God and the wisdom of God.

The word of the Lord.

GOSPEL: JOHN 3:13–17

The Holy Gospel according to John, the third chapter.

Jesus said:
¹³"No one has ascended into heaven
except the one who descended from heaven,
the Son of Man.
¹⁴And just as Moses lifted up the serpent in the wilderness,
so must the Son of Man be lifted up,
¹⁵that whoever believes in him may have eternal life.

¹⁶"For God so loved the world that he gave his only Son,
so that everyone who believes in him may not perish
but may have eternal life.
¹⁷Indeed, God did not send the Son into the world to condemn the world,
but in order that the world might be saved through him."

The Gospel of the Lord.

St. Matthew, Apostle and Evangelist

SEPTEMBER 21

FIRST READING: Ezekiel 2:8—3:11

A reading from Ezekiel:

8You, mortal, hear what I say to you;
do not be rebellious like that rebellious house;
open your mouth and eat what I give you.
9I looked, and a hand was stretched out to me,
and a written scroll was in it.
10He spread it before me;
it had writing on the front and on the back,
and written on it were words of lamentation and mourning and woe.

3:1He said to me, O mortal, eat what is offered to you;
eat this scroll, and go, speak to the house of Israel.
2So I opened my mouth, and he gave me the scroll to eat.
3He said to me, Mortal, eat this scroll that I give you
and fill your stomach with it.
Then I ate it; and in my mouth it was as sweet as honey.

4He said to me: Mortal, go to the house of Israel
and speak my very words to them.
5For you are not sent to a people of obscure speech and difficult language,
but to the house of Israel—
6not to many peoples of obscure speech and difficult language,
whose words you cannot understand.
Surely, if I sent you to them, they would listen to you.
7But the house of Israel will not listen to you,
for they are not willing to listen to me;
because all the house of Israel have a hard forehead and a stubborn heart.
8See, I have made your face hard against their faces,
and your forehead hard against their foreheads.
9Like the hardest stone, harder than flint, I have made your forehead;
do not fear them or be dismayed at their looks,
for they are a rebellious house.
10He said to me: Mortal, all my words that I shall speak to you
receive in your heart and hear with your ears;
11then go to the exiles, to your people, and speak to them.

Say to them, "Thus says the Lord GOD";
whether they hear or refuse to hear.

The word of the Lord.

PSALMODY: PSALM 119:33–40

SECOND READING: EPHESIANS 2:4–10

A reading from Ephesians:

[4]God, who is rich in mercy,
out of the great love with which he loved us
[5]even when we were dead through our trespasses,
made us alive together with Christ—by grace you have been saved—
[6]and raised us up with him
and seated us with him in the heavenly places in Christ Jesus,
[7]so that in the ages to come
he might show the immeasurable riches of his grace
in kindness toward us in Christ Jesus.
[8]For by grace you have been saved through faith,
and this is not your own doing;
it is the gift of God—
[9]not the result of works, so that no one may boast.
[10]For we are what he has made us,
created in Christ Jesus for good works,
which God prepared beforehand to be our way of life.

The word of the Lord.

The Holy Gospel according to Matthew, the ninth chapter.

9As Jesus was walking along,
he saw a man called Matthew sitting at the tax booth;
and he said to him, "Follow me."
And he got up and followed him.

10And as he sat at dinner in the house,
many tax collectors and sinners came
and were sitting with him and his disciples.
11When the Pharisees saw this, they said to his disciples,
"Why does your teacher eat with tax collectors and sinners?"
12But when he heard this, he said,
"Those who are well have no need of a physician,
but those who are sick.
13Go and learn what this means,
'I desire mercy, not sacrifice.'
For I have come to call not the righteous but sinners."

The Gospel of the Lord.

St. Michael and All Angels

SEPTEMBER 29

FIRST READING: Daniel 10:10–14; 12:1–3

A reading from Daniel:

¹⁰A hand touched me and roused me to my hands and knees.
¹¹He said to me, "Daniel, greatly beloved,
pay attention to the words that I am going to speak to you.
Stand on your feet, for I have now been sent to you."
So while he was speaking this word to me, I stood up trembling.
¹²He said to me, "Do not fear, Daniel,
for from the first day that you set your mind to gain understanding
and to humble yourself before your God,
your words have been heard, and I have come because of your words.
¹³But the prince of the kingdom of Persia opposed me twenty-one days.
So Michael, one of the chief princes, came to help me,
and I left him there with the prince of the kingdom of Persia,
¹⁴and have come to help you understand what is to happen to your people
at the end of days.
For there is a further vision for those days.

¹²:¹"At that time Michael, the great prince,
the protector of your people, shall arise.
There shall be a time of anguish,
such as has never occurred since nations first came into existence.
But at that time your people shall be delivered,
everyone who is found written in the book.
²Many of those who sleep in the dust of the earth shall awake,
some to everlasting life, and some to shame and everlasting contempt.
³Those who are wise shall shine like the brightness of the sky,
and those who lead many to righteousness,
like the stars forever and ever."

The word of the Lord.

PSALMODY: Psalm 103:1–5, 20–22

SECOND READING: Revelation 12:7–12

A reading from Revelation:

⁷War broke out in heaven;
Michael and his angels fought against the dragon.
The dragon and his angels fought back,
⁸but they were defeated, and there was no longer any place for them in heaven.
⁹The great dragon was thrown down,
that ancient serpent, who is called the Devil and Satan,
the deceiver of the whole world—
he was thrown down to the earth, and his angels were thrown down with him.

¹⁰Then I heard a loud voice in heaven, proclaiming,
    "Now have come the salvation and the power
        and the kingdom of our God
        and the authority of his Messiah,
    for the accuser of our comrades has been thrown down,
        who accuses them day and night before our God.
    ¹¹But they have conquered him by the blood of the Lamb
        and by the word of their testimony,
    for they did not cling to life even in the face of death.
    ¹²Rejoice then, you heavens
        and those who dwell in them!
    But woe to the earth and the sea,
        for the devil has come down to you
    with great wrath,
        because he knows that his time is short!"

The word of the Lord.

GOSPEL: Luke 10:17–20

The Holy Gospel according to Luke, the tenth chapter.

¹⁷The seventy returned with joy, saying,
"Lord, in your name even the demons submit to us!"
¹⁸He said to them,
"I watched Satan fall from heaven like a flash of lightning.
¹⁹See, I have given you authority to tread on snakes and scorpions,
and over all the power of the enemy;
and nothing will hurt you.
²⁰Nevertheless, do not rejoice at this,
that the spirits submit to you,
but rejoice that your names are written in heaven."

The Gospel of the Lord.

St. Luke, Evangelist

OCTOBER 18

FIRST READING: Isaiah 43:8–13

Or Isaiah 35:5–8, following

A reading from Isaiah:

⁸Bring forth the people who are blind, yet have eyes,
	who are deaf, yet have ears!
⁹Let all the nations gather together,
	and let the peoples assemble.
Who among them declared this,
	and foretold to us the former things?
Let them bring their witnesses to justify them,
	and let them hear and say, "It is true."
¹⁰You are my witnesses, says the Lord,
	and my servant whom I have chosen,
so that you may know and believe me
	and understand that I am he.
Before me no god was formed,
	nor shall there be any after me.
¹¹I, I am the Lord,
	and besides me there is no savior.
¹²I declared and saved and proclaimed,
	when there was no strange god among you;
	and you are my witnesses, says the Lord.
¹³I am God, and also henceforth I am He;
	there is no one who can deliver from my hand;
	I work and who can hinder it?

The word of the Lord.

OR: Isaiah 35:5–8

A reading from Isaiah:

⁵Then the eyes of the blind shall be opened,
	and the ears of the deaf unstopped;
⁶then the lame shall leap like a deer,
	and the tongue of the speechless sing for joy.

For waters shall break forth in the wilderness,
> and streams in the desert;
⁷the burning sand shall become a pool,
> and the thirsty ground springs of water;
the haunt of jackals shall become a swamp,
> the grass shall become reeds and rushes.

⁸A highway shall be there,
> and it shall be called the Holy Way;
the unclean shall not travel on it,
> but it shall be for God's people;
> no traveler, not even fools, shall go astray.

The word of the Lord.

PSALMODY: PSALM 124

SECOND READING: 2 TIMOTHY 4:5–11

A reading from Second Timothy:

⁵As for you, always be sober, endure suffering,
do the work of an evangelist, carry out your ministry fully.

⁶As for me, I am already being poured out as a libation,
and the time of my departure has come.
⁷I have fought the good fight,
I have finished the race,
I have kept the faith.
⁸From now on there is reserved for me the crown of righteousness,
which the Lord, the righteous judge, will give me on that day,
and not only to me but also to all who have longed for his appearing.

⁹Do your best to come to me soon,
¹⁰for Demas, in love with this present world,
has deserted me and gone to Thessalonica;
Crescens has gone to Galatia, Titus to Dalmatia.
¹¹Only Luke is with me.
Get Mark and bring him with you, for he is useful in my ministry.

The word of the Lord.

The Holy Gospel according to Luke, the first and twenty-fourth chapters.

Luke writes:
[1]Since many have undertaken to set down an orderly account
of the events that have been fulfilled among us,
[2]just as they were handed on to us
by those who from the beginning were eyewitnesses and servants of the word,
[3]I too decided, after investigating everything carefully from the very first,
to write an orderly account for you, most excellent Theophilus,
[4]so that you may know the truth concerning the things
about which you have been instructed.

[24:44]Before he ascended, Jesus said to the disciples and their companions:
"These are my words that I spoke to you while I was still with you—
that everything written about me in the law of Moses,
the prophets, and the psalms must be fulfilled."
[45]Then he opened their minds to understand the scriptures,
[46]and he said to them, "Thus it is written,
that the Messiah is to suffer and to rise from the dead on the third day,
[47]and that repentance and forgiveness of sins is to be proclaimed in his name
to all nations, beginning from Jerusalem.
[48]You are witnesses of these things.
[49]And see, I am sending upon you what my Father promised;
so stay here in the city until you have been clothed with power from on high."

[50]Then he led them out as far as Bethany,
and, lifting up his hands, he blessed them.
[51]While he was blessing them,
he withdrew from them and was carried up into heaven.
[52]And they worshiped him, and returned to Jerusalem with great joy;
[53]and they were continually in the temple blessing God.

The Gospel of the Lord.

ST. SIMON AND ST. JUDE, APOSTLES

OCTOBER 28

FIRST READING: JEREMIAH 26:[1–6] 7–16

A reading from Jeremiah:

[¹At the beginning of the reign of King Jehoiakim son of Josiah of Judah,
this word came from the LORD:
²Thus says the LORD:
Stand in the court of the LORD's house,
and speak to all the cities of Judah that come to worship in the house
        of the LORD;
speak to them all the words that I command you;
do not hold back a word.
³It may be that they will listen, all of them,
and will turn from their evil way,
that I may change my mind about the disaster
that I intend to bring on them because of their evil doings.
⁴You shall say to them:
Thus says the LORD: If you will not listen to me,
to walk in my law that I have set before you,
⁵and to heed the words of my servants the prophets
whom I send to you urgently—
though you have not heeded—
⁶then I will make this house like Shiloh,
and I will make this city a curse for all the nations of the earth.]

⁷The priests and the prophets and all the people
heard Jeremiah speaking these words in the house of the LORD.
⁸And when Jeremiah had finished speaking
all that the LORD had commanded him to speak to all the people,
then the priests and the prophets and all the people laid hold of him,
saying, "You shall die!
⁹Why have you prophesied in the name of the LORD, saying,
'This house shall be like Shiloh,
and this city shall be desolate, without inhabitant'?"
And all the people gathered around Jeremiah in the house of the LORD.

¹⁰When the officials of Judah heard these things,
they came up from the king's house to the house of the LORD
and took their seat in the entry of the New Gate of the house of the LORD.

¹¹Then the priests and the prophets said to the officials and to all the people,
"This man deserves the sentence of death
because he has prophesied against this city,
as you have heard with your own ears."

¹²Then Jeremiah spoke to all the officials and all the people, saying,
"It is the LORD who sent me to prophesy
against this house and this city all the words you have heard.
¹³Now therefore amend your ways and your doings,
and obey the voice of the LORD your God,
and the LORD will change his mind
about the disaster that he has pronounced against you.
¹⁴But as for me, here I am in your hands.
Do with me as seems good and right to you.
¹⁵Only know for certain that if you put me to death,
you will be bringing innocent blood upon yourselves
and upon this city and its inhabitants,
for in truth the LORD sent me to you to speak all these words in your ears."

¹⁶Then the officials and all the people said to the priests and the prophets,
"This man does not deserve the sentence of death,
for he has spoken to us in the name of the LORD our God."

The word of the Lord.

PSALMODY: PSALM 11

SECOND READING: 1 JOHN 4:1–6

A reading from First John:

¹Beloved, do not believe every spirit,
but test the spirits to see whether they are from God;
for many false prophets have gone out into the world.
²By this you know the Spirit of God:
every spirit that confesses that Jesus Christ has come in the flesh is from God,
³and every spirit that does not confess Jesus is not from God.
And this is the spirit of the antichrist,
of which you have heard that it is coming;
and now it is already in the world.

⁴Little children, you are from God, and have conquered them;
for the one who is in you is greater than the one who is in the world.
⁵They are from the world;
therefore what they say is from the world, and the world listens to them.

[6]We are from God.
Whoever knows God listens to us,
and whoever is not from God does not listen to us.
From this we know the spirit of truth and the spirit of error.

The word of the Lord.

GOSPEL: JOHN 14:21–27

The Holy Gospel according to John, the 14th chapter.

Jesus said to the disciples:
[21]"They who have my commandments and keep them are those who love me;
and those who love me will be loved by my Father,
and I will love them and reveal myself to them."
[22]Judas (not Iscariot) said to him,
"Lord, how is it that you will reveal yourself to us, and not to the world?"
[23]Jesus answered him,
"Those who love me will keep my word, and my Father will love them,
and we will come to them and make our home with them.
[24]Whoever does not love me does not keep my words;
and the word that you hear is not mine, but is from the Father who sent me.

[25]"I have said these things to you while I am still with you.
[26]But the Advocate, the Holy Spirit, whom the Father will send in my name,
will teach you everything,
and remind you of all that I have said to you.
[27]Peace I leave with you; my peace I give to you.
I do not give to you as the world gives.
Do not let your hearts be troubled, and do not let them be afraid."

The Gospel of the Lord.

REFORMATION DAY

OCTOBER 31

FIRST READING: JEREMIAH 31:31–34

A reading from Jeremiah:

³¹The days are surely coming, says the LORD,
when I will make a new covenant with the house of Israel
     and the house of Judah.
³²It will not be like the covenant that I made with their ancestors
when I took them by the hand to bring them out of the land of Egypt—
a covenant that they broke, though I was their husband, says the LORD.

³³But this is the covenant that I will make with the house of Israel
after those days, says the LORD:
I will put my law within them,
and I will write it on their hearts;
and I will be their God, and they shall be my people.
³⁴No longer shall they teach one another,
or say to each other, "Know the LORD,"
for they shall all know me,
from the least of them to the greatest, says the LORD;
for I will forgive their iniquity, and remember their sin no more.

The word of the Lord.

PSALMODY: PSALM 46

SECOND READING: ROMANS 3:19–28

A reading from Romans:

¹⁹Now we know that whatever the law says,
it speaks to those who are under the law,
so that every mouth may be silenced,
and the whole world may be held accountable to God.
²⁰For "no human being will be justified in his sight"
by deeds prescribed by the law,
for through the law comes the knowledge of sin.

21But now, apart from law, the righteousness of God has been disclosed,
and is attested by the law and the prophets,
22the righteousness of God through faith in Jesus Christ for all who believe.
For there is no distinction,
23since all have sinned and fall short of the glory of God;
24they are now justified by his grace as a gift,
through the redemption that is in Christ Jesus,
25whom God put forward as a sacrifice of atonement by his blood,
effective through faith.
He did this to show his righteousness,
because in his divine forbearance
he had passed over the sins previously committed;
26it was to prove at the present time that he himself is righteous
and that he justifies the one who has faith in Jesus.

27Then what becomes of boasting?
It is excluded.
By what law? By that of works?
No, but by the law of faith.
28For we hold that a person is justified by faith
apart from works prescribed by the law.

The word of the Lord.

GOSPEL: JOHN 8:31–36

The Holy Gospel according to John, the eighth chapter.

31Jesus said to the Jews who had believed in him,
"If you continue in my word, you are truly my disciples;
32and you will know the truth,
and the truth will make you free."
33They answered him,
"We are descendants of Abraham and have never been slaves to anyone.
What do you mean by saying, 'You will be made free'?"

34Jesus answered them,
"Very truly, I tell you, everyone who commits sin is a slave to sin.
35The slave does not have a permanent place in the household;
the son has a place there forever.

36"So if the Son makes you free, you will be free indeed."

The Gospel of the Lord.

ALL SAINTS DAY

NOVEMBER 1

ALL SAINTS SUNDAY: NOVEMBER 1, 1998   NOVEMBER 4, 2001   NOVEMBER 7, 2004

FIRST READING: DANIEL 7:1–3, 15–18

A reading from Daniel:

¹In the first year of King Belshazzar of Babylon,
Daniel had a dream and visions of his head as he lay in bed.
Then he wrote down the dream:
²I, Daniel, saw in my vision by night
the four winds of heaven stirring up the great sea,
³and four great beasts came up out of the sea, different from one another.

¹⁵As for me, Daniel, my spirit was troubled within me,
and the visions of my head terrified me.
¹⁶I approached one of the attendants to ask him the truth concerning all this.
So he said that he would disclose to me the interpretation of the matter:
¹⁷"As for these four great beasts, four kings shall arise out of the earth.
¹⁸But the holy ones of the Most High shall receive the kingdom
and possess the kingdom forever—forever and ever."

The word of the Lord.

PSALMODY: PSALM 149

SECOND READING: EPHESIANS 1:11–23

A reading from Ephesians:

[11]In Christ we have also obtained an inheritance,
having been destined according to the purpose of him
who accomplishes all things according to his counsel and will,
[12]so that we, who were the first to set our hope on Christ,
might live for the praise of his glory.
[13]In him you also, when you had heard the word of truth,
the gospel of your salvation,
and had believed in him,
were marked with the seal of the promised Holy Spirit;
[14]this is the pledge of our inheritance toward redemption as God's own people,
to the praise of his glory.

[15]I have heard of your faith in the Lord Jesus
and your love toward all the saints,
and for this reason [16]I do not cease to give thanks for you
as I remember you in my prayers.
[17]I pray that the God of our Lord Jesus Christ, the Father of glory,
may give you a spirit of wisdom and revelation as you come to know him,
[18]so that, with the eyes of your heart enlightened,
you may know what is the hope to which he has called you,
what are the riches of his glorious inheritance among the saints,
[19]and what is the immeasurable greatness of his power for us who believe,
according to the working of his great power.

[20]God put this power to work in Christ
when he raised him from the dead
and seated him at his right hand in the heavenly places,
[21]far above all rule and authority and power and dominion,
and above every name that is named,
not only in this age but also in the age to come.
[22]And he has put all things under his feet
and has made him the head over all things for the church,
[23]which is his body, the fullness of him who fills all in all.

The word of the Lord.

The Holy Gospel according to Luke, the sixth chapter.

[20]Then Jesus looked up at his disciples and said:
"Blessed are you who are poor,
    for yours is the kingdom of God.
[21]"Blessed are you who are hungry now,
    for you will be filled.
"Blessed are you who weep now,
    for you will laugh.
[22]"Blessed are you when people hate you,
and when they exclude you, revile you,
and defame you on account of the Son of Man.
[23]Rejoice in that day and leap for joy,
for surely your reward is great in heaven;
for that is what their ancestors did to the prophets.

[24]"But woe to you who are rich,
    for you have received your consolation.
[25]"Woe to you who are full now,
    for you will be hungry.
"Woe to you who are laughing now,
    for you will mourn and weep.
[26]"Woe to you when all speak well of you,
for that is what their ancestors did to the false prophets.

[27]"But I say to you that listen, Love your enemies,
do good to those who hate you,
[28]bless those who curse you,
pray for those who abuse you.
[29]If anyone strikes you on the cheek, offer the other also;
and from anyone who takes away your coat do not withhold even your shirt.
[30]Give to everyone who begs from you;
and if anyone takes away your goods, do not ask for them again.
[31]Do to others as you would have them do to you."

The Gospel of the Lord.

NEW YEAR'S EVE
DECEMBER 31

FIRST READING: ECCLESIASTES 3:1–13

A reading from Ecclesiastes:

¹For everything there is a season, and a time for every matter under heaven:
 ²a time to be born, and a time to die;
 a time to plant, and a time to pluck up what is planted;
 ³a time to kill, and a time to heal;
 a time to break down, and a time to build up;
 ⁴a time to weep, and a time to laugh;
 a time to mourn, and a time to dance;
 ⁵a time to throw away stones, and a time to gather stones together;
 a time to embrace, and a time to refrain from embracing;
 ⁶a time to seek, and a time to lose;
 a time to keep, and a time to throw away;
 ⁷a time to tear, and a time to sew;
 a time to keep silence, and a time to speak;
 ⁸a time to love, and a time to hate;
 a time for war, and a time for peace.

⁹What gain have the workers from their toil?
¹⁰I have seen the business that God has given to everyone to be busy with.
¹¹He has made everything suitable for its time;
moreover he has put a sense of past and future into their minds,
yet they cannot find out what God has done from the beginning to the end.
¹²I know that there is nothing better for them than to be happy
and enjoy themselves as long as they live;
¹³moreover, it is God's gift
that all should eat and drink and take pleasure in all their toil.

The word of the Lord.

PSALMODY: PSALM 8

SECOND READING: REVELATION 21:1–6a

A reading from Revelation:

[1]I saw a new heaven and a new earth;
for the first heaven and the first earth had passed away,
and the sea was no more.
[2]And I saw the holy city, the new Jerusalem,
coming down out of heaven from God,
prepared as a bride adorned for her husband.
[3]And I heard a loud voice from the throne saying,
    "See, the home of God is among mortals.
    He will dwell with them as their God;
    they will be his peoples,
    and God himself will be with them;
    [4]he will wipe every tear from their eyes.
    Death will be no more;
    mourning and crying and pain will be no more,
    for the first things have passed away."

[5]And the one who was seated on the throne said,
"See, I am making all things new."
Also he said,
"Write this, for these words are trustworthy and true."
[6a]Then he said to me,
"It is done! I am the Alpha and the Omega, the beginning and the end."

The word of the Lord.

GOSPEL: MATTHEW 25:31–46

The Holy Gospel according to Matthew, the 25th chapter.

Jesus said to the disciples:
[31]"When the Son of Man comes in his glory, and all the angels with him,
then he will sit on the throne of his glory.
[32]All the nations will be gathered before him,
and he will separate people one from another
as a shepherd separates the sheep from the goats,
[33]and he will put the sheep at his right hand and the goats at the left.

[34]"Then the king will say to those at his right hand,
'Come, you that are blessed by my Father,
inherit the kingdom prepared for you from the foundation of the world;
[35]for I was hungry and you gave me food,
I was thirsty and you gave me something to drink,
I was a stranger and you welcomed me,
[36]I was naked and you gave me clothing,
I was sick and you took care of me,

I was in prison and you visited me.'
37Then the righteous will answer him,
'Lord, when was it that we saw you hungry and gave you food,
or thirsty and gave you something to drink?
38And when was it that we saw you a stranger and welcomed you,
or naked and gave you clothing?
39And when was it that we saw you sick or in prison and visited you?'
40And the king will answer them,
'Truly I tell you,
just as you did it to one of the least of these who are members of my family,
you did it to me.'

41"Then he will say to those at his left hand,
'You that are accursed,
depart from me into the eternal fire prepared for the devil and his angels;
42for I was hungry and you gave me no food,
I was thirsty and you gave me nothing to drink,
43I was a stranger and you did not welcome me,
naked and you did not give me clothing,
sick and in prison and you did not visit me.'
44Then they also will answer,
'Lord, when was it that we saw you hungry or thirsty
or a stranger or naked or sick or in prison,
and did not take care of you?'
45Then he will answer them,
'Truly I tell you,
just as you did not do it to one of the least of these,
you did not do it to me.'
46And these will go away into eternal punishment,
but the righteous into eternal life."

The Gospel of the Lord.

Day of Thanksgiving

CANADA: OCTOBER 12, 1998   *OCTOBER 8, 2001*   *OCTOBER 11, 2004*
U.S.A.: NOVEMBER 26, 1998   *NOVEMBER 22, 2001*   *NOVEMBER 25, 2004*

FIRST READING: DEUTERONOMY 26:1–11

A reading from Deuteronomy:

¹When you have come into the land
that the LORD your God is giving you as an inheritance to possess,
and you possess it, and settle in it,
²you shall take some of the first of all the fruit of the ground,
which you harvest from the land that the LORD your God is giving you,
and you shall put it in a basket
and go to the place that the LORD your God will choose as a dwelling for his name.
³You shall go to the priest who is in office at that time, and say to him,
"Today I declare to the LORD your God
that I have come into the land that the LORD swore to our ancestors to give us."

⁴When the priest takes the basket from your hand
and sets it down before the altar of the LORD your God,
⁵you shall make this response before the LORD your God:
"A wandering Aramean was my ancestor;
he went down into Egypt and lived there as an alien, few in number,
and there he became a great nation, mighty and populous.
⁶When the Egyptians treated us harshly and afflicted us,
by imposing hard labor on us,
⁷we cried to the LORD, the God of our ancestors;
the LORD heard our voice and saw our affliction, our toil, and our oppression.
⁸The LORD brought us out of Egypt with a mighty hand and an outstretched arm,
with a terrifying display of power, and with signs and wonders;
⁹and he brought us into this place and gave us this land,
a land flowing with milk and honey.
¹⁰So now I bring the first of the fruit of the ground that you, O LORD, have
given me."
You shall set it down before the LORD your God
and bow down before the LORD your God.
¹¹Then you, together with the Levites and the aliens who reside among you,
shall celebrate with all the bounty
that the LORD your God has given to you and to your house.

The word of the Lord.

PSALMODY: PSALM 100

SECOND READING: PHILIPPIANS 4:4–9

A reading from Philippians:

[4]Rejoice in the Lord always;
again I will say, Rejoice.
[5]Let your gentleness be known to everyone.
The Lord is near.
[6]Do not worry about anything,
but in everything by prayer and supplication with thanksgiving
let your requests be made known to God.
[7]And the peace of God, which surpasses all understanding,
will guard your hearts and your minds in Christ Jesus.

[8]Finally, beloved, whatever is true, whatever is honorable,
whatever is just, whatever is pure,
whatever is pleasing, whatever is commendable,
if there is any excellence and if there is anything worthy of praise,
think about these things.
[9]Keep on doing the things that you have learned
and received and heard and seen in me,
and the God of peace will be with you.

The word of the Lord.

GOSPEL: JOHN 6:25–35

The Holy Gospel according to John, the sixth chapter.

[25]When they found him on the other side of the sea,
they said to him, "Rabbi, when did you come here?"
[26]Jesus answered them, "Very truly, I tell you,
you are looking for me, not because you saw signs,
but because you ate your fill of the loaves.
[27]Do not work for the food that perishes,
but for the food that endures for eternal life,
which the Son of Man will give you.
For it is on him that God the Father has set his seal."

[28]Then they said to him,
"What must we do to perform the works of God?"
[29]Jesus answered them, "This is the work of God,
that you believe in him whom he has sent."
[30]So they said to him,
"What sign are you going to give us then,
so that we may see it and believe you?
What work are you performing?
[31]Our ancestors ate the manna in the wilderness;
as it is written, 'He gave them bread from heaven to eat.' "
[32]Then Jesus said to them,
"Very truly, I tell you, it was not Moses who gave you the bread from heaven,
but it is my Father who gives you the true bread from heaven.
[33]For the bread of God is that which comes down from heaven
and gives life to the world."
[34]They said to him, "Sir, give us this bread always."

[35]Jesus said to them,
"I am the bread of life.
Whoever comes to me will never be hungry,
and whoever believes in me will never be thirsty."

The Gospel of the Lord.

APPENDIX A

SEMI-CONTINUOUS FIRST READINGS AND PSALMODY

FIRST READING: 1 KINGS 18:20–21 [22–29] 30–39

A reading from First Kings:

²⁰So Ahab sent to all the Israelites,
and assembled the prophets at Mount Carmel.
²¹Elijah then came near to all the people, and said,
"How long will you go limping with two different opinions?
If the LORD is God, follow him; but if Baal, then follow him."
The people did not answer him a word.

[²²Then Elijah said to the people,
"I, even I only, am left a prophet of the LORD;
but Baal's prophets number four hundred fifty.
²³Let two bulls be given to us;
let them choose one bull for themselves,
cut it in pieces, and lay it on the wood, but put no fire to it;
I will prepare the other bull and lay it on the wood, but put no fire to it.
²⁴Then you call on the name of your god
and I will call on the name of the LORD;
the god who answers by fire is indeed God."
All the people answered, "Well spoken!"
²⁵Then Elijah said to the prophets of Baal,
"Choose for yourselves one bull and prepare it first, for you are many;
then call on the name of your god, but put no fire to it."
²⁶So they took the bull that was given them, prepared it,
and called on the name of Baal from morning until noon,
crying, "O Baal, answer us!"
But there was no voice, and no answer.
They limped about the altar that they had made.
²⁷At noon Elijah mocked them, saying,
"Cry aloud! Surely he is a god;
either he is meditating, or he has wandered away, or he is on a journey,
or perhaps he is asleep and must be awakened."
²⁸Then they cried aloud and, as was their custom,
they cut themselves with swords and lances until the blood gushed out over
        them.
²⁹As midday passed,
they raved on until the time of the offering of the oblation,
but there was no voice, no answer, and no response.]

³⁰Then Elijah said to all the people, "Come closer to me";
and all the people came closer to him.
First he repaired the altar of the LORD that had been thrown down;
³¹Elijah took twelve stones,
according to the number of the tribes of the sons of Jacob,
to whom the word of the LORD came, saying, "Israel shall be your name";
³²with the stones he built an altar in the name of the LORD.
Then he made a trench around the altar,
large enough to contain two measures of seed.
³³Next he put the wood in order, cut the bull in pieces, and laid it on the wood.
He said, "Fill four jars with water
and pour it on the burnt offering and on the wood."
³⁴Then he said, "Do it a second time"; and they did it a second time.
Again he said, "Do it a third time"; and they did it a third time,
³⁵so that the water ran all around the altar, and filled the trench also with water.

³⁶At the time of the offering of the oblation,
the prophet Elijah came near and said,
"O LORD, God of Abraham, Isaac, and Israel,
let it be known this day that you are God in Israel,
that I am your servant, and that I have done all these things at your bidding.
³⁷Answer me, O LORD, answer me,
so that this people may know that you, O LORD, are God,
and that you have turned their hearts back."
³⁸Then the fire of the LORD fell
and consumed the burnt offering, the wood, the stones, and the dust,
and even licked up the water that was in the trench.
³⁹When all the people saw it, they fell on their faces and said,
"The LORD indeed is God; the LORD indeed is God."

The word of the Lord.

PSALMODY: PSALM 96

Readings continue on p. 193

FIRST READING: 1 KINGS 17:8–16 [17–24]

A reading from First Kings:

⁸Then the word of the LORD came to Elijah, saying,
⁹"Go now to Zarephath, which belongs to Sidon, and live there;
for I have commanded a widow there to feed you."
¹⁰So he set out and went to Zarephath.
When he came to the gate of the town,
a widow was there gathering sticks;
he called to her and said,
"Bring me a little water in a vessel, so that I may drink."
¹¹As she was going to bring it, he called to her and said,
"Bring me a morsel of bread in your hand."
¹²But she said,
"As the LORD your God lives, I have nothing baked,
only a handful of meal in a jar, and a little oil in a jug;
I am now gathering a couple of sticks,
so that I may go home and prepare it for myself and my son,
that we may eat it, and die."

¹³Elijah said to her,
"Do not be afraid; go and do as you have said;
but first make me a little cake of it and bring it to me,
and afterwards make something for yourself and your son.
¹⁴For thus says the LORD the God of Israel:
The jar of meal will not be emptied
and the jug of oil will not fail
until the day that the LORD sends rain on the earth."

¹⁵She went and did as Elijah said,
so that she as well as he and her household ate for many days.
¹⁶The jar of meal was not emptied, neither did the jug of oil fail,
according to the word of the LORD that he spoke by Elijah.

[¹⁷After this the son of the woman, the mistress of the house, became ill;
his illness was so severe that there was no breath left in him.
¹⁸She then said to Elijah, "What have you against me, O man of God?
You have come to me to bring my sin to remembrance,

and to cause the death of my son!"
¹⁹But he said to her, "Give me your son."
He took him from her bosom,
carried him up into the upper chamber where he was lodging,
and laid him on his own bed.
²⁰He cried out to the Lord, "O Lord my God,
have you brought calamity even upon the widow with whom I am staying,
by killing her son?"
²¹Then he stretched himself upon the child three times,
and cried out to the Lord,
"O Lord my God, let this child's life come into him again."
²²The Lord listened to the voice of Elijah;
the life of the child came into him again, and he revived.
²³Elijah took the child,
brought him down from the upper chamber into the house,
and gave him to his mother;
then Elijah said, "See, your son is alive."
²⁴So the woman said to Elijah,
"Now I know that you are a man of God,
and that the word of the Lord in your mouth is truth."]

The word of the Lord.

PSALMODY: Psalm 146

Readings continue on p. 196

FIRST READING: 1 KINGS 21:1–10 [11–14] 15–21a

A reading from First Kings:

¹Later the following events took place:
Naboth the Jezreelite had a vineyard in Jezreel,
beside the palace of King Ahab of Samaria.
²And Ahab said to Naboth, "Give me your vineyard,
so that I may have it for a vegetable garden, because it is near my house;
I will give you a better vineyard for it;
or, if it seems good to you, I will give you its value in money."
³But Naboth said to Ahab,
"The LORD forbid that I should give you my ancestral inheritance."

⁴Ahab went home resentful and sullen
because of what Naboth the Jezreelite had said to him;
for he had said, "I will not give you my ancestral inheritance."
He lay down on his bed, turned away his face, and would not eat.
⁵His wife Jezebel came to him and said,
"Why are you so depressed that you will not eat?"
⁶He said to her,
"Because I spoke to Naboth the Jezreelite and said to him,
'Give me your vineyard for money;
or else, if you prefer, I will give you another vineyard for it';
but he answered, 'I will not give you my vineyard.' "
⁷His wife Jezebel said to him, "Do you now govern Israel?
Get up, eat some food, and be cheerful;
I will give you the vineyard of Naboth the Jezreelite."

⁸So she wrote letters in Ahab's name and sealed them with his seal;
she sent the letters to the elders and the nobles who lived with Naboth in
        his city.
⁹She wrote in the letters,
"Proclaim a fast, and seat Naboth at the head of the assembly;
¹⁰seat two scoundrels opposite him,
and have them bring a charge against him, saying,
'You have cursed God and the king.'

Then take him out, and stone him to death."
[¹¹The men of his city, the elders and the nobles who lived in his city,
did as Jezebel had sent word to them.
Just as it was written in the letters that she had sent to them,
¹²they proclaimed a fast and seated Naboth at the head of the assembly.
¹³The two scoundrels came in and sat opposite him;
and the scoundrels brought a charge against Naboth,
in the presence of the people, saying,
"Naboth cursed God and the king."
So they took him outside the city, and stoned him to death.
¹⁴Then they sent to Jezebel, saying, "Naboth has been stoned; he is dead."]

¹⁵As soon as Jezebel heard that Naboth had been stoned and was dead,
Jezebel said to Ahab,
"Go, take possession of the vineyard of Naboth the Jezreelite,
which he refused to give you for money;
for Naboth is not alive, but dead."
¹⁶As soon as Ahab heard that Naboth was dead,
Ahab set out to go down to the vineyard of Naboth the Jezreelite,
to take possession of it.

¹⁷Then the word of the LORD came to Elijah the Tishbite, saying:
¹⁸Go down to meet King Ahab of Israel, who rules in Samaria;
he is now in the vineyard of Naboth, where he has gone to take possession.
¹⁹You shall say to him,
"Thus says the LORD: Have you killed, and also taken possession?"
You shall say to him, "Thus says the LORD:
In the place where dogs licked up the blood of Naboth,
dogs will also lick up your blood."

²⁰Ahab said to Elijah, "Have you found me, O my enemy?"
He answered, "I have found you.
Because you have sold yourself to do what is evil in the sight of the LORD,
²¹I will bring disaster on you."

The word of the Lord.

PSALMODY: PSALM 5:1–8

Readings continue on p. 200

FIRST READING: 1 KINGS 19:1–4 [5–7] 8–15a

A reading from First Kings:

¹Ahab told Jezebel all that Elijah had done,
and how he had killed all the prophets with the sword.
²Then Jezebel sent a messenger to Elijah, saying,
"So may the gods do to me, and more also,
if I do not make your life like the life of one of them by this time tomorrow."
³Then he was afraid;
he got up and fled for his life, and came to Beer-sheba,
which belongs to Judah;
he left his servant there.
⁴But he himself went a day's journey into the wilderness,
and came and sat down under a solitary broom tree.
He asked that he might die:
"It is enough; now, O LORD, take away my life,
for I am no better than my ancestors."

[⁵Then he lay down under the broom tree and fell asleep.
Suddenly an angel touched him and said to him, "Get up and eat."
⁶He looked, and there at his head was a cake baked on hot stones,
and a jar of water.
He ate and drank, and lay down again.
⁷The angel of the LORD came a second time, touched him, and said,
"Get up and eat,
otherwise the journey will be too much for you."]

⁸He got up, and ate and drank;
then he went in the strength of that food
forty days and forty nights to Horeb the mount of God.
⁹At that place he came to a cave, and spent the night there.
Then the word of the LORD came to him, saying,
"What are you doing here, Elijah?"
¹⁰He answered,
"I have been very zealous for the LORD, the God of hosts;
for the Israelites have forsaken your covenant,

thrown down your altars, and killed your prophets with the sword.
I alone am left, and they are seeking my life, to take it away."
¹¹He said, "Go out and stand on the mountain before the L ORD,
for the L ORD is about to pass by."
Now there was a great wind, so strong that it was splitting mountains
and breaking rocks in pieces before the L ORD,
but the L ORD was not in the wind;
and after the wind an earthquake, but the L ORD was not in the earthquake;
¹²and after the earthquake a fire, but the L ORD was not in the fire;
and after the fire a sound of sheer silence.
¹³When Elijah heard it, he wrapped his face in his mantle
and went out and stood at the entrance of the cave.
Then there came a voice to him that said,
"What are you doing here, Elijah?"
¹⁴He answered, "I have been very zealous for the L ORD, the God of hosts;
for the Israelites have forsaken your covenant,
thrown down your altars, and killed your prophets with the sword.
I alone am left, and they are seeking my life, to take it away."
¹⁵Then the L ORD said to him,
"Go, return on your way to the wilderness of Damascus."

The word of the Lord.

PSALMODY: P SALM 42 and 43

Readings continue on p. 204

SUNDAY BETWEEN
JUNE 26 AND JULY 2 INCLUSIVE

PROPER 8

JUNE 28, 1998   JULY 1, 2001   JUNE 27, 2004

FIRST READING: 2 KINGS 2:1–2, 6–14

A reading from Second Kings:

¹Now when the LORD was about to take Elijah up to heaven by a whirlwind,
Elijah and Elisha were on their way from Gilgal.
²Elijah said to Elisha, "Stay here; for the LORD has sent me as far as Bethel."
But Elisha said, "As the LORD lives, and as you yourself live,
I will not leave you."
So they went down to Bethel.

⁶Then Elijah said to him,
"Stay here; for the LORD has sent me to the Jordan."
But he said, "As the LORD lives, and as you yourself live,
I will not leave you."
So the two of them went on.
⁷Fifty men of the company of prophets also went,
and stood at some distance from them,
as they both were standing by the Jordan.
⁸Then Elijah took his mantle and rolled it up, and struck the water;
the water was parted to the one side and to the other,
until the two of them crossed on dry ground.

⁹When they had crossed, Elijah said to Elisha,
"Tell me what I may do for you, before I am taken from you."
Elisha said, "Please let me inherit a double share of your spirit."
¹⁰He responded, "You have asked a hard thing;
yet, if you see me as I am being taken from you,
it will be granted you;
if not, it will not."
¹¹As they continued walking and talking,
a chariot of fire and horses of fire separated the two of them,
and Elijah ascended in a whirlwind into heaven.
¹²Elisha kept watching and crying out, "Father, father!
The chariots of Israel and its horsemen!"
But when he could no longer see him,
he grasped his own clothes and tore them in two pieces.

¹³He picked up the mantle of Elijah that had fallen from him,
and went back and stood on the bank of the Jordan.
¹⁴He took the mantle of Elijah that had fallen from him,
and struck the water, saying,
"Where is the LORD, the God of Elijah?"
When he had struck the water,
the water was parted to the one side and to the other,
and Elisha went over.

The word of the Lord.

PSALMODY: PSALM 77:1–2, 11–20

Readings continue on p. 207

SUNDAY BETWEEN
JULY 3 AND 9 INCLUSIVE

PROPER 9

JULY 5, 1998   *JULY 8, 2001*   *JULY 4, 2004*

FIRST READING: 2 KINGS 5:1–14

A reading from Second Kings:

¹Naaman, commander of the army of the king of Aram,
was a great man and in high favor with his master,
because by him the LORD had given victory to Aram.
The man, though a mighty warrior, suffered from leprosy.
²Now the Arameans on one of their raids
had taken a young girl captive from the land of Israel,
and she served Naaman's wife.
³She said to her mistress,
"If only my lord were with the prophet who is in Samaria!
He would cure him of his leprosy."
⁴So Naaman went in
and told his lord just what the girl from the land of Israel had said.
⁵And the king of Aram said,
"Go then, and I will send along a letter to the king of Israel."

He went, taking with him ten talents of silver,
six thousand shekels of gold, and ten sets of garments.
⁶He brought the letter to the king of Israel, which read,
"When this letter reaches you,
know that I have sent to you my servant Naaman,
that you may cure him of his leprosy."
⁷When the king of Israel read the letter, he tore his clothes and said,
"Am I God, to give death or life,
that this man sends word to me to cure a man of his leprosy?
Just look and see how he is trying to pick a quarrel with me."

⁸But when Elisha the man of God heard that the king of Israel had torn his
        clothes,
he sent a message to the king, "Why have you torn your clothes?
Let him come to me, that he may learn that there is a prophet in Israel."
⁹So Naaman came with his horses and chariots,
and halted at the entrance of Elisha's house.
¹⁰Elisha sent a messenger to him, saying,

"Go, wash in the Jordan seven times,
and your flesh shall be restored and you shall be clean."
[11]But Naaman became angry and went away, saying,
"I thought that for me he would surely come out,
and stand and call on the name of the LORD his God,
and would wave his hand over the spot, and cure the leprosy!
[12]Are not Abana and Pharpar, the rivers of Damascus,
better than all the waters of Israel?
Could I not wash in them, and be clean?"
He turned and went away in a rage.
[13]But his servants approached and said to him,
"Father, if the prophet had commanded you to do something difficult,
would you not have done it?
How much more, when all he said to you was, 'Wash, and be clean'?"
[14]So he went down and immersed himself seven times in the Jordan,
according to the word of the man of God;
his flesh was restored like the flesh of a young boy, and he was clean.

The word of the Lord.

PSALMODY: PSALM 30

Readings continue on p. 210

FIRST READING: Amos 7:7–17

A reading from Amos:

[7]This is what he showed me:
the Lord was standing beside a wall built with a plumb line,
with a plumb line in his hand.
[8]And the LORD said to me, "Amos, what do you see?"
And I said, "A plumb line." Then the Lord said,
    "See, I am setting a plumb line
        in the midst of my people Israel;
        I will never again pass them by;
    [9]the high places of Isaac shall be made desolate,
        and the sanctuaries of Israel shall be laid waste,
        and I will rise against the house of Jeroboam with the sword."

[10]Then Amaziah, the priest of Bethel, sent to King Jeroboam of Israel,
saying, "Amos has conspired against you in the very center of the house
        of Israel;
the land is not able to bear all his words.
[11]For thus Amos has said,
    'Jeroboam shall die by the sword,
        and Israel must go into exile
        away from his land.' "
[12]And Amaziah said to Amos,
"O seer, go, flee away to the land of Judah,
earn your bread there, and prophesy there;
[13]but never again prophesy at Bethel,
for it is the king's sanctuary, and it is a temple of the kingdom."

[14]Then Amos answered Amaziah,
"I am no prophet, nor a prophet's son;
but I am a herdsman, and a dresser of sycamore trees,
[15]and the LORD took me from following the flock,
and the LORD said to me, 'Go, prophesy to my people Israel.'
    [16]"Now therefore hear the word of the LORD.
    You say, 'Do not prophesy against Israel,
        and do not preach against the house of Isaac.'

[17]Therefore thus says the L ORD:
'Your wife shall become a prostitute in the city,
and your sons and your daughters shall fall by the sword,
and your land shall be parceled out by line;
you yourself shall die in an unclean land,
and Israel shall surely go into exile away from its land.' "

The word of the Lord.

PSALMODY: P SALM 82

Readings continue on p. 213

FIRST READING: AMOS 8:1–12

A reading from Amos:

¹This is what the Lord GOD showed me—a basket of summer fruit.
²He said, "Amos, what do you see?"
And I said, "A basket of summer fruit."
Then the LORD said to me,
    "The end has come upon my people Israel;
        I will never again pass them by.
    ³The songs of the temple shall become wailings in that day,"
                                        says the Lord GOD;
    "the dead bodies shall be many,
        cast out in every place. Be silent!"

⁴Hear this, you that trample on the needy,
    and bring to ruin the poor of the land,
⁵saying, "When will the new moon be over
    so that we may sell grain;
and the sabbath,
    so that we may offer wheat for sale?
We will make the ephah small and the shekel great,
    and practice deceit with false balances,
⁶buying the poor for silver
    and the needy for a pair of sandals,
    and selling the sweepings of the wheat."

⁷The LORD has sworn by the pride of Jacob:
Surely I will never forget any of their deeds.
⁸Shall not the land tremble on this account,
    and everyone mourn who lives in it,
and all of it rise like the Nile,
    and be tossed about and sink again, like the Nile of Egypt?

⁹On that day, says the Lord GOD,
    I will make the sun go down at noon,
    and darken the earth in broad daylight.

¹⁰I will turn your feasts into mourning,
 and all your songs into lamentation;
I will bring sackcloth on all loins,
 and baldness on every head;
I will make it like the mourning for an only son,
 and the end of it like a bitter day.

¹¹The time is surely coming, says the Lord GOD,
 when I will send a famine on the land;
not a famine of bread, or a thirst for water,
 but of hearing the words of the LORD.
¹²They shall wander from sea to sea,
 and from north to east;
they shall run to and fro, seeking the word of the LORD,
 but they shall not find it.

The word of the Lord.

PSALMODY: PSALM 52

Readings continue on p. 216

SUNDAY BETWEEN
JULY 24 AND 30 INCLUSIVE

PROPER 12

JULY 26, 1998   *JULY 29, 2001*   *JULY 25, 2004*

FIRST READING: HOSEA 1:2–10

A reading from Hosea:

²When the LORD first spoke through Hosea,
the LORD said to Hosea,
"Go, take for yourself a wife of whoredom and have children of whoredom,
for the land commits great whoredom by forsaking the LORD."
³So he went and took Gomer daughter of Diblaim,
and she conceived and bore him a son.
⁴And the LORD said to him, "Name him Jezreel;
for in a little while I will punish the house of Jehu for the blood of Jezreel,
and I will put an end to the kingdom of the house of Israel.
⁵On that day I will break the bow of Israel in the valley of Jezreel."

⁶She conceived again and bore a daughter.
Then the LORD said to him, "Name her Lo-ruhamah,
for I will no longer have pity on the house of Israel or forgive them.
⁷But I will have pity on the house of Judah,
and I will save them by the LORD their God;
I will not save them by bow,
          or by sword, or by war, or by horses, or by horsemen."

⁸When she had weaned Lo-ruhamah, she conceived and bore a son.
⁹Then the LORD said, "Name him Lo-ammi,
for you are not my people and I am not your God."

¹⁰Yet the number of the people of Israel shall be like the sand of the sea,
which can be neither measured nor numbered;
and in the place where it was said to them, "You are not my people,"
it shall be said to them, "Children of the living God."

The word of the Lord.

PSALMODY: PSALM 85

Readings continue on p. 219

FIRST READING: HOSEA 11:1–11

A reading from Hosea:

¹When Israel was a child, I loved him,
   and out of Egypt I called my son.
²The more I called them,
   the more they went from me;
they kept sacrificing to the Baals,
   and offering incense to idols.

³Yet it was I who taught Ephraim to walk,
   I took them up in my arms;
   but they did not know that I healed them.
⁴I led them with cords of human kindness,
   with bands of love.
I was to them like those
   who lift infants to their cheeks.
   I bent down to them and fed them.

⁵They shall return to the land of Egypt,
   and Assyria shall be their king,
   because they have refused to return to me.
⁶The sword rages in their cities,
   it consumes their oracle-priests,
   and devours because of their schemes.
⁷My people are bent on turning away from me.
   To the Most High they call,
   but he does not raise them up at all.

⁸How can I give you up, Ephraim?
   How can I hand you over, O Israel?
How can I make you like Admah?
   How can I treat you like Zeboiim?
My heart recoils within me;
   my compassion grows warm and tender.
⁹I will not execute my fierce anger;
   I will not again destroy Ephraim;

for I am God and no mortal,
>   the Holy One in your midst,
>   and I will not come in wrath.
[10]They shall go after the LORD,
>   who roars like a lion;
when he roars,
>   his children shall come trembling from the west.
[11]They shall come trembling like birds from Egypt,
>   and like doves from the land of Assyria;
>   and I will return them to their homes, says the LORD.

The word of the Lord.

PSALMODY: PSALM 107:1–9, 43

Readings continue on p. 222

SUNDAY BETWEEN
AUGUST 7 AND 13 INCLUSIVE

PROPER 14

AUGUST 9, 1998   AUGUST 12, 2001   AUGUST 8, 2004

FIRST READING: ISAIAH 1:1, 10–20

A reading from Isaiah:

¹The vision of Isaiah son of Amoz,
which he saw concerning Judah and Jerusalem
in the days of Uzziah, Jotham, Ahaz, and Hezekiah, kings of Judah.

> ¹⁰Hear the word of the LORD,
>   you rulers of Sodom!
> Listen to the teaching of our God,
>   you people of Gomorrah!
> ¹¹What to me is the multitude of your sacrifices?
>   says the LORD;
> I have had enough of burnt offerings of rams
>   and the fat of fed beasts;
> I do not delight in the blood of bulls,
>   or of lambs, or of goats.
>
> ¹²When you come to appear before me,
>   who asked this from your hand?
>   Trample my courts no more;
> ¹³bringing offerings is futile;
>   incense is an abomination to me.
> New moon and sabbath and calling of convocation—
>   I cannot endure solemn assemblies with iniquity.
> ¹⁴Your new moons and your appointed festivals
>   my soul hates;
> they have become a burden to me,
>   I am weary of bearing them.
> ¹⁵When you stretch out your hands,
>   I will hide my eyes from you;
> even though you make many prayers,
>   I will not listen;
>   your hands are full of blood.
> ¹⁶Wash yourselves; make yourselves clean;
>   remove the evil of your doings
>   from before my eyes;

cease to do evil,
   ¹⁷learn to do good;
seek justice,
   rescue the oppressed,
defend the orphan,
   plead for the widow.

¹⁸Come now, let us argue it out,
   says the LORD:
though your sins are like scarlet,
   they shall be like snow;
though they are red like crimson,
   they shall become like wool.
¹⁹If you are willing and obedient,
   you shall eat the good of the land;
²⁰but if you refuse and rebel,
   you shall be devoured by the sword;
   for the mouth of the LORD has spoken.

The word of the Lord.

PSALMODY: PSALM 50:1–8, 22–23

Readings continue on p. 225

SUNDAY BETWEEN
AUGUST 14 AND 20 INCLUSIVE

PROPER 15

AUGUST 16, 1998   AUGUST 19, 2001   AUGUST 15, 2004

FIRST READING: Isaiah 5:1–7

A reading from Isaiah:

[1]Let me sing for my beloved
    my love-song concerning his vineyard:
My beloved had a vineyard
    on a very fertile hill.
[2]He dug it and cleared it of stones,
    and planted it with choice vines;
he built a watchtower in the midst of it,
    and hewed out a wine vat in it;
he expected it to yield grapes,
    but it yielded wild grapes.

[3]And now, inhabitants of Jerusalem
    and people of Judah,
judge between me
    and my vineyard.
[4]What more was there to do for my vineyard
    that I have not done in it?
When I expected it to yield grapes,
    why did it yield wild grapes?

[5]And now I will tell you
    what I will do to my vineyard.
I will remove its hedge,
    and it shall be devoured;
I will break down its wall,
    and it shall be trampled down.
[6]I will make it a waste;
    it shall not be pruned or hoed,
    and it shall be overgrown with briers and thorns;
I will also command the clouds
    that they rain no rain upon it.

[7]For the vineyard of the Lord of hosts
    is the house of Israel,
and the people of Judah

are his pleasant planting;
he expected justice,
    but saw bloodshed;
righteousness,
    but heard a cry!

The word of the Lord.

PSALMODY: PSALM 80:1–2, 8–19

Readings continue on p. 228

SUNDAY BETWEEN
AUGUST 21 AND 27 INCLUSIVE

PROPER 16

AUGUST 23, 1998   *AUGUST 26, 2001*   *AUGUST 22, 2004*

FIRST READING: JEREMIAH 1:4–10

A reading from Jeremiah:

⁴Now the word of the LORD came to me saying,
   ⁵"Before I formed you in the womb I knew you,
   and before you were born I consecrated you;
   I appointed you a prophet to the nations."
⁶Then I said, "Ah, Lord GOD!
Truly I do not know how to speak, for I am only a boy."
⁷But the LORD said to me,
   "Do not say, 'I am only a boy';
   For you shall go to all to whom I send you,
   and you shall speak whatever I command you.
   ⁸Do not be afraid of them,
   for I am with you to deliver you, says the LORD."
⁹Then the LORD put out his hand and touched my mouth;
and the LORD said to me,
   "Now I have put my words in your mouth.
   ¹⁰See, today I appoint you over nations and over kingdoms,
   to pluck up and to pull down,
   to destroy and to overthrow,
   to build and to plant."

The word of the Lord.

PSALMODY: PSALM 71:1–6

Readings continue on p. 231

SUNDAY BETWEEN
AUGUST 28 AND SEPTEMBER 3
INCLUSIVE

PROPER 17

AUGUST 30, 1998   *SEPTEMBER 2, 2001*   *AUGUST 29, 2004*

FIRST READING: JEREMIAH 2:4–13

A reading from Jeremiah:

⁴Hear the word of the LORD, O house of Jacob,
and all the families of the house of Israel.
⁵Thus says the LORD:
    What wrong did your ancestors find in me
        that they went far from me,
    and went after worthless things, and became worthless themselves?
⁶They did not say, "Where is the LORD
        who brought us up from the land of Egypt,
    who led us in the wilderness,
        in a land of deserts and pits,
    in a land of drought and deep darkness,
        in a land that no one passes through,
        where no one lives?"
⁷I brought you into a plentiful land
        to eat its fruits and its good things.
But when you entered you defiled my land,
        and made my heritage an abomination.
⁸The priests did not say, "Where is the LORD?"
        Those who handle the law did not know me;
the rulers transgressed against me;
        the prophets prophesied by Baal,
        and went after things that do not profit.

⁹Therefore once more I accuse you,
                says the LORD,
    and I accuse your children's children.
¹⁰Cross to the coasts of Cyprus and look,
        send to Kedar and examine with care;
        see if there has ever been such a thing.
¹¹Has a nation changed its gods,
        even though they are no gods?
But my people have changed their glory
        for something that does not profit.

^{12}Be appalled, O heavens, at this,
 be shocked, be utterly desolate,
     says the LORD,
^{13}for my people have committed two evils:
 they have forsaken me,
the fountain of living water,
 and dug out cisterns for themselves,
cracked cisterns
 that can hold no water.

The word of the Lord.

PSALMODY: PSALM 81:1, 10–16

Readings continue on p. 234

SUNDAY BETWEEN
SEPTEMBER 4 AND 10 INCLUSIVE

PROPER 18

SEPTEMBER 6, 1998 *SEPTEMBER 9, 2001* *SEPTEMBER 5, 2004*

FIRST READING: JEREMIAH 18:1–11

A reading from Jeremiah:

¹The word that came to Jeremiah from the LORD:
²"Come, go down to the potter's house,
and there I will let you hear my words."
³So I went down to the potter's house,
and there he was working at his wheel.
⁴The vessel he was making of clay was spoiled in the potter's hand,
and he reworked it into another vessel, as seemed good to him.

⁵Then the word of the LORD came to me:
⁶Can I not do with you, O house of Israel,
just as this potter has done? says the LORD.
Just like the clay in the potter's hand,
so are you in my hand, O house of Israel.
⁷At one moment I may declare concerning a nation or a kingdom,
that I will pluck up and break down and destroy it,
⁸but if that nation, concerning which I have spoken, turns from its evil,
I will change my mind about the disaster that I intended to bring on it.
⁹And at another moment I may declare concerning a nation or a kingdom
that I will build and plant it,
¹⁰but if it does evil in my sight, not listening to my voice,
then I will change my mind about the good that I had intended to do to it.
¹¹Now, therefore, say to the people of Judah and the inhabitants of Jerusalem:
Thus says the LORD:
Look, I am a potter shaping evil against you and devising a plan against you.
Turn now, all of you from your evil way,
and amend your ways and your doings.

The word of the Lord.

PSALMODY: PSALM 139:1–6, 13–18

Readings continue on p. 237

SUNDAY BETWEEN
SEPTEMBER 11 AND 17 INCLUSIVE
PROPER 19

SEPTEMBER 13, 1998   *SEPTEMBER 16, 2001*   *SEPTEMBER 12, 2004*

FIRST READING: JEREMIAH 4:11–12, 22–28

A reading from Jeremiah:

¹¹At that time it will be said to this people and to Jerusalem:
A hot wind comes from me out of the bare heights in the desert
toward my poor people,
not to winnow or cleanse—
¹²a wind too strong for that.
Now it is I who speak in judgment against them.

> ²²"For my people are foolish,
>   they do not know me;
> they are stupid children,
>   they have no understanding.
> They are skilled in doing evil,
>   but do not know how to do good."
>
> ²³I looked on the earth, and lo, it was waste and void;
>   and to the heavens, and they had no light.
> ²⁴I looked on the mountains, and lo, they were quaking,
>   and all the hills moved to and fro.
> ²⁵I looked, and lo, there was no one at all,
>   and all the birds of the air had fled.
> ²⁶I looked, and lo, the fruitful land was a desert,
>   and all its cities were laid in ruins
>   before the LORD, before his fierce anger.

²⁷For thus says the LORD:
The whole land shall be a desolation;
yet I will not make a full end.
> ²⁸Because of this the earth shall mourn,
>   and the heavens above grow black;
> for I have spoken, I have purposed;
>   I have not relented nor will I turn back.

The word of the Lord.

PSALMODY: PSALM 14

Readings continue on p. 240

Readings continue on p. 240

FIRST READING: JEREMIAH 8:18—9:1

A reading from Jeremiah:

¹⁸My joy is gone, grief is upon me,
    my heart is sick.
¹⁹Hark, the cry of my poor people
    from far and wide in the land:
"Is the LORD not in Zion?
    Is her King not in her?"
("Why have they provoked me to anger with their images,
    with their foreign idols?")
²⁰"The harvest is past, the summer is ended,
    and we are not saved."
²¹For the hurt of my poor people I am hurt,
    I mourn, and dismay has taken hold of me.

²²Is there no balm in Gilead?
    Is there no physician there?
Why then has the health of my poor people
    not been restored?
⁹:¹O that my head were a spring of water,
    and my eyes a fountain of tears,
so that I might weep day and night
    for the slain of my poor people!

The word of the Lord.

PSALMODY: PSALM 79:1–9

Readings continue on p. 243

FIRST READING: JEREMIAH 32:1–3a, 6–15

A reading from Jeremiah:

¹The word that came to Jeremiah from the LORD
in the tenth year of King Zedekiah of Judah,
which was the eighteenth year of Nebuchadrezzar.
²At that time the army of the king of Babylon was besieging Jerusalem,
and the prophet Jeremiah was confined in the court of the guard
that was in the palace of the king of Judah,
³where King Zedekiah of Judah had confined him.

⁶Jeremiah said, The word of the LORD came to me:
⁷Hanamel son of your uncle Shallum is going to come to you and say,
"Buy my field that is at Anathoth,
for the right of redemption by purchase is yours."
⁸Then my cousin Hanamel came to me in the court of the guard,
in accordance with the word of the LORD, and said to me,
"Buy my field that is at Anathoth in the land of Benjamin,
for the right of possession and redemption is yours; buy it for yourself."
Then I knew that this was the word of the LORD.

⁹And I bought the field at Anathoth from my cousin Hanamel,
and weighed out the money to him, seventeen shekels of silver.
¹⁰I signed the deed, sealed it, got witnesses, and weighed the money on scales.
¹¹Then I took the sealed deed of purchase, containing the terms and conditions,
and the open copy;
¹²and I gave the deed of purchase to Baruch son of Neriah son of Mahseiah,
in the presence of my cousin Hanamel,
in the presence of the witnesses who signed the deed of purchase,
and in the presence of all the Judeans who were sitting in the court of the guard.
¹³In their presence I charged Baruch, saying,
¹⁴Thus says the LORD of hosts, the God of Israel:
Take these deeds, both this sealed deed of purchase and this open deed,
and put them in an earthenware jar,
in order that they may last for a long time.

[15]For thus says the Lord of hosts, the God of Israel:
Houses and fields and vineyards shall again be bought in this land.

The word of the Lord.

PSALMODY: Psalm 91:1–6, 14–16

Readings continue on p. 246

FIRST READING: LAMENTATIONS 1:1–6

A reading from Lamentations:

¹How lonely sits the city
  that once was full of people!
How like a widow she has become,
  she that was great among the nations!
She that was a princess among the provinces
  has become a vassal.
²She weeps bitterly in the night,
  with tears on her cheeks;
among all her lovers
  she has no one to comfort her;
all her friends have dealt treacherously with her,
  they have become her enemies.

³Judah has gone into exile with suffering
  and hard servitude;
she lives now among the nations,
  and finds no resting place;
her pursuers have all overtaken her
  in the midst of her distress.
⁴The roads to Zion mourn,
  for no one comes to the festivals;
all her gates are desolate,
  her priests groan;
her young girls grieve,
  and her lot is bitter.
⁵Her foes have become the masters,
  her enemies prosper,
because the LORD has made her suffer
  for the multitude of her transgressions;
her children have gone away,
  captives before the foe.

⁶From daughter Zion has departed
  all her majesty.

Her princes have become like stags
    that find no pasture;
they fled without strength
    before the pursuer.

The word of the Lord.

PSALMODY: LAMENTATIONS 3:19–26 or PSALM 137

Readings continue on p. 249

SUNDAY BETWEEN
OCTOBER 9 AND 15 INCLUSIVE

PROPER 23

OCTOBER 11, 1998   *OCTOBER 14, 2001*   *OCTOBER 10, 2004*

FIRST READING: JEREMIAH 29:1, 4–7

A reading from Jeremiah:

¹These are the words of the letter that the prophet Jeremiah sent
    from Jerusalem
to the remaining elders among the exiles,
and to the priests, the prophets, and all the people,
whom Nebuchadnezzar had taken into exile from Jerusalem to Babylon.

⁴Thus says the LORD of hosts, the God of Israel,
to all the exiles whom I have sent into exile from Jerusalem to Babylon:
⁵Build houses and live in them;
plant gardens and eat what they produce.
⁶Take wives and have sons and daughters;
take wives for your sons, and give your daughters in marriage,
that they may bear sons and daughters;
multiply there, and do not decrease.
⁷But seek the welfare of the city where I have sent you into exile,
and pray to the LORD on its behalf,
for in its welfare you will find your welfare.

The word of the Lord.

PSALMODY: PSALM 66:1–12

Readings continue on p. 253

SUNDAY BETWEEN
OCTOBER 16 AND 22 INCLUSIVE

PROPER 24

OCTOBER 18, 1998   *OCTOBER 21, 2001*   *OCTOBER 17, 2004*

FIRST READING: JEREMIAH 31:27–34

A reading from Jeremiah:

²⁷The days are surely coming, says the LORD,
when I will sow the house of Israel and the house of Judah
with the seed of humans and the seed of animals.
²⁸And just as I have watched over them to pluck up and break down,
to overthrow, destroy, and bring evil,
so I will watch over them to build and to plant, says the LORD.
²⁹In those days they shall no longer say:
    "The parents have eaten sour grapes,
       and the children's teeth are set on edge."
³⁰But all shall die for their own sins;
the teeth of everyone who eats sour grapes shall be set on edge.

³¹The days are surely coming, says the LORD,
when I will make a new covenant with the house of Israel and the house of Judah.
³²It will not be like the covenant that I made with their ancestors
when I took them by the hand to bring them out of the land of Egypt—
a covenant that they broke,
though I was their husband, says the LORD.
³³But this is the covenant that I will make with the house of Israel
      after those days,
says the LORD:
I will put my law within them,
and I will write it on their hearts;
and I will be their God, and they shall be my people.
³⁴No longer shall they teach one another,
or say to each other, "Know the LORD,"
for they shall all know me,
from the least of them to the greatest, says the LORD;
for I will forgive their iniquity,
and remember their sin no more.

The word of the Lord.

PSALMODY: PSALM 119:97–104

Readings continue on p. 255

Readings continue on p. 255

SUNDAY BETWEEN
OCTOBER 23 AND 29 INCLUSIVE

PROPER 25

OCTOBER 25, 1998   OCTOBER 28, 2001   OCTOBER 24, 2004

FIRST READING: JOEL 2:23–32

A reading from Joel:

²³O children of Zion, be glad
    and rejoice in the LORD your God;
for he has given the early rain for your vindication,
    he has poured down for you abundant rain,
    the early and the later rain, as before.
²⁴The threshing floors shall be full of grain,
    the vats shall overflow with wine and oil.

²⁵I will repay you for the years
    that the swarming locust has eaten,
the hopper, the destroyer, and the cutter,
    my great army, which I sent against you.

²⁶You shall eat in plenty and be satisfied,
    and praise the name of the LORD your God,
    who has dealt wondrously with you.
And my people shall never again be put to shame.
²⁷You shall know that I am in the midst of Israel,
    and that I, the LORD, am your God and there is no other.
And my people shall never again
    be put to shame.

²⁸Then afterward
    I will pour out my spirit on all flesh;
your sons and your daughters shall prophesy,
    your old men shall dream dreams,
    and your young men shall see visions.
²⁹Even on the male and female slaves,
    in those days, I will pour out my spirit.

³⁰I will show portents in the heavens and on the earth,
blood and fire and columns of smoke.
³¹The sun shall be turned to darkness, and the moon to blood,

before the great and terrible day of the LORD comes.
³²Then everyone who calls on the name of the LORD shall be saved;
for in Mount Zion and in Jerusalem there shall be those who escape,
as the LORD has said,
and among the survivors shall be those whom the LORD calls.

The word of the Lord.

PSALMODY: PSALM 65

Readings continue on p. 259

FIRST READING: HABAKKUK 1:1–4; 2:1–4

A reading from Habakkuk:

¹The oracle that the prophet Habakkuk saw.

²O LORD, how long shall I cry for help,
    and you will not listen?
Or cry to you "Violence!"
    and you will not save?
³Why do you make me see wrong-doing
    and look at trouble?
Destruction and violence are before me;
    strife and contention arise.
⁴So the law becomes slack
    and justice never prevails.
The wicked surround the righteous—
    therefore judgment comes forth perverted.
²:¹I will stand at my watchpost,
    and station myself on the rampart;
I will keep watch to see what he will say to me,
    and what he will answer concerning my complaint.

²Then the LORD answered me and said:
Write the vision;
    make it plain on tablets,
    so that a runner may read it.
³For there is still a vision for the appointed time;
    it speaks of the end, and does not lie.
If it seems to tarry, wait for it;
    it will surely come, it will not delay.
⁴Look at the proud!
    Their spirit is not right in them,
    but the righteous live by their faith.

The word of the Lord.

PSALMODY: PSALM 119:137–144

Readings continue on p. 262

SUNDAY BETWEEN
NOVEMBER 6 AND 12 INCLUSIVE

PROPER 27

NOVEMBER 8, 1998   *NOVEMBER 11, 2001*   *NOVEMBER 7, 2004*

FIRST READING: HAGGAI 1:15b—2:9

A reading from Haggai:

¹:¹⁵ᵇIn the second year of King Darius, ²:¹in the seventh month,
on the twenty-first day of the month,
the word of the LORD came by the prophet Haggai, saying:
²Speak now to Zerubbabel son of Shealtiel, governor of Judah,
and to Joshua son of Jehozadak, the high priest,
and to the remnant of the people, and say,
³Who is left among you that saw this house in its former glory?
How does it look to you now?
Is it not in your sight as nothing?
⁴Yet now take courage, O Zerubbabel, says the LORD;
take courage, O Joshua, son of Jehozadak, the high priest;
take courage, all you people of the land, says the LORD;
work, for I am with you, says the LORD of hosts,
⁵according to the promise that I made you when you came out of Egypt.
My spirit abides among you; do not fear.
⁶For thus says the LORD of hosts:
Once again, in a little while,
I will shake the heavens and the earth and the sea and the dry land;
⁷and I will shake all the nations,
so that the treasure of all nations shall come,
and I will fill this house with splendor, says the LORD of hosts.
⁸The silver is mine, and the gold is mine, says the LORD of hosts.
⁹The latter splendor of this house shall be greater than the former,
says the LORD of hosts;
and in this place I will give prosperity, says the LORD of hosts.

The word of the Lord.

PSALMODY: PSALM 145:1–5, 17–21 or PSALM 98

Readings continue on p. 264

SUNDAY BETWEEN
NOVEMBER 13 AND 19 INCLUSIVE
PROPER 28

NOVEMBER 15, 1998   NOVEMBER 18, 2001   NOVEMBER 14, 2004

FIRST READING: ISAIAH 65:17–25

A reading from Isaiah:

¹⁷For I am about to create new heavens
    and a new earth;
the former things shall not be remembered
    or come to mind.
¹⁸But be glad and rejoice forever
    in what I am creating;
for I am about to create Jerusalem as a joy,
    and its people as a delight.
¹⁹I will rejoice in Jerusalem,
    and delight in my people;
no more shall the sound of weeping be heard in it,
    or the cry of distress.
²⁰No more shall there be in it
    an infant that lives but a few days,
    or an old person who does not live out a lifetime;
for one who dies at a hundred years will be considered a youth,
    and one who falls short of a hundred will be considered accursed.
²¹They shall build houses and inhabit them;
    they shall plant vineyards and eat their fruit.
²²They shall not build and another inhabit;
    they shall not plant and another eat;
for like the days of a tree shall the days of my people be,
    and my chosen shall long enjoy the work of their hands.
²³They shall not labor in vain,
    or bear children for calamity;
for they shall be offspring blessed by the LORD—
    and their descendants as well.
²⁴Before they call I will answer,
    while they are yet speaking I will hear.
²⁵The wolf and the lamb shall feed together,
    the lion shall eat straw like the ox;
    but the serpent—its food shall be dust!

They shall not hurt or destroy
  on all my holy mountain,
      says the LORD.

The word of the Lord.

PSALMODY: Isaiah 12

Readings continue on p. 267

CHRIST THE KING

Last Sunday after Pentecost[†]

PROPER 29

NOVEMBER 22, 1998　　　*NOVEMBER 25, 2001*　　　*NOVEMBER 21, 2004*

FIRST READING: JEREMIAH 23:1–6

A reading from Jeremiah:

[1]Woe to the shepherds who destroy and scatter the sheep of my pasture!
says the LORD.
[2]Therefore thus says the LORD, the God of Israel,
concerning the shepherds who shepherd my people:
It is you who have scattered my flock,
and have driven them away,
and you have not attended to them.
So I will attend to you for your evil doings, says the LORD.
[3]Then I myself will gather the remnant of my flock
out of all the lands where I have driven them,
and I will bring them back to their fold,
and they shall be fruitful and multiply.
[4]I will raise up shepherds over them who will shepherd them,
and they shall not fear any longer, or be dismayed,
nor shall any be missing, says the LORD.

[5]The days are surely coming, says the LORD,
when I will raise up for David a righteous Branch,
and he shall reign as king and deal wisely,
and shall execute justice and righteousness in the land.
[6]In his days Judah will be saved and Israel will live in safety.
And this is the name by which he will be called:
"The LORD is our righteousness."

The word of the Lord.

PSALMODY: LUKE 1:68–79

Readings continue on p. 270

[†]*Sunday between November 20 and 26 inclusive*

APPENDIX B

READINGS FROM THE APOCRYPHAL BOOKS

FIRST READING: BARUCH 5:1–9

A reading from Baruch:

¹Take off the garment of your sorrow and affliction, O Jerusalem,
   and put on forever the beauty of the glory from God.
²Put on the robe of the righteousness that comes from God;
   put on your head the diadem of the glory of the Everlasting;
³for God will show your splendor everywhere under heaven.
⁴For God will give you evermore the name,
   "Righteous Peace, Godly Glory."

⁵Arise, O Jerusalem, stand upon the height;
   look toward the east,
and see your children gathered from west and east
   at the word of the Holy One,
   rejoicing that God has remembered them.
⁶For they went out from you on foot,
   led away by their enemies;
but God will bring them back to you,
   carried in glory, as on a royal throne,
⁷For God has ordered that every high mountain and the everlasting hills be
      made low
   and the valleys filled up, to make level ground,
   so that Israel may walk safely in the glory of God,
⁸The woods and every fragrant tree
   have shaded Israel at God's command.
⁹For God will lead Israel with joy,
   in the light of his glory,
   with the mercy and righteousness that come from him.

The word of the Lord.

PSALMODY: LUKE 1:68–79

Readings continue on p. 5

SECOND SUNDAY AFTER CHRISTMAS

JANUARY 4, 1998   JANUARY 4, 2004

FIRST READING: Sirach 24:1–12

A reading from Sirach:

[1]Wisdom praises herself,
    and tells of her glory in the midst of her people.
[2]In the assembly of the Most High she opens her mouth,
    and in the presence of his hosts she tells of her glory:

[3]"I came forth from the mouth of the most High,
    and covered the earth like a mist.
[4]I dwelt in the highest heavens,
    and my throne was in a pillar of cloud.
[5]Alone I compassed the vault of heaven
    and traversed the depths of the abyss.
[6]Over waves of the sea, over all the earth,
    and over every people and nation I have held sway."
[7]Among all these I sought a resting place;
    in whose territory should I abide?

[8]"Then the Creator of all things gave me a command,
    and my Creator chose the place for my tent.
He said, 'Make your dwelling in Jacob,
    and in Israel receive your inheritance.'
[9]Before the ages, in the beginning, he created me,
    and for all the ages I shall not cease to be.
[10]In the holy tent I ministered before him,
    and so I was established in Zion.

[11]"Thus in the beloved city he gave me a resting place,
    and in Jerusalem was my domain.
[12]I took root in an honored people,
    in the portion of the Lord, his heritage."

The word of the Lord.

PSALMODY: Wisdom of Solomon 10:15–21

Readings continue on p. 26

EIGHTH SUNDAY AFTER THE EPIPHANY
PROPER 3

FIRST READING: SIRACH 27:4–7

A reading from Sirach:

⁴When a sieve is shaken, the refuse appears;
    so do a person's faults when he speaks.
⁵The kiln tests the potter's vessels;
    so the test of a person is in his conversation.
⁶Its fruit discloses the cultivation of a tree;
    so a person's speech discloses the cultivation of his mind.
⁷Do not praise anyone before he speaks,
    for this is the way people are tested.

The word of the Lord.

PSALMODY: PSALM 92:1–4, 12–15

Psalm 92:1–4, 11–14, LBW/BCP

Readings continue on p. 58

THE RESURRECTION OF OUR LORD
VIGIL OF EASTER

APRIL 11, 1998   APRIL 14, 2001   APRIL 10, 2004

SIXTH READING: BARUCH 3:9–15, 32—4:4

A reading from Baruch:

⁹Hear the commandments of life, O Israel;
    give ear, and learn wisdom!
¹⁰Why is it, O Israel, why is it that you are in the land of your enemies,
    that you are growing old in a foreign country,
that you are defiled with the dead,
    ¹¹that you are counted among those in Hades?
¹²You have forsaken the fountain of wisdom.
¹³If you had walked in the way of God,
    you would be living in peace forever.
¹⁴Learn where there is wisdom,
    where there is strength,
    where there is understanding,
so that you may at the same time discern
    where there is length of days, and life,
    where there is light for the eyes, and peace.

¹⁵Who has found her place?
    And who has entered her storehouses?

³²But the one who knows all things knows her,
    he found her by his understanding.
The one who prepared the earth for all time
    filled it with four-footed creatures;
³³the one who sends forth the light, and it goes;
    he called it, and it obeyed him, trembling;
³⁴the stars shone in their watches, and were glad;
    he called them, and they said, "Here we are!"
    They shone with gladness for him who made them.
³⁵This is our God;
    no other can be compared to him.
³⁶He found the whole way to knowledge,
    and gave her to his servant Jacob
    and to Israel, whom he loved.
³⁷Afterward she appeared on earth
    and lived with humankind.

4:1She is the book of the commandments of God,
  the law that endures forever.
All who hold her fast will live,
  and those who forsake her will die.
2Turn, O Jacob, and take her;
  walk toward the shining of her light.
3Do not give your glory to another,
  or your advantages to an alien people.
4Happy are we, O Israel,
  for we know what is pleasing to God.

The word of the Lord.

RESPONSE: PSALM 19

Readings continue on p. 135

SUNDAY BETWEEN
MAY 24 AND 28 INCLUSIVE
(if after Trinity Sunday)

PROPER 3

FIRST READING: Sɪʀᴀᴄʜ 27:4–7

A reading from Sirach:

⁴When a sieve is shaken, the refuse appears;
    so do a person's faults when he speaks.
⁵The kiln tests the potter's vessels;
    so the test of a person is in his conversation.
⁶Its fruit discloses the cultivation of a tree;
    so a person's speech discloses the cultivation of his mind.
⁷Do not praise anyone before he speaks,
    for this is the way people are tested.

The word of the Lord.

PSALMODY: Psᴀʟᴍ 92: 1–4, 12–15   *Psalm 92:1–4, 11–14* LBW/BCP

Readings continue on p. 190

Sunday between
August 28 and September 3
Inclusive

PROPER 17

AUGUST 30, 1998   SEPTEMBER 2, 2001   AUGUST 29, 2004

FIRST READING: Sirach 10:12–18

A reading from Sirach:

¹²The beginning of human pride is to forsake the Lord;
    the heart has withdrawn from its Maker.
¹³For the beginning of pride is sin,
    and the one who clings to it pours out abominations.
Therefore the Lord brings upon them unheard-of calamities,
    and destroys them completely.
¹⁴The Lord overthrows the thrones of rulers,
    and enthrones the lowly in their place.
¹⁵The Lord plucks up the roots of the nations,
    and plants the humble in their place.
¹⁶The Lord lays waste the lands of the nations,
    and destroys them to the foundations of the earth.
¹⁷He removes some of them and destroys them,
    and erases the memory of them from the earth.
¹⁸Pride was not created for human beings,
    or violent anger for those born of women.

The word of the Lord.

PSALMODY: Psalm 112

Readings continue on p. 234

SUNDAY BETWEEN
OCTOBER 23 AND 29 INCLUSIVE

PROPER 25

OCTOBER 25, 1998   OCTOBER 28, 2001   OCTOBER 24, 2004

FIRST READING: SIRACH 35:12–17

A reading from Sirach:

¹²Give to the Most High as he has given to you,
    and as generously as you can afford.
¹³For the Lord is the one who repays,
    and he will repay you sevenfold.
¹⁴Do not offer him a bribe, for he will not accept it;
    ¹⁵and do not rely on a dishonest sacrifice;
for the Lord is the judge,
    and with him there is no partiality.
¹⁶He will not show partiality to the poor;
    but he will listen to the prayer of one who is wronged.
¹⁷He will not ignore the supplication of the orphan,
    or the widow when she pours out her complaint.

The word of the Lord.

PSALMODY: PSALM 84:1–7   *Psalm 84:1–6,* LBW/BCP

Readings continue on p. 259

INDEX